'*The Last English Poachers* moves along at a cracking pace and offers a platform to a section of the British population that is rarely admitted into print . . . A note at the end suggests it was ghosted for the Toveys by a professional writer called John MacDonald. If so, he has done a masterly job, brilliantly capturing a tone of voice that is at once threatening and droll, comical and surly, belligerent and rustic. And lyrical too.' *Mail on Sunday*

'This skilfully ghosted account has the rakish charm of a "Burglar Bill" for adults - with the added frisson that it's non-fiction. The Toveys' dislike of the ruling classes is matched by their passionate love of the natural world. "I've never engaged in cruelty of any kind," Bob claims. "I has no truck with them who does."'
Intelligent Life magazine

'. . . the rollicking good tales they tell . . . are frequently hilarious, sometimes violent and always illuminating' *Country Life*

'Welcome to the gnarly undergrowth of the real countryside . . . A work of important social history' *Sunday Times*

'There is a scandalous charm to *The Last English Poachers*. An odd importance too; it is as rare as hens' teeth that the rural underclass gets the lamplight' *The Times*

'The darker side of country living comes to light' Must Reads, *Sunday Times*

'Doesn't give a "fiddler's feck"' *Guardian*

'Sincere and unambiguous . . . a brilliant narrative . . .'
Literary Review

Bob and Brian Tovey are father and son, born 1938 and 1963 respectively, who have lived their whole lives in the Gloucestershire countryside. Their knowledge of the woodlands, fields and streams close to them – and the birds and animals found there – is comparable to that of indigenous peoples in pre-industrial societies. Their way of life – taking what they need to feed themselves from the land around them – is fast dying out. They are the last English poachers. Bob Tovey died in February 2015.

THE LAST ENGLISH POACHERS

BOB AND BRIAN TOVEY

With John F. McDonald

SIMON & SCHUSTER

London · New York · Sydney · Toronto · New Delhi

A CBS COMPANY

First published in Great Britain by Simon & Schuster UK Ltd, 2015
This paperback edition first published in Great Britain by
Simon & Schuster UK Ltd, 2016
A CBS COMPANY

1 3 5 7 9 10 8 6 4 2

Simon & Schuster UK Ltd
1st Floor
222 Gray's Inn Road
London WC1X 8HB

www.simonandschuster.co.uk

Simon & Schuster Australia, Sydney
Simon & Schuster India, New Delhi

The author and publishers have made all reasonable efforts to
contact copyright-holders for permission, and apologise for
any omissions or errors in the form of credits given.
Corrections may be made to future printings.

A CIP catalogue record for this book
is available from the British Library

Paperback ISBN: 978-1-47113-568-2
Ebook ISBN: 978-1-47113-569-9

Printed and bound by CPI Group (UK) Ltd, Croydon, CR0 4YY

To Robert Seward Tovey, who was a proper countryman,
and Beatrice Frances Tovey, who died too young.

Also Francis George Neal, who died on HMS *Monmouth*
at the naval battle of Coronel on 1 November 1914,
and Jane Ellen Neal, who was a lovely woman.

Contents

1. Bob – The Deer Hunt   1
2. Bob – The Early Years   11
3. Bob – The Navy   28
4. Bob – The Poacher   43
5. Brian – The Panther   53
6. Brian – The Early Years   66
7. Bob – The Enemy   82
8. Bob – Hare Coursing   94
9. Brian – The Law   105
10. Bob – Lamping and Other Stories   119
11. Bob – Long-Netting   131
12. Brian – Poacher vs Landowner   146
13. Brian – Prison   159
14. Brian – Poaching Tricks   171
15. Bob – Eccentric Characters   184
16. Brian – Greyhounds   199
17. Bob – Drag Coursing   212
18. Brian – Country Activities   226
19. Brian – Into the Wild   240
20. Brian – The Last English Poachers   256

A Poacher's Glossary   269
Cora's Game Recipes   273
Afterword   275

1

Bob – The Deer Hunt

A light March drizzle is sticking to the windscreen of the Austin A35 as we drive in the rare hours, without headlights, up to the high brick wall that marks the boundary of the Berkeley Estate. We park the car in the narrow lane, under cover of some trees, and camouflage it with undergrowth that we've used before on many occasions. Then we scale the wall, with me legging Brian up first and him fixing a rope round the overhanging branch of an oak tree. Even though he's no more than seven years old, the boy knows what it's all about. He's been coming out with me since he was four and he's as good a watcher as any man I've known.

I picks this spot whenever we comes out here from our village because it's easy to get over the wall. I pull myself up by the rope now and drop down the other side, into the estate. I catch Brian when he jumps from the top and set him down, before we move off, after making sure the rope ain't visible from either side of the wall. The ghost of a moon is shining through the thin cloud as me and the boy makes our way across the fields to the edge of the woodland. It's as quiet as a graveyard, with the scurrying of the night animals and the odd hoot of a tawny owl the only sounds. And it's times like this I loves the most, an hour before daylight, with my son on my heels and the feel of the land under my feet and the fresh breeze blowing agin' my face.

It's darker once we gets inside the tree line and we need to take cover and wait for first light to break over the hills to the east. I has a flask of strong sweet tea and I gives the boy a drink from the plastic cup first and then I takes myself a slug – just to keep out the chill that's trying to creep in through our clothes and make us shiver and shake. I'm carrying a .22 rifle and we waits for the sickly pale rays of sunlight to come shafting through the leaves.

Brian drinks the tea and grins back at me because I'm the man he looks up to most in the world. I gives him this – this freedom from all the other stuff – and it sometimes feels like we're part of each other. Every son is part of his father, but few of 'em feels it like Brian does.

I'm wearing my long army coat and boots and Brian has a thick corduroy jacket and trousers and a woolly hat on his head. The colours of our clothes being brown and green to blend in with the woodland vegetation and keep us from getting spotted by some keen-eyed keeper with a pair of binoculars.

The light creeps up like a ghostly spectre in the distance to the east. And once we can see with some clarity, we starts off on our hunt for a suitable deer. The estate's a big place, maybe ten thousand acres altogether, with five or six hundred acres of parkland alongside farmland and fisheries and small hilly woods dotted about over six or seven miles, where the deer take refuge.

We keep low to the ground when we has to break from the

cover of the trees to get from one thicket to another. Them gamekeepers ain't beyond giving poachers a good kicking and taking our guns away from us. And I hope they don't come upon us all sudden like, because I'll want to fight 'em and probably get beaten and I hates to see them kick the boy away when he tries to help me. But we've been here before and know the escape routes well enough to make a run for it, as long as we're alert and don't let 'em get too close to us.

We can see the outline of the old Norman castle silhouetted agin' the skyline to the north of us. It's a dark and demonic-looking place, where they murdered King Edward II by sticking a red-hot poker up his arse so there'd be no sign of any wound on his body. And every September, on the equinox, he can be heard screaming. I know that because I hears him sometimes, even though we lives a fair distance away – his voice comes floating and finds its way into our house and I tells it to go leave me and mine alone. And it does.

And Dickie Pearce, the last court jester in England, died there after falling from the minstrels' gallery, and Queen Matilda came and killed all the deer in revenge for Roger de Berkeley not supporting her in the war they called 'the anarchy'. So it's a foreboding place with a blood-flecked pedigree, and it growls at us now as we cross its land in search of its game.

There's about two hundred red and fallow deer on the estate and we start to see 'em as the early spring sun climbs to a low slant in the milky sky. We wants a big stag, not a hind or an albino, or a fawn. I want to joint it up and keep what we need for ourselves, then sell some and give what's left to the poorer people of our village. I does this all the time and gives away a lot of what we hunts because there's too much for me and Brian and my daughter June and there's just the three of us now, since their mother left when they was younger. Though Cora says she'll be moving in soon to take care of us all. Very soon, I hope.

And then I sees him – a big proud fella with maybe twelve or fifteen points to his antlers. I signal the boy to be still and quiet because I has to get close to him to make a clean kill and, if I spook the herd, he'll run with them. The deer is alert, even at this time of morning, but they're used to humans on this estate. They're semi-tame and not as flighty as truly wild deer that you'd get on the high hills of Scotland so, as long as we keeps downwind of 'em with the low light behind us and in their eyes, we'll be alright. We move silently, stealthily, like we was animals ourselves and this was our natural habitat – which, in a way, it is.

The .22 bolt action has a decent range for about a hundred yards; after that the bullet can fall away at a rapid rate and not hit the target, but I wants to get closer than that, to make sure I drops the animal with one shot. We might get away with the one round not being heard by the keepers, but not two or three. I make my silent signals and Brian knows I want to get as close as possible to make the kill – maybe as close as thirty yards. The boy's job is to keep watch while I do my job and shoot the quarry, which is what I call whatever it is I'm hunting. So he turns away from me and keeps his eyes peeled and I can concentrate without worrying about someone creeping up behind me. The gamekeepers will have shotguns and they won't think twice about using them. If they pepper one of us, they can always claim it was in self-defence because we pointed the rifle at them. And who's going take the word of a poacher and his seven-year-old son agin' that lot?

The big stag's getting frisky now – he senses something, maybe the adrenaline that's filling the air, or the spectres of the poachers that's been hung here over the years, drifting past us in the half-light – and I'll have to take the shot soon. I don't have telescopic sight on the rifle, but I got a good and well-practised eye. A deer is a big animal, but the vital areas for clean kills are small. I always aim for the heart or lungs rather than the head. I've known idiots in the woods to hit an animal in the mouth instead of the brain and shatter its jaw and it runs off and starves to death because it can't feed no more. Clobheads like that needs beating with the butts of their own guns.

Brian's waiting for the sound of the shot. He don't know when it'll come because he's turned away from me. I know he'll be saying to hisself 'any second now' and 'be prepared', but it always makes him start, no matter how ready he is. Always.

I gets into a good position to take the shot and I know the boy's watching out behind me to see if any sneaking keeper sticks his big ugly head up when I pulls the trigger. I takes the aim and can almost see the anticipation in the animal's eye as I squeeze off the round. The bullet flies through the air and strikes the stag in the heart, a split second before it hears the sound of the shot. The animal drops to the ground and the rest of the herd takes off across the open part of the estate towards another copse of trees and scrub. We wait, to see if there's any shouting in the distance, because the gamekeepers are like lumbering bulls and, even if we can't see 'em, we can hear 'em coming a mile off.

There's no sound, so we move forward until we comes to the stag. Its eyes are wild with panic and it's making low, baying sounds of distress. So I takes out my hunting knife and slices its throat and lets it bleed out, because venison can go off quicker than some other meat if you don't get the blood out straight away. The smell will soon attract fox and stoat and reclusive badger and birds of prey, and they'll circle and hover round us to see if we'll leave anything for them when we move off. When the predators and carcass pillagers come, they'll make a lot of fuss and I know they'll attract the keepers if we ain't quick.

Brian's still watching while I tend to my work. He knows what I'm doing – it's bloody and brutal to some, but it's the way of things with us. After bleeding the beast, I open the carcass and gralloch it, which means dragging out the guts, and I leaves the pluck in the undergrowth for the scavengers. A stag's heavy enough to drag over a distance, without pulling the insides along too.

Me and the boy then gets hold of the antlers and starts to drag him back to the wall. It's a long way and we need to stick to the woodland and heavy undergrowth, rather than risk being seen in hazy daylight across the open fields. Brian's only young and not strong enough yet to pull his full weight, so most of the work's down to me. He's trying to help me as best he can, but the beast is heavy and it's hard going through the rough woodland. He's sweating, even though the early morning's cool, and he takes off his woolly hat and stuffs it into his pocket.

I'm telling him all the time how good a lad he is and how he's always such fine company for me when it's dark and cold at some cock-crow hour, with the wind sharp as a knife between our ribs, or when circling rooks is signalling rain, or the tawny owl calls for a starlit night and a morning fair. We're dragging for half an hour and it's taking too long and soon the keepers will be coming round with their 12-bores, maybe shooting vermin like crows and squirrels and being on the lookout for the likes of us to aim at too. So I props up the stag as best as I can agin' a tree and gives the gun to Brian to carry. Then I gets underneath the animal and lifts him up across my shoulders. The beast's a dead weight and heavier than myself and my muscles are aching from the dragging and my legs are tired, but I manage to keep going without stumbling and we finally reach the edge of the tree line where we came in. The wall's in sight, a couple of hundred yards away, but it's across open ground and we'll have to move fast.

Just then I hear the low growl of voices approaching the edge of the wood. I drops the deer into some bushes and signals for Brian to follow me. We hide a couple of yards away in good cover and wait. If the keepers find the stag, they won't find us with it, but we'll still have to make a good getaway and all our hard work will be for nothing. They come close – two of them – and I could reach over and tap 'em on the shoulder if I wanted to. Luckily there ain't no dog with them to sniff out the kill. They stop walking not more than a few feet away from us and decide to have a chinwag and smoke a cigarette. I signal to the boy not to make a sound. He's holding his breath, still as a stalk-ing fox, with my hand on his shoulder to steady him. We're crouched down and it won't be long before the pins and needles make our knees go giddy. We can hear the keepers talking.

'Bit of a racket down in that gully.'

'What you think? Poachers?'

'Don't know. Not much left by the time we got there.'

'Could've been foxes, maybe killed a hare or a hedgehog.'

'Yeah, I suppose. Nothing over this side.'

We keep crouching. Motionless as mice, with the foliage all around us and sweat from the exertion of carrying the carcass running into our eyes. We're as close as Siamese twins, me and Brian, neither of us moving a muscle and barely letting the breath come out of our mouths. The keepers are standing on the edge of the tree line, cracking jokes and laughing, with their shotguns broken over their arms. They're close enough to smell. If they find us now we'll never get away. We're too near them to run and Brian's too young, so I'll have to fight 'em and it'll be bloody. I hope they bugger off soon, because I'm an impatient man and I might let loose at any second.

Brian's holding on to my coat and the only thing that's keeping us hidden is the knowing that he'll get hurt if I has a go. The time passes slowly, minute by heavy minute. I feel my knee joints stiffening and I need to move, but can't. The boy's motionless beside me, hardly breathing. Smoke from their cigarettes drifts towards us and up my nose and I hope it don't make Brian cough. Insects are crawling over us, spiders and beetles and little biting flies. I feel the boy move lightly agin' my shoulder and I think maybe he might be about to flag. I turn my head slowly and see him smile up at me, even though I knows he's in pain from the crouching position, just the same as myself.

At last the keepers move off. We wait until there's no sound other than our slow breathing, then wait a bit longer, just to be sure. Brian tries to stand, but his legs buckle from the numbness. I rub his calves until the blood begins to flow again, then I puts my arm under his shoulder to support him until the feeling comes back into his wobbly limbs. We watch the keepers away in the distance and wait until they're completely out of sight, then I lifts the stag onto my shoulders again and stumble off at a jogging gait across the open parkland to the wall.

We're moving fast over the ground, the boy running with the

gun behind and me ahead of him with the deer. I wait for the shouts of 'stop' to come after us, but they don't, and then we're at the wall and almost away. I leg Brian up and tie the end of the rope round the deer's antlers. Then I pull myself up onto the wall and loosen the rope knot and use the tree branch as a pulley, checking the lane to make sure nobody's about. I swing myself down, using the force of the drop and my weight to pull the kill up level with the top of the wall. Brian pushes the dead animal until it swings, more and more, until it's pitching out over the wall. I choose my moment and let go of the rope and the stag drops down on the outside.

Brian loops the rope off the branch and I help him down off the wall. We drag the camouflage off the car and I drive it over to the dead deer. But the stag's too big to get in the boot. We can get the body in, but not the head and antlers. I consider cutting the head off, but it'll take too long and, any minute now, some yawney from the estate might come along the lane.

There's no other option: I has to drive along the back roads with the stag's head sticking out of the boot and the antlers scraping along the ground. This is alright in the narrow byways, but I also has to drive for a short while along the A38, the old main Bristol to Gloucester road, to get back home. There's no other choice and I've got to take the chance. It's an odd sight, us two in the little old Austin motor and the stag looking out from the boot with its antlers sparking off the road. And I'm smiling at the faces in the windows of the cars that pass us – them all with their mouths open speechless to catch the flies and their jaws dropping and their eyes not believing what they're seeing. The boy's laughing too, at them giving us their frowning stares as they come close, as much as to say, 'Look at them cheeky poachers', and they'll probably stop at the first telephone box to grass us up. But the luck's with us and we don't pass no police and we makes it home safely.

I has a cool shed set up in the yard behind my house and we drag the stag in there and hangs him and then goes in to take our rest. It's dinnertime, because we always has dinner in the middle of the day, which is proper, with supper in the evenings. Cora and my young daughter June's cooked us pheasant and potatoes and mashed-up swede, that we grows ourselves, and we wolfs it down because we're starving with the hunger of our exertions. Then I drive down to the village pub for a well-earned drink. Brian leaves Cora and June to clear up and goes out to tend to the dogs.

We has eight greyhounds here at the house and they need walking for five miles on a hard surface to keep their pads up. Later, when they're fed and watered, and the spaniels too, he'll go back inside and wait for me to come home from the pub. June knows I'll be a bit belligerent, like I sometimes gets after twenty pints, so she slopes off to bed. But Brian waits to hear about the arguments and the aftermath of the rows and ructions and to stop me from breaking up the furniture. Again.

Next day, after I sobers up, I skins the stag and dresses it and cuts its head off. Brian gets rid of the head and antlers by dumping them somewhere secluded, far away from the house. The keepers on the estate know all their beasts and it won't be long before they notice this big fella's missing. Then the coppers will be snooping round and we don't want 'em finding his head and antlers anywhere near us.

The day after, the animal is jointed up and the meat sold and distributed among the people who owns that deer just as much as the earls of bloody Berkeley Castle.

2

Bob – The Early Years

My name is Bob Tovey and I'm a poacher. I was born on 21 February 1938 in the Royal Infirmary, Bristol. My parents were Robert and Beatrice Tovey and they came from a small village in South Gloucestershire and that's where I grew up. My father was a poacher before me, along with being a butcher and slaughterman. He had a small shop called 'R S Tovey – Butcher' opposite the town hall clock in the High Street. The clock was very old and the only one like it in the world. The mechanism was operated by a rope and, in wet weather, it would run three minutes slow – it ran three minutes fast in summer, because of the tautness of the rope. So it only ever told the right time in the spring and in the autumn.

My father taught me many things about animals: how to castrate a cat and de-bristle a pig and shoot a dog and kill a sheep with a piece of rope. Now, you might be thinking these things is cruel and inhumane but, in the ways of the countryside, they ain't. If the tomcat don't get castrated, he goes about trying to service the queans in heat and howling his head off at night and spraying everywhere and roaming and fighting and getting stud-tailed and blood poisoned – which is probably what he deserves. But it's kinder to castrate him.

Pigs is de-bristled after they're dead, so that ain't cruel now, is it? My father would lay a bed of straw and get the pig onto it and shoot it with a humane killer. He'd cut its throat and tip it up to get the blood out, then sprinkle straw all over the carcass and burn it. It was a lovely smell. I used to help clean the chitlin, then boil and plait 'em, so nothing got wasted, not even the trotters. He'd cut the pig in half and lay it on two flat tombstones that he'd nicked from the local churchyard and rub a mixture of salt, saltpetre and brown sugar into it. The liquor would run down and be collected underneath and he'd pour it back over the bacon – over and over. Then he'd joint it and wrap it in muslin cloth and it'd keep for ages. Mother would soak it before cooking and make Lazarus pie from bits of backbone the size of your fist with the meat still on, cooked with stock and pastry on top – and I never tasted nothing like it in my whole life.

Butchering a sheep was done with a rope; he'd tie two back legs and one front leg and put his fingers up the animal's nose, then he'd pull its head back and cut its throat, tip it up to get the blood out and gut it and skin it. It was quick and considerate and, despite what people might think, my father taught me to respect life and to do what was needed to be done without getting all sentimental over it. During and after the war, when there was rationing, he'd go round the farms and I'd keep watch while he slaughtered and butchered black-market animals that the farmers hadn't declared to the ministry men. He'd be paid sometimes with money and other times with meat.

One time he killed a pig for a farmer and carried it a mile and a half on his shoulders back to the slaughterhouse and went to hang it up, but there was a woman already hanging there on the hook. She'd killed herself. The old man dropped the pig and cut her down and checked she was dead and went to get her husband. Nobody knew why she did it, apart from her husband being a miserable bastard and maybe she just couldn't stick living with him no longer.

So I knew a bit about death and animals right from an early age. All kinds of animals, including dogs. And dogs to me is for working, not for pets. If a dog can't earn its keep it needs to go. Better to shoot it than ill-treat it or turn it out to starve to death like some does. Shooting's more humane than taking a dog to the vets – it's quicker and the dog don't know what's coming until it's over. You take a dog to the vet and it knows something bad's going to happen. It gets to fretting long before the injection kills it. So there's no use saying to me I got no appreciation of animals. It ain't true – I got more than you!

But this book ain't about domestic animals, nor farm animals neither. It's about wild animals and the kinship between a poacher like me and the creatures that live and roam wild in this country we calls ours.

The village where I grew up was a small place before people spilled out here from Bristol and other towns besides. It was just one street and butts for archery surrounded by land – farmland and big estates belonging to the aristocracy, earls and lords and dukes and the like. There was no television back in my boyhood days, just newspapers and radio, and I could tell whose horse it was by the sound of the hooves coming down the street.

We had a Christmas party in the village hall every year and all the children got a little present, along with jelly and ice cream.

And celebrating on Saint Stephen's Day with a wren dangling from a stick and the lads dressed like Morris men and calling and carousing with a dance and a dingle and a little jingle or two:

I followed the wren three miles or more,
Three miles or more, three miles or more.
I followed the wren three miles or more
At six o'clock in the morning.
Up with the kettle and down with the pan
And give us a penny to bury the wren.

They'd be waving a bunch of bee nettles and blind-eyes and creeping jinny. And the robin would whistle-call to its little chicks in the snow and the grown-ups had bellies full of whisky and warm feelings.

Everybody knew everybody else and there were village fêtes in summer and outings to the seaside and fairs and sporting days, and nothing much changed for years and years. But it's all gone now, except for the odd memory and melancholy.

Most work came from farming or from the Arnold Perrett Brewery, which had been around since 1820 and brewed ale until 1924, when it became a cider factory. They stopped making the cider in 1970 and started making the ale again, and they still do to this day. Some villagers travelled the short distance over to Yate, to work for the Parnall Aircraft Company. The site there was built in 1917 by German prisoners-of-war, and it were originally the home of the Royal Flying Corps. There were camps and hostels to cater for the thousands of workers and, on market days, they'd have to plough their way through the sheep and cows teeming the streets. They made 'planes like the Parnall

Pike and the Pipit and the Perch and the Parnall Pixie in the years between the wars. When the Second World War came, they made gun turrets for bombers like the Wellington and the Lancaster and the Blenheim and airframes for Spitfires. And there were craters all around the local countryside, where them German blackguards used to lighten their loads before heading home – if they hadn't got rid of all their bombs upon the industrial towns of Coventry and Sheffield and Nottingham.

As a boy, I'd ramble the land all around and I knew every inch of it. I'd climb to the top of the Nibley Monument, built in honour of William Tyndale, who translated the New Testament Bible and who used to pray, on a Sunday morning, for the souls of all those still in bed, fornicating. Up a spiral staircase of a hundred and twenty steps and look down over the world to the north, south, east and west. Then there was the Somerset Monument, over near Hawkesbury in honour of Lord Edward Somerset, who was the son of the Duke of Beaufort and fought at Waterloo and was, by all accounts, said to have three testicles. It was on the lands of the Beaufort Estate and other estates like it that I did my poaching.

The art and craft of poaching goes back before the history books began. It goes back to when a few people believed they owned all the land and others had no right to the game that ran and flew on that land. But a wild animal or a bird is nobody's property – it's 'fair game', and them who thinks different thinks they own the very air. They no more own the land nor the air than they own the sun or the moon or the stars. Men have always been hunters, long before they became farmers or carpenters or office workers or lorry drivers. We hunted with dogs not too far removed from their wolf ancestors and we used spears and arrows and snares. We hunted to eat and we needed to eat to live.

A lot of people who complain about poachers and the ways of the wild countryside eat meat that comes from factory farms and is mass-produced and distressing to the animals that live lives of continuous cruelty and die undignified deaths on blood-covered concrete. But, as long as it's out of their sensitive sight, it's alright. Everything I hunts and kills as a poacher dies humanely and is eaten or sold on and nothing's wasted nor thrown away.

To stop people like us poachers, the lords and ladies and bishops and bigwigs employed roughnecks to do their dirty work for them. They called them 'foresters' in olden times and now they're called gamekeepers. They were brutal lackeys who beat and killed ordinary folk who tried to feed their families by poaching a bird or a beast. In later times, they used the law to fine and imprison poachers, which they still do to some extent today. So, you can see how there was never no love lost between the poacher and the gamekeeper.

Nowadays a lot of the land belongs to farmers and syndicates who runs shoots for rich businessmen and foreign fat-cats who think, like the lost sailor, that they can buy the wind. And they employ their own bully boys to keep the likes of me away from their game birds and the other wild animals that run on their property. But I've never been afraid of any man who takes wages to keep his own kind away from what's rightfully theirs to hunt and eat, if they're of a mind to do it. And I've faced and fought gamekeepers and wardens as often as I've run from 'em.

Anyway, to get back to my story, I was an only child and I found that to be a disadvantage because you don't learn about other people and how to deal with this bear-baiting bastard of a world. You don't know what it's like to go hungry, or what to do when they're all about you with big sticks, trying to break your bloody neck. I'm not saying it was all plums and soft-pedal; I had plenty of jobs to do for my father – sawing railway sleepers for firewood and carrying the coal and digging in the big garden. I had to carry water using a yoke, a wooden beam that fitted over my shoulders, with a chain each end and buckets attached to the chain, like a medieval milkmaid. But the work made me strong and I went everywhere with my father. He hunted with whippets and terriers, and he taught me to poach and how to work the dogs. But the first thing he taught me was how to be quiet.

'You'll never get nothin' talking.'

And he was right. I was young then and full of fidgeting like youngsters is and I couldn't keep still. But he never lost his temper with me and I learned from his example.

I got my first greyhound when I was about six or seven and I'd take it out with a terrier. The terrier would work the hedges and the greyhound would stalk the outside and catch anything that bolted. This was pre-myxomatosis and there'd be thousands of rabbits quatting in the grass in frosty weather. I learned how to move quietly and creep up on them, which ain't easy because a rabbit can see backwards as well as forwards. And it was a jumping joy to kick up a hare and have the dog catch it and bring it back without chewing it up and spoiling the meat, and I'd be out every chance I got, roaming the land and breathing the free fresh air of this wild west country.

My first dog was called Queenie and I loved her like the leaves on the trees. Me and her was inseparable when I was a young 'un. I remember being out with her one rainy day and she caught a rabbit in a small field. She brought it back and, as I leaned over to take it from her, I noticed a hare about two yards in front of me. It was quiet in the grass and not moving. I took some mud off one of my boots and threw it at the hare and it ran. Queenie saw it and took off after it. It made for the hedge to escape, but the dog ran round and forced it back into the field. She was clever enough to keep it in the field until it got tired. Then she killed it. And to see this spectacle – dog after hare, this wild battle of wits – was one of the finest sights in the world.

The rain eased on the way home and it was just me and Queenie out there under a jet-black sky, with the moon trying to peep out of its cloud pocket and a warm satisfaction round my heart at the young knowing inside me.

I learned from my father how to read tracks: what's been this way and that way and how long ago. A boy can learn a lot from early cobwebs across a path or flattened grass or a snapped branch. I learned how to lure pheasants with a drop or two of aniseed in the corn, because they likes it a lot, and how to work with ferrets and how to set snares and traps and nets and lures. Some Gypsies made me a catapult when I was young, with a metal frame and thick, strong, square-shaped rubber and a leather pocket. That thing could do serious damage at close range with a clear view and it was silent and stealthy. I some-times shot four pheasants in a row with it, and plenty of pigeons at roost in the trees.

One dull drizzly evening, just as it's getting dark, I leaves my bicycle in a ditch and creeps out onto the Berkeley Estate. I sees a pheasant at roost and shoots it with my catapult. The bird falls, but gets stuck in a blackthorn bush. I'm about to go in after it, when I sees a keeper approaching. I legs it back to the bike and takes the chain off. The keeper follows me and comes over.

'What you up to, Tovey?'

They all know me by my name.

'Bike chain's broken.'

He looks me up and down to make sure I ain't carrying nothing. Then he laughs.

'Have to walk home then, won't you?'

I wheels the bike until I'm out of sight, then puts the chain back on and comes back after dark for the pheasant. And it was a pure joy to get one over on them keepers and I'd whistle and sing about it, like my father was always doing. I asked him once, 'Why you always whistling and singing?'

'I'm happy, ain't I.'

And that was his nature; he was a happy man. But he could never stray far over the poaching line; because he ran a butcher's shop he depended on the gentry and the farmers and the people who worked on the land, and he couldn't afford to go agin' them too much. He had to tug his forelock to 'em like the rest of the village. But I didn't, and I got hooked on it – the poaching. It grew on me like a new skin and I couldn't sleep at night for the urge to be out there in the wild openness. I loved it – the skill of it, the joy of it, the excitement of it.

That ain't to say my father was a yes-man, he weren't. He was a very gentle man – until someone upset him, then he could mix it with the best of 'em. And he always warned me about the monkey-men I'd meet going through life, even if I never took much notice of him at the time.

He kept ferrets – three Jills and a Hob – and he taught me to hunt with them using hemp purse nets. We'd put the nets over the entrances to rabbit warrens and send the ferrets in. The nets'd close on a draw cord when the rabbits bolted into 'em to get away from the ferrets. We'd set up long nets to cut across where we thought the rabbits would bolt if they got through the purse nets and the animals would get tangled in the loose bagging. The old man would bring his whippets with us and they'd run down any rabbits that escaped the nets. Sometimes the ferrets would kill rabbits underground. When that happened, we'd have to listen with our ears to the ground to hear where they was doing the killing, then we'd dig down with a ditching spade.

We ate what we needed and my father sold the rest in his shop. The pluck was fed to the dogs and the ferrets, and the skins were sold off to be cured and tanned and used for hats and the collars of coats. Those we caught live were used for spot coursing, to give the dogs a run and keep them up for it – and it ain't cruel, if that's what you think, because a greyhound will kill a rabbit quickly, a lot quicker than it rotting away for months from some man-made disease.

I learned how to set hingles for hares and rabbits, with a noose made of copper wire attached by a cord to a stake driven firmly into the ground. A pricker stick would hold the noose about six inches off the ground for a hare and four fingers for a rabbit. Another stick would be bent over the hingle to make the animal lower its head. Hares run, so the position of the snare weren't never a big fuss, but rabbits hop and there's daps in the run. The wire had to be set about three inches above the dap, so the forepaws went under the wire and the head went through, breaking the neck for a quick kill. Them who didn't know how often set the snares wrong and the forepaws went through and the rabbit was caught round the stomach and it tore all the fur and flesh off itself trying to get free.

I'd run down my snares in the daytime, in case they was spotted. I'd take the wires off the pricker sticks and hide them in the grass and I'd reset 'em of an evening. But having to visit the snares twice a day was dangerous – double the chance of getting caught. As well as that, if I got a kill, a fox, stoat or badger might take it before I got to collect it. Predators like that would always be out hunting in the dark and would take one or two of my rabbits. So I had to go round a couple of times during the night, take out what I'd caught and reset the wire.

I could even catch a quatting hare by hand. I was so stealthy I'd pretend not to see it, then snatch it up by the loose skin on its side and back and break its neck. I could catch a pheasant with a slip snare, which was similar to a hingle. I'd set the snare and start tapping further down the hedge. When the pheasant went to its run, it got caught in the snare and the lot went up and left the bird dangling in the air.

As I grew older, I learned my own lessons – like, never to drink alcohol and poach at the same time. Never to take on something that didn't seem right. Always to work alone – until Brian was old enough to come out with me. I learned to have contempt for landowners and their lackeys and to believe I had as much right to the wild game of this country as any lord or freemason or vicar or magistrate or billionaire businessman. And I became a bit of a wild boy, roaming the land with my dog and my catapult and ferrets, catching rabbits and hares and pheasants and white-fronted geese and widgeon and duck and anything that moved and could be eaten. What we couldn't eat got put into my father's little butcher shop and sold to the passing pilgrims.

Of course, the people who owned the land and the estates and who thought they owned the wild animals as well didn't take kindly to me and I was often on the receiving end of a beating from a warden or a gamekeeper. If it was a man they caught, they might not try it on and just take his name and address and set the law on him, but a boy like me was good for a hiding instead of the courthouse and I sometimes came back home bleeding and bruised.

I had to go to school, too, and keep going till I got an education. But I hated every day of it and I regret ever going to school at all. I went to the local Primary and a nearby Grammar after that, but I mitched from there regularly and I was always taking off across the fields whenever I could get away without anyone seeing me. Maybe if I'd took to the learning a bit better, I might've been something different – gone to work in the cider factory or been a farmer's boy or a drayman like my grandfather. But I never wanted to be nothing other than what I became – a professional poacher!

I didn't just stick to the land. I poached fish with gaffs and four-pronged spears. My father taught me how to make the spears by cutting a tall straight sapling that weren't too thick. Then he'd split one end with a knife, carefully, just tapping the blade so the split didn't run the full length of the wood. He'd make another split across the first 'un, so the end of the sapling was divided into four. At that point, he'd lash some jute twine around the wood, about eighteen inches from the split end, to make sure the splits didn't travel down the shaft as he cut 'em right up to the lashing. I'd find two twigs for him that were a couple of inches longer than the width of the sapling and he'd slide them up as close to the lashing as possible, spreading out the four prongs. Then he'd lash the twigs into place with more jute twine. All that was left to be done was to sharpen the end of each prong and you had your spear. If a keeper came along, you could just throw it away because it cost nothing but a bit of time, and you could fetch it back or make another 'un later.

I took the fish from the private streams and lakes for miles around. I mean, how can a man say a fish is his, as it swims upstream from one estate to another? Or, if one bank is on private land and the other's on public land? It's codswallop. I'd use night lines and funnel nets and even tickle the trout. If you knew the water well enough, like I did, you'd find where the fish rested, under rocks and out of the current. I'd lie face down and lower an arm into the stream – slowly, very slowly. I'd let my fingers brush up agin' the trout's side. The fish would move away at first, but my fingers would follow it until it got used to the brushing sensation. Then I'd work along its body to the gills, the only place a big trout can be gripped without it slipping away. I'd hook it out and it was mine!

Catching salmon by hand was a bit more difficult. I'd operate in shallow water on dark nights, wading upstream with a hand-held torch and a hessian bag over my shoulder. I'd flash the torch into the salmon's lie and the curious fish would rise towards the light. I'd have to be quick and grab it by the gills and heave it into the bag.

I was ten years old when my Uncle Ted died. He left me his gun and seventeen cartridges and I went to the post office and got a licence for ten shillings. It was a .410 shotgun, a small gun which used to fire a little two-inch cartridge with not much lead, so's not to do too much damage to the meat when you shot a pheasant in the head with it. With a three-inch cartridge, the .410 can shoot nearly as far as a 12-bore and it don't make a lot of noise, neither, not like the bigger bore guns, so it's less likely to be heard by a prowling gamekeeper. A 12-bore would put a big hole in an elephant's head and they're favoured by the keepers, but not by us poachers.

Once I had the gun I could go lamping of a night for pheasants, using a handheld torch with an easy beam. I'd shoot the quarry and the spaniel would fetch 'em back to me and I'd reward him with a biscuit. Pheasants roost facing the wind, so's not to get their feathers ruffled the wrong way. I'd move downwind through the wood and see 'em silhouetted agin' the sky. After shooting them, I'd try to collect all the feathers where they dropped, so the keepers never even knew I'd been there.

I learned how to use the weather – on wet, dark, windy nights it was always better to work the open country; on still, clear nights I took to the woods. A short duck's frost in the morning was dangerous, because footprints showed up clear for a while – and you couldn't set snares nor use ferrets in the snow – and it was easy to get lost in a mist and hard to spot a roosting pheasant, but it muffled the report of the gun. All these things I learned as I made my way through my early little life.

There were skills to be practised too; you has to have a good eye to be a poacher. You must be able to see game at a distance, camouflaged in a field or hidden behind trees or blending in with the bushes. And be a good shot, and a good bluffer. If I was out with my gun in daylight I'd always keep to the public ways, like paths or lanes. As long as I had a licence, I was legal to carry the gun and, if I saw a bird, I'd take a shot at it and come back for it after dark. That way, if I was suddenly come upon, I'd be carrying nothing and, no matter how suspicious I looked, there was bugger all a keeper or a landowner or a farmer could do. So you can see, in the early days I grew up setting snares and traps and hunting with ferrets and dogs, but once I got my first gun, I always preferred it to anything else, as it was the easiest way to get game.

I remember one time going down to a private stretch of water on the Earl of Ducie's land. It's about two in the morning and I'm wearing nothing but a pair of plimsolls and old shorts and carrying my .410 shotgun. I hides myself quietly until I hears the quacking of the ducks I know is there, then I slip waist-deep into the water. I wade along through the reeds and rushes, keeping out of sight as much as possible, because ducks can see in the dark and they has good eyes. I know I'll only get one shot in and it'll have to be a good 'un. I come across a whole paddling of them – maybe seven or eight. I'm so close the shot kills three of them and the rest fly away, feathers everywhere. I get the three dead 'uns and make a run for it, in case the shot brings the keepers, even at this hour of the night.

When I gets to the road, I sees one of the ducks that flew away running about between the hedges, wounded. So I catches it and puts it out of its misery. I goes down a quiet lane and hides the four dead birds and the gun and slopes back to the water, to see if there's any more 'runners'. Many a poacher's been caught chasing a runner and it's better to leave 'em, but I hates to see an animal suffer, or a bird for that matter. There's nobody about – the keepers is too lazy to get out of their warm beds, even if they hear the shot. So I search the rushes and the area about, but there ain't no more wounded birds. I goes back and collects my bag. Four ducks with the one shot; not bad for a night's work.

I'm only fourteen.

And so, as a boy, I hunted and poached and beat out for long-netters all over the countryside around my village, which was in a rural diocese that was surrounded by land belonging to the lords and earls of England: the estates of the Earl of Ducie and the Duke of Beaufort and the Earl of Berkeley and Lord Moreton and the Codrington Estate – whose family were slave-traders in the West Indies – and the Slimbridge Wildfowl and Wetland Reserve, and around Dursley, which means 'Deer's Lay', and was owned by the Seymour family, descendants of Sir John Seymour, who was a nephew of Jane Seymour, who married Henry VIII. There was also Badminton and Gatcombe and Sherbourne and many other places besides. I wore a long coat with deep poachers' pockets, until later when I traded a few pheasants for postbags, and I used my .410 bolt-action shotgun and my greyhound and spaniel. I was never convicted of a crime in all my days as a poacher, apart from being fined a fiver once, and I never will be now. They tried to do me many times, but I was always too clever for 'em and one step ahead.

Some things I never had much to do with, like fox-hunting and badger-baiting. Hunting a fox was alright if you killed the animal cleanly. It was the poncey bastards on the horses I had a problem with – the 'get out of my way' types; the saddle-bumpers who weren't satisfied with the chase, and who had to dig the fox out when it went to ground and let their pack dogs tear it apart. That wasn't for me. So I never got involved. And, anyway, hunting foxes was for the toffs – they'd go round the houses and show the old people their dogs and horses, when it was legal. I'd watch 'em prancing about in their get-up and tooting their silly horns and stuff. It was supposed to be symbolic or something, but I never did like that word – especially the bolic bit.

Badger-baiting ain't nothing more than pointless bloodshed. Alright, people ate badgers years ago, when it was legal to kill 'em; they called 'em 'pigs' and had badger roasts and they called the meat 'ham', but that ain't nothing to do with badger-digging and -baiting and no one eats 'em now. I never used gin traps neither, because they can catch an animal and hold it by its feet instead of killing it outright.

I learned respect for the countryside and for all the wild things that roamed through it and flew over it and it made me into a man. What my father taught me I taught to my sons, and there's more they learned for themselves, just like I did. And all those skills that's been handed down will be lost when the last of the old-fashioned poachers hangs up their guns and turns their dogs into docile housepets.

Bob's father, Robert Tovey, 1920s   Bob, circa 1942

3

Bob – The Navy

When I turned sixteen, I joined the Navy. My father was agin' it, because he knew it wouldn't suit me, but there was a history of Navy in the family – my grandfather, George Neal, went down with the HMS *Monmouth* when it was sunk during the battle of Coronel in 1914. I thought the Navy would lead to a life of freedom, travelling the world, so I signed on as a junior stoker at Victoria Street in Bristol and was sent to HMS *Raleigh* Basic Training Facility at Torpoint in Cornwall. But I never did like authority in any shape or form – always agin' orders and officers and the high holy born-again freemasons and all their fundamental friends and pointy-hatted partners, on account of them being a dangerous shower of shit-stirrers and nuisance-causers. So I was always going to be in trouble for one thing or another, right from the start.

After basic training, I was assigned to HMS *Sluys*, a battle-class destroyer in reserve – that's where I learned all about being a stoker and finished my training. But my feet was itching to be off and I couldn't wait to be given a posting so I could get going round the world to see all the sights and sleep under all the stars. My first real ship was HMS *Pickle*, a minesweeper based at Harwich, and I was drafted to her when I knew what I was supposed to be doing. Some sailor asked me if I had a rubber when I first came aboard and I thought he was talking about a French letter. Now, I'd heard a bit about buggery and stuff like that going on in the Navy and I was worried. The big burlys could see I was shaking in my shoes and they all had a good laugh, because a 'rubber' was a pound note in Navy slang and a half-sheet was a ten-bob note, and nothing at all to do with sodomy or shirt-lifting.

But I had to start growing up, fast. I might have been Bob Tovey the poacher in my village, but nobody knew that in the Navy, and nobody cared. I was given a bucket, and that was for washing myself and my clothes. We slept in hammocks and I thought that was the bee's knees because I was always upright, no matter how the ship rolled. We had to lash 'em up in the morning and put 'em away and, on the first morning after I got up, I went to the mess hall and made myself a bacon sandwich. The next thing I knows, some bloke hits me and knocks me out. There was this big Scouse stoker called Tommo, and he helped me up and told me it was because I didn't wash before I went to get the grub. He told me I had to be very clean onboard ship – before I got in my hammock I had to wash myself and my clothes and take 'em to the boiler room to dry. I had to wash again after I got up, before breakfast, and it was all because of living and eating in such close quarters – to prevent illness and infections. If you didn't keep yourself clean, you got walloped. I was to find out the importance of this when I served on the *Ark Royal*, later on. Anyway, Tommo took me under his wing and I soon learned the ropes. It was a rough place, down in the stoke-hold, and it wasn't long before I got into a fight with another stoker. I can't even remember what the argument was all about, but they were a short-tempered crew and it didn't take much to spark off a row. I was lucky to have Tommo on my side, but nobody totally looks after you in the Navy, so I still had to learn how to look after myself. I grew up in the Navy – I was a boy going in, but I was a man coming out.

HMS *Pickle* went down to Portsmouth for repairs first, before going to sea. Repairing a ship throws the compass off; even if you put three rivets in a bulkhead, it'll offset some bloody thing. So, when the work was done, we had to steam round and round in the Solent till I nearly got dizzy from the circling. This was to get the compass right and, once it was reset, we sailed up to Invergordon, in the Cromarty Firth on the west coast of Scotland. When we got up there, Tommo told me to get my wash-bucket and take it across to the dockyard canteen and fill it with beer – which I did. The two of us took it down to the stoke-hold and kept dipping our glasses into the bucket until I got so drunk I couldn't see for several hours. But Tommo kept drinking until all the beer was gone. And that's how I learned to be a heavy boozer.

In the Navy.

My first real voyage was across the Norwegian Sea to Tromsø in Norway, over 200 miles north of the Arctic Circle. The weather was rough going over and I was sick as a spaniel and spewed yards from the afterdeck, with my legs wobbling like jelly and my guts as green as my gullet. I was alright after we got to Tromsø and, from there, we traversed up and down the fjords in lovely calm waters – all the way round northern Norway, through the Arctic Ocean to Vardo in the Barents Sea. Our mission was supposed to be fishery protection, but we were really keeping an eye on what the Russians were getting up to.

And it was as cold as a gamekeeper's heart, even down in the stoke-hold. Now, some people would think it would be nice and warm down there, but we was over the Arctic Circle, remember, and it was freezing because there were big fans all the time blowing on the furnaces. And the minesweeper was only a little ship, so it was rough again every time we came down a fjord and went back out into open sea. But I survived.

On the way out of Tromsø, we passed the island of Hakoya, where the *Tirpitz*, the biggest battleship built in Germany during the Second World War, was sunk by Lancaster bombers dropping Tallboy bombs on her in 1944. We sailed close to where she was being broken up by a joint Norwegian and German salvage operation and it was something to see, for a country lad like me.

You might be saying this has nothing to do with poaching, but the Norwegian fjords are very deep, so we could sail close to the land as we went up and down them. I noticed that the areas beyond the shoreline were covered with birch and pine forests and, I thought to myself, there must be plenty of game in there, just waiting to be trapped. And there was – mountain hares and willow grouse and moose and all sorts of other animals.

Now, the grub on board ship weren't much to get giddy about, so I thought if I could only get over there I could bag a few birds and we could have a treat for once. So when we anchored off the island of Seiland I decided to do a bit of poaching. We promised the watch we'd bring something back for him and lowered a lifeboat in the middle of the night and me and Tommo rowed across to the island. I'd already made some wire snares and we took bits of bacon and porridge oats as bait, hoping to catch some game during the course of the night-time.

Seiland is mostly uninhabited, apart from a few remote areas, and I might have known my way round the English West Country, but I didn't know my way round this place. I decided, not knowing the terrain and where the animals run, it might be better to set the snares near water. So we searched till we found a small stream and, once the wires were in place, we moved away downwind to wait. Tommo had a bottle of Norwegian *hjemme-brent*, which is a local moonshine made from potatoes and sugar and is said to be strong enough to stun a moose. And that don't surprise me, seeing as back then Norway was said to have one of the highest rates of alcoholism in the world. We drank it to keep out the cold while we were waiting and, sometime later, I heard a sound like I ain't never heard before. It was a soft howling, not like a dog, but more like a yodelling coyote – low and muted.

We made our unsteady way back to the traps but, instead of finding a mountain hare or a big grouse, like I expected, we found a beaver caught up in one of the wires. It looked like an old animal and I soon put it out of its pain and gutted it there on the spot. By now, it's time to be getting back to the ship, but the *hjemmebrent* had really kicked in and we were both disorientated. We stumbled about for a while in the darkness with the dead beaver, before collapsing into a stupefied coma.

The captain of HMS *Pickle* sent out a search party the next morning and they found us still snoring close to the boat we'd rowed ashore the night before. We were taken back and given two days in the brig. I gave the beaver to one of the men who came after us and told him to make sure it got to the cook in the mess hall. When I got out, I went along to see if there was any of it left. And there was – the whole thing. None of the sailors would skin it and the captain told the cook to keep it for me and make me eat it as a punishment. They all gathered round to watch, thinking I'd be sick, like I was on the voyage through the Norwegian Sea. I skinned the animal myself and threw it into a pot and boiled it for a while. Then I cut it up and fried it in a pan. It tasted a bit like beef to me, maybe a bit stronger and more sinewy. But it was as good as anything else I'd eaten on board the HMS *Pickle*. I cured the pelt with salt and made a hat out of it, with the tail hanging down the back of my neck, and they called me 'Beaver Bob' after that. I had that hat until I went aboard the *Ark Royal* and some thieving bugger stole it.

Once we got round to Vardo in the Barents Sea, we was given some shore leave. Now, there was nothing much to do in Vardo, but it did have the northernmost illegal boozer in the world – so where do you think we went? It was just a wooden shack, really, and the choice of drinks was very limited. It was mostly stuff called akvavit and it tasted like petrol. We was drinking this akvavit for a couple of hours when an Eskimo came in. He started giving it the big 'un about how he'd been six hundred miles over the polar ice cap with his reindeer and how he'd hunted sea-lions and bears and narwhales on the way. I was very drunk by then, so I called him a liar. He turned to me with a serious scowl on his scarred face.

'Who call me liar?'

'I did.'

With that, he had me by the neck and a hunting knife up to my throat.

'You be dead if you not just a boy.'

'I'm a better hunter than you.'

Tommo and some of the other sailors stood up and the Eskimo put me down. He laughed.

'We see.'

He drank with us and, during the course of the session, I must've agreed to go out hunting with him the next day, even though I couldn't remember doing any such thing.

We slept on the floor of the hut and, as it's winter time and mostly dark, it's difficult to tell whether it's day or night. The Eskimo wakes me after a few hours.

'We hunt.'

'Where?'

'Mainland.'

We goes across a stretch of water between the island of Vardoya and the Varanger Peninsula in a boat called an *umiak*, made out of driftwood and waterproofed with seal oil. We paddle it, one of us either side, in the twilight of the northern winter and with him at the bow. He has an old over/under combo-gun, which combines a .22mag rifle barrel on the bottom, with a 12-bore shotgun barrel on the top, and I has nothing but a knife.

We tether the boat when we gets across and starts to trek inland. The country's flat, without much cover, and I can't see how we're going to bag anything. The sun's scarce at this time of year when, suddenly, we puts up a brace of grouse. The Eskimo's a crack shot and he brings down both birds with his hybrid gun. We trek on, with me carrying the grouse, and the terrain becoming more marshy, with trees now and brown gorse, and I catch glimpses of animals in the distance – reindeer and wolverine and arctic fox, along with all kinds of birds, many of which I ain't never seen before and can't identify.

The Eskimo gives me the gun to test me out and I shoot an arctic goose. But the sound of that shot attracts the attention of some men across a stretch of water. They start to shout and wave their fists at us.

'What's up with them?'

'Better to go now.'

'Are they gamekeepers?'

'What is gamekeeper?'

He starts to jog back in the direction we came from. I jog after him, carrying the dead birds. I find out later that some species on the peninsula, like arctic fox, are protected because they're being hunted to extinction for their pelts. I also find out there's territorial rivalry between some Inuit tribes and the Sami. So the people who are shouting at us might be some kind of rangers or other native types. I never get to know for sure.

Anyway, we're running back towards the boat but, just before we gets to it, we disturb a brown bear that's feeding on a reindeer carcass. Well, this animal's a good eight feet tall when it stands up on its hind legs and growls at us. The Eskimo unslings his gun and takes aim, but it jams when he pulls the trigger. The bear's about fifty feet away and begins coming towards us. The Eskimo backs away. Slowly. I follow him, walking backwards and keeping my eyes on the bear at all times. We're close to the boat when the bear starts its run towards us. It's moving fast and can easily outstrip us. The Eskimo turns and flees at full pelt. I throw the dead birds at the bear and run after him. The bear stops to sniff the birds and that's enough time for us to jump into the *umiak* and paddle as fast as we can, out into the stretch of the Barents Sea between the peninsula and the island of Vardoya.

We laughed about it when we got back to the hut and drank a few glasses of akvavit – we were laughing with relief, not because we thought it was funny. But the Eskimo didn't brag about hunting musk ox and walrus and moose no more, because I saw the way he ran when the big bear came after us.

We stayed up in Norway on the HMS *Pickle* for quite a while and I had my sea legs by the time we sailed back over the Norwegian Sea. On the way back, we came across a trawler with fresh cod and the officers wanted some. So I was sent with a few other sailors to get the fish. We had to row across to the trawler and the cod was all frozen when they threw it down to us. It was like concrete blocks landing in the water and we had to fish 'em in with nets and take 'em back to the *Pickle*.

When we finally got back to Portsmouth, I found out my mother had died. She had an abscess up her nose and the doctor dropped the scalpel when he was lancing it. This caused an infection, which spread to her brain. She had to have her head cut in half and her eyes taken out for them to get at the damage they done to her. She went through a terrible time and then she died. I was about eighteen. They gave me leave to visit her grave and I thought about not coming back. But they'd only have come and got me and threw me in the brig again.

In September 1957, Operation Strikeback was happening off the coast of Norway and I was transferred to the *Ark Royal*, an Audacious-class aircraft carrier. Strikeback was a major NATO naval exercise to simulate an all-out Soviet attack. It involved two hundred warships and six hundred aircraft and seventy-five thousand men from America and Britain and Canada and Europe. It was the largest peacetime operation and the most ships assembled together since the Second World War. But we were struck with an epidemic of Asian flu and some men died because of contagion. The messes were converted into emergency isolation wards and ventilation systems turned on at full power. We also had to go onto the flight deck for physical exercises every day because the officers and medics believed this would keep the lurgy at bay. I managed to escape infection because I slept on the upper deck on a camp bed, instead of going below, and because of the keeping clean routine I learned the hard way early on. The epidemic had run its course by the end of the operation and the *Ark Royal* was sent on patrol in the Mediterranean.

While serving in the Mediterranean, I got to visit places like Naples and Genoa and Rimini and Capri and Malta, and I remember going to see an active volcano on an island called Stromboli, off the north coast of Sicily. There was a group of us, including this big queer able-seaman called Arthur. After watching the lava eruption for a few minutes, Arthur turned to the rest of us and said, 'I've seen brighter lights in a stoker's eyes.'

And I wasn't all that impressed either – or with any of the places I went. I longed for the fields and woods of south Gloucestershire and the hunting and poaching, which was the only life I really wanted to know. I realised then that joining the Navy was a mistake, but I was in now and couldn't get out. I was put on canteen duty in the Med and one of my jobs was to take all the accumulated rubbish across to the shipyard when we docked. The bin was heavy and I got fed up lugging it back and forth, so one day I just threw the lot overboard into the sea, bin and all. I got charged with losing one of Her Majesty's bins and was fined £2/10s. But I was getting into trouble all the time for fighting and not being properly turned out and the Navy was losing its patience with me.

After the *Ark Royal*, I got transferred to HMS *Belfast*, a light cruiser in the reserve fleet. It could do 30 knots and, when it fired a broadside, it went right over in the water and we got thrown about like rag dolls if we didn't hang on to something. But the food was good, better than any other boat I'd been on. She was due to go on a tour of the Far East in 1959 and I fancied having a go at hunting water buffalo in Borneo and sambar in Ceylon, before they became endangered species. The thing is, I just couldn't behave myself and I was transferred off the *Belfast* before she went on tour and was sent aboard HMS *Jutland*, a battle-class destroyer, searching for unexploded mines round the Channel Islands.

Sometimes bombs got washed up on the beaches and we had to go and investigate. On one particular day, the ship was running slowly and we were being lowered in a motorboat. I was on the engine, under the canopy, because I was a stoker. But the shackles didn't slip properly and we all got tipped into the water. I came up from under in a bubble and grabbed on to a floating diesel can. The rest of them, a midshipman and a load of able-seamen, were all round one lifebelt. An officer was screaming at us from the deck, 'Don't panic, men! Don't panic!'

We all got hauled back aboard eventually and I went straight up to the officer and smacked him on the jaw.

'No one was panicking except you, you bloody idiot!'

I got three months in the brig for that, and it wasn't long after I got out when I came offshore drunk and being abusive. So this same officer got them to put me in a straitjacket and hung me from the deckhead on an eyebolt and I was twisting round and round and round all night. Next morning they let me down and I had to sit on a coil of rope for half an hour to get my bearings, before going up some stairs to the upper deck. Well, the officer who had me hung up was coming behind me and I turned round and kicked him in the mouth and knocked all his teeth out. They put me in the spud locker for a few hours, before taking me to the captain. I said it was an accident, but I got forty days in pompey, in solitary confinement, and I had to pick oakum from big pieces of rope. They used the oakum to caulk the planks on the upper decks and sealed it with pitch. Anyway, they got fed up with me on the *Jutland* and I was transferred to HMS *Rothesay*, a frigate, which took me over to Gibraltar.

I was ashore in Gib on my birthday and everyone was giving me rum. I was drinking heavy by then and wanted to get to the bars in town quick from the dockyard. So I stole a motorbike and was speeding along when I ran into a naval lorry and got thrown into the air. I wasn't wearing a crash helmet and I suffered multiple injuries, including a fractured skull and a broken arm, and I was messed up fairly bad. I came to in a military hospital and I was in a hell of a state – all plastered and strapped up. After a while, a military doctor came to see me.

'Have you ever thought about your drinking, Tovey?'

'Yes, sir, it's all I thinks about.'

'We pumped a washbowl full of rum out of your stomach.'

'Waste of time drinking that, then.'

I was in a rehabilitation centre for a year, where they gave me electric shocks to the deltoid muscle to keep it alive and, while I was there, there was an inspection by the brass. I was told to sit to attention in a chair at the end of the bed, with back straight and eyes forward. I was having none of that. The RSM came over, screaming at me to sit up and poking me in the ribs with his fancy stick. I grabbed it and broke it in two and threw it at him.

'If you do that again, I'll shove your stick up your arse sideways!' I cheeked him.

He growled away and I thought I'd be in for it. But he never came back and nobody said nothing about it.

When I was well enough, I was flown back in handcuffs on a Vickers Viscount aeroplane to a naval prison in England. There was me and another stoker on the plane and an officer in charge of us.

'If I remove the handcuffs, you won't try to escape, will you?'

What a clobhead – we're thirty thousand feet in the air, going at three hundred miles an hour, without a parachute between us. What did he expect we'd do, try to hijack the plane? We landed for some reason at Biarritz and us two prisoners made a run for it when the doors opened. But we were grabbed by a couple of armed Gendarmes and thrown back onto the plane. At Gatwick, we were handed over to an officer called Commander De'Ath. He scowled at us.

'My name is De'Ath. Remove the comma and that's what will happen to you if there's any messing about.'

It was the spring of 1960 and I'd just turned twenty-two. I remember Princess Margaret got married at the time, and they took us first to Notting Hill in London, where I was put in a police holding cell, before sending me down to Portsmouth naval prison. I had to strip naked when I went into Portsmouth and shave off all my body hair. Then I was de-loused with DDT powder, which is banned now. My bed was three wooden planks and a hollowed-out piece of wood for a pillow. I had a metal piss-pot that I had to use for shaving as well – washed out and shined with brick dust and soap. Breakfast was half a cup of tea and two hardtack biscuits; dinner was bread and gruel and, in the evening, we had more gruel with the other half of the cup of tea from breakfast time. They put bromide in the tea to stop us getting frisky and we had to go round an assault course every day.

Everything was done on the run – you double-timed outside and they threw a cigarette at you and you had to catch it. A marine would hold a taper and you had to jump up to get a light off it while you were running round and you had two minutes to smoke it on the double. It was a hard place, but it got me fit again after the accident. I was like a whippet with a big head when I finally come out of there.

But I still couldn't do what I was told. A short while after getting out of Portsmouth, I hit a mouthy officer and, when he went down on the deck, I pissed on him and I was given sixty days in Dorchester Prison. Dorchester was civvy jail and a doddle after Portsmouth. They put me on an outside working party and I was chopping up trees near Chantmarle Police Training Centre in Dorset. One of the trainees was a bloke I served with on the *Jutland*. He saw me and came over.

'What are you doing here, Bob?'

'I'm doing time, what d'you think!'

He told me to volunteer to clean the toilets at the centre, which I did, and every morning he'd leave a flat bottle of rum and twenty cigarettes on top of a cistern. I'd get the rum down me quick and I wouldn't care about anything after that for the rest of the dibby day.

Once I did my time in Dorchester, I was dishonourably discharged from the Navy. I'd already sold my uniform because I knew I wouldn't need it no more. They kept me on the mess deck before the dismissal ceremony and the sailors were giving me rum there. I was drunk when they marched me onto the upper deck of the *Rothesay* in bare feet and overalls with marines each aside of me, and I can't even remember the captain reading the discharge order. But I was out!

I'll always be glad I joined the Navy, because it made me hard and world-wise after being an only child and I got to go to places I never would have seen otherwise. But I'm also glad I got kicked out.

Bob, second left, as a 16-year-old boy sailor

4

Bob – The Poacher

My grandfather was a big man, round the middle. Not the same grandfather who went down on HMS *Monmouth*, the other 'un. He used to drive a dray for the Arnold Perrett Brewery and he needed three horses to get it up over the steep village hill from the brewery at the bottom. The dray was always piled high with big barrels that he could lift on his own, because he was a very strong man as well as being burly. Once over the hill, he'd let one of the horses go off the chains and it would find its own way back down to the brewery – then he'd be gone for days, delivering to all the pubs for miles around. He got free beer at every stop and he could drink a great quantity of pints.

One day he was going up a steep incline called Anchor Hill and another drayman was coming down. They crashed into each other, with barrels rolling everywhere and horses neighing and rearing in the shafts and the two men cursing and blaming each other. More than likely they was both pissed. My grandfather had to go to court and the magistrate said, 'Were you drunk, Tovey?'

'Impossible, your worship. I'd only had two gallons.'

So, you see, I didn't lick it up off the ground – the drinking.

I married Violet Mayer in 1962 in a register office in Plymouth, while I was still in the Navy. She was pregnant when she came back to my village with me after I got thrown out and we went to live with my father at his butcher shop. My son Brian was born in 1963 and my daughter June was born in 1965. Violet and me was constantly rowing and the marriage didn't work out. She took off in 1969 and, when she went, I was left to bring up two young children on my own. I was a hard-drinking man in them days, having learned how to booze in the Navy. I could drink twenty pints of ale in a single sitting – or standing at the bar for that matter. Then I'd have a fight in the street with some idiot who looked at me crooked. There didn't have to be no reason for me to fight; it could come over anything – a remark, or a laugh, or a cough. Or nothing at all. I broke a bloke's jaw once who'd spilled my beer and never said sorry. It's not something I'm proud of now, but it was the way I was back then. Sometimes I'd drink so much I couldn't see and I'd turn into a different man with the alcohol inside me. My eyes would turn cold and hard like marbles and I didn't know what I was doing, even though I thought I did.

I was hard on the kids back then, too, shouting at them when I was drunk and smashing up the furniture and drinking all the money. One of the men I drank with hung hisself at the end of the garden – he had the shakes and the tremens and was in a bad state. And I might have ended up like that myself, if I hadn't met Cora.

Now you'd think, being that violent, I'd have been put away – and some of the times I deserved to be put away. But, whenever

I was had up, the police always helped me out and made sure I had a good solicitor. The reason being, the coppers round here back then all lived in new houses that was built specially for 'em and I nicked a lot of stuff whenever I got some work on the buildings to earn a bit of extra cash – slabs and paint and bricks and all that sort of thing. They were as partial to a bit of knocked-off gear as anyone else, the police. One copper said to me, 'If you carry on like this, Bob, we'll all be doing time.'

So they looked after me when I got hauled up for fighting and I never went down for none of it – or anything else for that matter. I used to drink with this big Irishman in a pub beside a coalyard and we'd nick the bags of coal when we came out drunk and then nick bags of potatoes from outside the green-grocer's up the road. And I was never done for nothing. But they didn't like me poaching, because that was taking from the gentry and couldn't be tolerated. It might lead to people thinking they was as good as the lords and ladies.

Even back then there were very few true poachers. Lots talked about poaching but never done it. There was plenty of 'em in the pubs, but you'd never come across them in the fields or the woods when you was out there of a night on your own. They was as full of shit as a Christmas turkey! That's what really got my goat when I was drinking: people talking about shooting this and trapping that and netting the other. I'd got past the stage of talking about it long ago and actually went out and done it – and kept on doing it. Mostly what I loved was shooting the pheasants and that's the thing the lords hated me most for – taking their game birds. I'd take hundreds and either eat 'em or sell 'em, and it was my way of sticking two fingers up at the powers that be – at the people who'd ruled the land for centuries.

By taking their pheasants I was showing them I couldn't be controlled like the rest of the knee-benders. I was a law unto myself – part of my own little kinship, expecting nothing from the outside world and acting on the spur of the moment instead of making pathetic plans. Spitting on authority, with its coppers and courthouses and awful bloody conceit. And everyone knew me for my swagger and classed me by my contrariness – and me all the time playing my small part in the black bartering of a hostile society, but keeping well apart from it.

There was many ways to poach what I needed. I used to snare rabbits and set traps for pheasants as well as shoot 'em back in them days, using corn as bait for the traps. I'd use a little bit of corn on the outside and a lot on the inside. But the foxes and badgers round this area would take the rabbits out of the snare wires, and the trouble with traps is you has to go check them every day and that makes it easy for someone to see you and set an ambush for you. Another way I used to get pheasants at night, if I didn't want to make a noise, was with a long stick with a wire snare fixed to the end of it and plenty of baler twine. I'd slowly reach up and put the loop over the bird's head and tug on the twine. I also used clap nets to catch birds. You lay a trail of corn for bait that leads into the clap net – which is a spring-loaded net that can vary in size. The net's kept in a furled position and when the bird follows the feed into it, I pull on a draw cord that releases the spring and the net gets thrown over the bird. All that was OK, but by far the best way was always with the .410 shotgun. Job done. No messing about. A lot of other ways is only fit for tall tales in the pub. But if you wants birds, lead's the best way.

Poaching was essential to life for me back then – me with a family to rear and never having much money to do it with. I remember once when I was broke – no money and no food and only four cartridges – I went out with my dog into a small wood. A pheasant got up and I shot it with one cartridge. Then the dog put a rabbit out of a hedge and I shot that with my second cartridge. I shot a wood pigeon with the third cartridge and a hare with the fourth. Four cartridges, four meals. But there's two sides to poaching: there's the sheer necessity of it for a man like me, to eat, to survive. Then there's the love of it, the sport of it, the beauty of it. It's a man alone, in hostile territory, with a dog or a gun – a man agin' the elements, agin' the keepers, agin' the law. Can't you feel it? The rawness of it, the adrenaline pumping, the heart beating. The sound of a twig snapping, the hoot of an owl, the flap of a wing. There's nothing like it in the whole world. It's a true kind of freedom, to be doing what's in your nature to do since the dawn of time.

It was always inside me, from the day I was born – the shadowy tradition of the poaching game. It was something I understood, following after the old woodsmen, slipping along the path of their profession. I felt it touch my heart; watched it claim me as its own. Until it was all I knew or wanted to know. From snaring and trapping to shooting and hunting with the dogs. I reigned over my crooked little kingdom like a cock pheasant – crowing out from the saddle of a hill, colours flaunting and feathers flaring and a closed fist shaking at the scowling world around me.

But the toffs didn't give up their game easy. In the 1960s, the gamekeepers could give you a hiding and confiscate your gun if they caught you and they'd not be done for assault or anything because they had the police and the judges and the courts on their side. So I had to be nifty on my feet to keep out of their clutches. I'd roam all over the land with my gun and dogs, and the long poacher's coat with deep pockets to stash whatever I bagged.

Brian started coming poaching with me from the age of four. He was expelled from every school he went to because the teachers weren't able to control him. They said he was 'feral', whatever that means, and I was always having the truant officer coming round.

'Where's Brian today?'

'You tell me.'

'I've never met people like you Toveys.'

'I'm glad to hear that.'

'How did *you* get educated, Bob?'

'Reading the Bible!'

But he was alright, the truant officer. There was nothing he could do, and he knew it. Brian had no interest in lessons and he'd be sent out to help the groundsmen, because he was a disruptive influence in the classroom. I could understand that; I hated school myself and never had no time for book-learning, even though I did get educated. I learned what I really needed to know out in the fields and the woods. I learned how to survive outside the system. I went to work on building sites when I needed to, if I wanted a bit of quick cash for something special. But I jacked it in as soon as I had enough money to get whatever I was after. It was a means to an end, not an end in itself, like it is with most people. Most people are slaves to their jobs and bosses, making millions and billions for them who does nothing to deserve it. I was never going to fall into that trap after I got kicked out of the Navy. I'd had enough of authority by then and was determined to live a free life, accountable to no man nor master. If Brian wanted to do the same, I'd have been a hypocrite to try and stop him.

I think I already told you that I always used a long poacher's coat with deep pockets, until one day the postman came by while I was plucking a pheasant outside on the step.

'How much do you want for the bird, Bob?'

'I'll swap you for your postbag.'

He took out all the letters and we swapped over. Ever since then I've used postbags for stuffing game in – they're even better than the long pockets in a poacher's coat. Country people ate game and wild animals back then, rather than go to the shops. I was a supplier of that food and I traded it for whatever I could. There was a gunmaker who used to take game for cartridges; a coal man who'd take a bit of venison for a bag of anthracite; the man in the petrol station liked a goose every now and then, and you could always get a few free pints in the pub for a brace of rabbits or a widgeon or two. It was like in the old days of the barter – as good a system as any in the country-side.

Like I said, lots of people talked about poaching, but never done it; they'd catch plenty in the pub when they was full of beer. But the police knew who could do it and who couldn't. Back in them days, if your name was Tovey, you was constantly being harassed and questioned by gamekeepers and landowners and stopped in the lanes if you had a dog with you. I was the most notorious poacher in south Gloucestershire. Even the local vicar badmouthed me behind my back and said I would rustle and steal anything that moved – take the whites from your eyes and pop back for the pupils. But I never gave a fiddler's feck what none of them thought. They was all happy to come looking for a pheasant or two at Christmas to put on their yuletide tables. I kept myself to myself and never mixed nor socialised with none of 'em – the ones who thought they was above the likes of me. I had a few mates who were ordinary men and who weren't members of the stinkless-shit club, but the rest I kept well clear of and wished that they'd keep well clear of me.

I remember once being out shooting rabbits with a mate called Clifford. Clifford had shooting rights on a piece of land from the farmer. So, when this man came up shouting at us, I told him to 'piss off'. What I didn't know was, the farmer had died and this bigmouth was now in charge. Well, me and Clifford ended up before the magistrates, charged with taking game. Of course, rabbits ain't game, they're 'coneys' – classed as vermin. So the charge was wrong and, once Clifford pointed this out, the case would've been kicked out on a point of law. As Clifford had the original shooting rights, it was up to him to do the talking. I nudged him forward and he pointed out the prob- lem. The prosecutor turned round and smiled at him and said, 'Sorry about that, do you mind if we carry on?'

Clifford should have said, 'Not bloody likely!' But, instead, the idiot said, 'Carry on, sir. It's perfectly alright.'

The prosecutor changed the charge; we got fined ten pounds and Clifford was lucky I didn't kill him outside the courthouse. But it just goes to show the deference with which these legal people were treated by blokes like Clifford. Not by me. They all had arses they farted through and that meant they was no dif- ferent to me, so why should I think they were?

After the court, I goes out into the fields to relax with the greyhound. It's drifting into evening when I comes upon some old Gypsies with lurchers who're looking for a hare or two. We puts a few up and I gives my dog a run agin' their dogs and the greyhound comes best every time. I was never a betting man, but the Gypsies are, and a bit of money is made and lost in the long-shadowed fields, with always an ear open for the game-keepers and farmers and estate workers who don't know how to live like us and begrudge us our freedom from the land-owner's whip.

In the later hours, we sits by the sheltered edge of a field and one of the Gypsies cooks up a hedgehog, which they calls a *hotchi*. He kills the animal first and cuts it off at the top of its head and slices right the way around to its tail. He then puts his fingers slightly in underneath the belly and keeps pulling until the spiky skin comes away. He leaves the feet on because, he says, he likes it that way – although you can snip 'em off if you prefers. He rolls the animal up in a ball with good clay, digs a shallow hole with plenty of dead leaf and tends a little fire on top. And while the *hotchi* cooks away and moths flicker in the flame-glow, the sparks from the embers drift up into the night air like fireflies.

And they say the meat's very good for the baldness.

I'm easy on the way home, with the stars winking down at me and the taste of hedgehog still in my mouth and the low growl of their voices fading away across the stillness. The Gypsies talked of learning new ways and reading and writing and how asking a traveller to spell the words of his language is like asking a stone to speak. And how it's getting harder and harder to get a touch these days and a story about this woman who had a house but had to get planning permission to park a trailer on her own land, simply because she was a Gypsy. And the farmers can give them twenty-eight days to move on if they're working on the land for 'em, but no longer – and how the Children's Act could sometimes prevent evictions but not always. And then they're gone, like ghosts in the gloom, as I looks up at the infinite sky and thanks my lucky stars.

For the life I leads.

Bob's grandfather, the drayman, seated with apron, outside The Lion pub in Yate, 1919

5

Brian – The Panther

My name is Brian Tovey and I'm a poacher. I was born on 4 October 1963, but I don't know much about my mother because she left home when I was six years of age. I have very few memories of her, apart from the rows with my father and a lot of shouting and screaming and that sort of shenanigans. Me and my sister June were brought up by my father, Bob and, because he was a poacher, I became a poacher too. To me, poaching means more than killing wild animals for food; it's an inclusive way of life that incorporates conservation and a dislike, bordering on hatred, of the ruling elite and their cap-tippers. Just like in Bob's time before me, once my name was Tovey and I was seen with a greyhound or a gun, I'd be constantly stopped and harassed by farmers and keepers and lords and earls. I was known for trespassing and not giving a flying fart about anything or anybody.

You may think Bob's influence made me what I am today, and that might be true to some extent. But I've always had my own free will and could've found something else to do if I'd wanted to – tried a training course in reality television, or become a mugger or a murderer and sold my story to the tabloids. But who's to say what's a safe bet in these days of media manipulation and misinformation and every silly bugger buying lottery tickets in a futile attempt to join the echelons of the upper classes.

I was about ten when a friend of my father's bought some farmland from the Earl of Ducie. The land was beside the earl's Tortworth Estate and the farmer gave us permission to shoot and hunt and lamp and do whatever we liked on his land. Now, there's no pheasants to speak of on the farmland, so we set up some feed-bins hanging low in the trees to draw them in from the earl's neighbouring estate. We get these five-gallon drums and cut thin slits in the bottoms – maybe half-an-inch by four inches – and we cover the slits with metal gauze. Then we fill them with corn and tie them up to the trees and nutbushes. We lay a trail of corn from the edge of the estate to the feed-bins and the earl's pheasants all follow the trail and peck at the bottoms of the bins to get more corn out. Pheasants get clever during the shooting season; they don't like getting driven over guns and shot at every week, so they spread out to the edges of the estates where they're warm and dry and think they're safe – and that's where we get them. They keep coming and coming all the time and Bob and me hide and he shoots them before it gets dark. Or, if he wants a sporting shot, he'll send in our spaniel to flush them up to flight.

This area of farmland, where me and Bob set up our feed-bins, has good cover that naturally draws game birds, and they soon learn that pecking at the bottoms or sides of the bins will release more corn for them. We have a steady supply of birds and Bob uses what he wants for our own little family and sells the rest or distributes them among those whose need is greatest. Now, the Earl of Ducie ain't taking too kindly to us having his birds like that. One day, me and Bob are out there shooting with the long coats that have the big pockets, and we're watching the pheasants feed from the corn bins and then flying back to their release pens, and we think we might just nip onto the estate and get a bit of other game and then nip quickly back to where we have permission if anyone hears the shots. You see, if they can't get us bang to rights actually trespassing, then they can't do anything to us. So me and Bob skips across the fields and fallow land and shoots a few rabbits and we're laughing at the sport we're having and the game we're taking at the earl's expense.

Anyway, Ducie and his gamekeepers are hiding down by the local quarry and they see us getting the rabbits. Ducie goes off to get the police while the gamekeepers come after us. But by now we're back where we have permission. We have four pheasants and a few rabbits in the coats when the keepers start bawling at us. We can see them coming about fifty yards away and normally we'd be off running and they probably wouldn't catch us. But this time it's different. I drop the game where it can't be seen in the long grass and we stand and wait for them.

'Come with us!'

'Where?'

'The earl is on his way with the police.'

Bob winks at me and we say nothing, but go with them towards the quarry, where Earl Ducie has arrived with the coppers. The earl always has a loaded double-barrelled 12-bore shotgun with him. Always. And he gets away with it because of who he is. A big smirk comes all across his aristocratic puss. He thinks he has us.

'Got you at last!'

Bob faces up to him.

'Break your gun.'

He hesitates for a second or two, not used to being spoken to in that tone, but he does what he's told. Then the coppers step in and take Bob's gun.

'Been poaching, have we?'

'No.'

'What's this, then?'

They search our long coats and find nothing, but the keepers have a dog with them and it sniffs out the game I dropped in the grass. Ducie's nearly doing a double-jig he's so pleased with himself.

'What about these, then?'

'We has permission to shoot here.'

'From who?'

'The farmer. Go get him and he'll tell you.'

The grin on Ducie's face turns to a growl. He orders the police to hold us while he and one of his keepers go to find the farmer. When they come back, the earl's fuming and his well-fed chops are as purple as a peacock's bum. He's shouting at the farmer.

'You'll never buy land from me again!'

But they have to let us go and the coppers ain't too well pleased for having their time wasted like that. And Bob has a big grin on his face and he asks the earl if he'd like one of the rabbits for his tea. But this is the game between us poachers and the gentry – it's one up for us and one over on them. And it's what the sweet sketch of life's all about – getting one over on them who think they run the world, along with their gamekeeper bullies. Nobody owns the animals and birds that run free over this land, and Bob says we have as much right to hunt them as any other man or boy.

Later that night we go over onto the earl's Tortworth Estate again – lamping this time – and we're moving quietly through some fields of maize towards a wood called The Withybeds, because it's full of withy trees. There's been a lot of rain lately, so the maize is too wet to be harvested and we have to go through it to get to the wood, where we know there are pheasants roosting. The earl takes a great interest in the management of his estate, particularly his woodlands, and spends a lot of money on game preservation. Anti-poaching laws are rigorously enforced and, more often than not, the magistrate you're facing is the very man whose land you're hunting. But, the stricter the penalties for poaching, the more determined we are to outwit them and the cleverer us poachers become.

We've come out on bicycles tonight, not in the car, with the gun tied to the crossbar. Bikes are quieter than cars and easy to hide in a ditch or hedge. Every place that's keepered well is looking for a parked-up motor someplace suspicious and that's when you get clobbered. But if the gamekeepers find the bikes, they'll either wait for us to come back or slash the tyres – which is something we'd do if we found bicycles or cars belonging to other poachers who came into our area. If we get other people coming onto land around here, it can make it worse for us. For instance, if we've taken pheasants out of a wood, we'll leave it alone for a while and let it quieten down. If you got other people poaching there as well, they may be careless and leave drops –

feathers on the ground where the birds dropped – so the keepers are watching, watching, watching the whole time. And our worst enemies are the bum-lickers who'll ring the police on us when we're out of a night – people who're frightened to do it themselves and begrudge us doing it, who ain't afraid. Legal shooters will do it too, who have the money to pay for a bit of shooting. They might get one or two birds in a season where they can legally shoot, but we go anywhere we want and get hundreds of birds in a season. They'll grass us up if they see us. Jealous spineless buggers. That's why I hate them all, just like Bob does – cap-tippers and shit-kickers and saddle-bumpers and lords and ladies and bishops and big wigs and ponces that are no good for getting off their bums, except to scratch them.

I'm still a boy and Bob's teaching me the ways of the poacher – like how to avoid traps set by the keepers. Things like a line stretched across a ride with fish-hooks hanging every eighteen inches, to tangle you up or catch you in the face – or a camouflaged pitfall, or a thick branch crossing a marshy ditch sawn most of the way through. But Bob knows the land better than any gamekeeper and we can leap across and avoid such traps and the chasers sometimes forget about them and get caught themselves. And we laugh while we're making our easy getaway. It's always been a battle like that, for as long as some people have owned land and others haven't. Sometimes a battle of wits, and sometimes life or death. The estates of Beaufort and Berkeley and Tortworth all border each other and they used to unite to protect each other's game. In the nineteenth century, people went poaching in big groups for protection and the keepers were always mob-handed as well. Labour was cheap, so a landowner could have ten or twenty keepers, compared to one or two now, and it was very violent, with people getting clubbed and stabbed and shot. Bob tells me stories sometimes, that he's heard from his father and his father's heard from his father before him, going back into the dim and distant past, about men being hanged in the courtyard of Berkeley Castle just for poaching a few rabbits.

One such tale comes into my young mind now, as we move through the dark night, and it gives me a strange sense of foreboding, because it happened on the very land we're walking. The year is 1816 and a poacher is killed by a forester's spring-gun in these woods, then belonging to Lord Ducie, the present earl's great-grandfather. A spring-gun's another man-trap – a shotgun rigged to fire when a string is tripped that 'springs' the trigger, so that anyone stumbling over it discharges the gun. The killing angers other poachers in the area so much that a group of them come up here to confront a gang of foresters belonging to Lord Ducie and Colonel Berkeley. In the fight that follows, an assistant keeper's shot dead and five others are badly injured. The poachers have their faces blackened, so nobody can recognise them, but that don't stop the head keeper from saying he knew one of them to be a young man called John Allen. The coroner issues a verdict of wilful murder against all the poachers who were in the woods that night, but no such verdict against the forester who set the spring-gun. Colonel Berkeley and some of his men go to John Allen's house and arrest him. Allen gives himself up without a fight, saying he's innocent of any crime, but the colonel strikes him to the ground with a cudgel.

During the days that follow fifteen men are rounded up to be sent for trial, even though no one can identify any of them for sure. Four of them manage to escape – two to America, one to the West Indies, and one to Ireland. The trial of the other eleven is held at the Lent Assizes in Gloucester and lasts three days. The prisoners are all found guilty, even though there's no hard evidence against any of them. John Allen and another man called John Penny are hanged at Gloucester Gaol and the other nine transported for life to Van Diemen's Land in one of the harshest parts of Australia. Most people at the time believe this to be a grave miscarriage of justice, but Colonel Berkeley and Lord Ducie don't care much about that – the colonel even has a painting made, showing the 'heroic' foresters clashing with the 'evil' poachers, and he hangs it in the breakfast room at Berkeley Castle. Some of the men convicted are young, almost as young as I am now, but neither the law nor the lords care about such things. A poacher's neither a boy nor a man – he's just a dirty poacher. As far as I know, John Allen's buried in the churchyard of the village of Stone, near the Little Avon River.

Thoughts like this come crossing my mind and I know the earl will be hopping mad for us getting one over on him earlier. So if he or his men come upon us, it'll go hard on us and we'll most likely be laid up in hospital for a few days. And there'll be no point bringing charges for assault because the village police have nothing better to do than to arrest us poachers and bring us in front of the magistrates. So, if we get caught and beat up, which is likely because Bob has a temper and won't back down from no man, if we complain about it we'll get charged with poaching and brought to court and the keepers will get off scot-free and the police will get a pat on the back and a nice warm feeling that they've done something to please the lord.

We're carrying two postbags apiece, one over each shoulder. Bob gets them from the postman for a couple of rabbits. They're canvas-made and big and deep and as good as the deep pockets in a poacher's coat. And you can hide them easy if you have to make a run for it. As we come out of the fields of maize and make our way into the woods, I hear an unusual sound, like a deep meowing – a sound like a feral cat makes, only more of a growl – hollow, low-pitched. I touch Bob's shoulder and whisper.

'Did you hear that?'

'Aye.'

'What is it?'

'Don't know.'

We move forward quietly, to where the pheasants are roosting. They're up in some blackthorn bushes and Bob shines his small torch up there. That's all he needs. A powerful lamp's like a searchlight in the sky and can be seen for miles, so all he needs is this small torch to find them. We have no dog with us tonight and, when he shoots a bird, I have to retrieve it from the bushes. I got to be careful and not get ripped and torn by the thorns and not to cry out if I do. The .410's a small shotgun and only makes a little noise, not like a 12-bore or a big 10-bore used for wild-fowling, so we're hoping we won't be heard until we have our bag and are away. I've already been out here before it got dark, finding where the birds are roosting. I marked the spots with scrunched-up bits of paper – something a gamekeeper won't notice as a marker. Now Bob knows the trees and bushes the pheasants are in and he can shoot them quick and be away before anyone's the wiser.

I'm retrieving the birds, but it's dark and I run straight into a blackberry bush and get tangled up in it. Bob puts down the gun and helps me out by cutting the bushes away with his knife. It's another lesson I've learned: to be careful and not be too quick to rush in. The four postbags are full with about two-dozen pheasant and it's time to make our way back to the bicycles. Woods are different in the dark than they are during the day; it's easy to get disorientated and lose your way. But Bob's an excellent poacher and he has a great sense of direction, just like an animal, and he's always able to find his way home. I follow close behind him and we come out of the trees and back into the field of maize, close to a small pond. There's something about this night – something eerie. It's unnaturally quiet. Normally the nocturnal noises would be all around us: the hoot of an owl, the bark of a fox, the churr of a badger, the night-time call of a sedge warbler, the clicking and buzzing of insects. But tonight there's nothing in the maize field. And I don't like it.

We move forward, slowly. Bob's cautious as well, although he says nothing. I can feel his apprehension, the way his eyes are watchful. There may be a gamekeeper lying in wait, or several gamekeepers, who'll attack us and beat us to the ground. So we proceed carefully, stealthily, surrounded by the silent maize field. Suddenly there's the sound again – growling, guttural. It's a most unusual sound, not like anything I've ever heard before. The pond has thorn trees round it and we take cover there. Bob crouches and signals for me to do the same. I whisper to him, almost inaudibly.

'Fox?'

'That ain't no fox.'

Bob starts to squeak the animal in, if it is an animal, making a sound like a dying rabbit. We wait. Something's moving towards us through the uncut maize. Bob squeaks it closer. And closer. We only have the little single-shot .410, with a two-inch cartridge, which is alright for the pheasants but not for anything bigger. When it's almost upon us, he shines his torch into its eyes – eyes that are big and round, shining back. But it's not a fox; it's a black panther, as big as an Alsatian dog! It frightens the wits out of us and we take out to run, through the maize and out into a ploughed field. We're both wearing hob-nailers and the ploughed earth's thick on the bottoms of the boots, making it hard to move fast.

After some distance of running, I look over my shoulder, but the panther ain't following us. We slow down, breathing heavily; the postbags full of pheasants weighing like lead from our shoulders. Bob speaks through his fast, steamy breath.

'It must've got just as big a fright as us.'

'I expect so.'

'Fancy coming through a field of maize, thinking you're going to find an injured rabbit.'

'And instead . . .'

'Instead you find two poachers who jump up shouting and waving their arms.'

We both laugh and look round to get our bearings. We've run away from the bikes instead of towards them and now we must make our way back. But we don't believe the panther will come near us again.

We have to get back to the bikes by a roundabout way, as running from the panther has taken us off course. Bob's in front and I'm behind him. Suddenly he's not there any more and I wonder what's happened to him. Then I see some bubbles on the ground and water churning and gurgling. He's gone down in a trap dug by the keepers, water up to his chin. The postbags have filled up and they're dragging him down further. He can't get the straps from around his neck. I throw off my own postbags and go to help him, firstly by shoving over a broken tree branch for him to hold on to. Then I take out my knife and cut the straps to his postbags, so they sink down into the water and Bob's able to haul himself out, with my help. We've lost half our pheasants, but at least he ain't drowned. It's cold and we need to get back to the bikes quickly and be away, which we do.

Now, I've always held a dislike for cats, big or small, feral or tame. They're a useless animal. They kill just for the sake of it — skylark chicks, when they're coming out of the long grass, feathered, before they can fly properly and are lying out in the short grass getting the sun on them. That's when the cats will have them. I soon put paid to that by shooting them with Bob's gun and chucking them in a ditch where a fox will find them and eat them. A lot of townie people who've moved into the village have cats and they might not appreciate me killing their little moggies, but I hate the things; they're horrible buggers, killing just for fun, not out of necessity, and I'll shoot them any chance I get. Sometimes I catch them in cage traps that I've set for a fox or a badger. If that happens, I'll kill them and chuck them in the ditch, so it looks like they've been hit by a car.

There's several other sightings of the big black panther in the area after that and Mrs Cox, a farmer's wife, is overheard saying to her son, 'I hope you don't think I'm mad, but I seen a wildcat going across the fields.'

'A wild cat?'

'No, a wildcat.'

And there's scratches on a fowl-house door that looks like they were made with six-inch nails, with such force that they move the fowl-house two or three feet along. There's quite a few acres of maize round The Withybeds, so it's safe in there, the panther. Probably has a lair, living on rabbits or muntjac; maybe escaped from a wildlife park or released by some idiot who keeps such an animal as a pet.

After the maize gets cut, the panther disappears and is never seen again.

Young Brian with white-fronted geese, shot 25 December 1981 on the Dumbles at Slimbridge

6

Brian – The Early Years

When I was born we lived in the butcher shop with my grandfather. My grandmother died a long time before and I never really knew my mother's parents. I was four years old when we moved to our own house, where we live now, and that's when my earliest memories begin. I used to go back up to the butcher shop a lot back then and I found my grandfather dead up there one day in 1968, when I was very young. He was sixty-nine and he'd had a heart attack or stroke or something and just fell over. I found him lying there, but he didn't look dead and I could hear him in my head, giving out his advice, like he used to.

'Never compromise with none of the buggers, young Brian, because they're all only in it for themselves and they'll disappoint you in the end.' And saying how the world was full of unscrupulous shysters and political poltroons and sinister shadowmen.

I was but a boy and really didn't understand what he was saying, nor what was wrong with him now. I ran back down the road to get Bob but sometimes I think I should have said something to him. A few final words, like, 'Hello, why did you have to go?' Or, 'Goodbye, why did you have to die?'

I was brought up poaching from when I could walk and I just wanted to be out across the fields and in the woods with Bob, hunting day and night. And that's where it begins for me, when I'm four years old and we're on a right-of-way footpath with greyhounds and we're approached by two policemen – a sergeant and a constable. We're on public land, so there's nothing they can do us for, but they like to harass us every chance they get. You see, the coppers just want to wait by roads or pathways. They don't really want to be out there in the first place, and they don't like getting their boots dirty running across mucky fields after poachers they won't be able to catch. They want to get back to the warm station and have a cup of tea. Anyway, Bob sees them coming and he whispers to me, 'Tell 'em to piss off.'

The sergeant's trying to look all stern and official-like.

'What have you two been doing?'

'Piss off!'

They laugh at a four-year-old like me saying something like that to them. But if Bob said it they'd probably haul him in to the station on some pretext or other and let him out of the cells later, after wasting his time for a few hours. There's nothing they can do to me, so they let us on our way. I told them to 'piss off' many times after that.

I remember once in those days when I was young, maybe about four or five, I saw this woman pushing an old man in an invalid chair. She was struggling a bit, so I went up and asked her if she wanted some help. Her name was Mrs Rocket and she was the sister-in-law of Archibald Vowden, a local vicar and the man in the chair. She gave me a few pennies for my trouble and we'd go for walks on a regular basis after that and I used to push the old vicar around in his wheelchair.

This was to save me from a long stretch in prison later in life. But after my mother left when I was six, Bob's dislike of all authority was handed down to me.

He was a very violent man with the drink in him, a chronic alcoholic, and he'd come home lathered on a Sunday and there'd be trouble if his dinner wasn't on the table. Or, if the fire wasn't to his liking he'd smash up the furniture and burn it. If I wasn't out of bed quick enough in the morning I'd have to walk the fifteen miles down to Bradley Stoke, where he rented kennels and looked after about a hundred greyhounds for people who ran them on independent tracks. He charged £3 a week for looking after a dog and it was my job to clean out the kennels. If I wasn't up in time, he'd drive off and make me walk. I'd have no grub in me and I'd be nicking apples off the trees on the way.

Bob made me work hard all my young life and he made my brother Robert work hard too, when he came along in 1973. If we were weeding the garden and he looked out the window and saw us taking a break, he be roaring down at us and threatening us with the belt. He was generally a nasty violent individual back then, always shouting and screaming at us, but it wouldn't be right to say I hated him – it wasn't like that. The drunkenness and violence were normal for me when I was a boy. I knew no other life, so I couldn't say I did or didn't like my father then. It was a sad illness he had and I don't hold it against him now. I don't judge him and he never judged me neither. A father–son friendship is a peculiar sort of thing – we have our name in common and the tradition of our trade. Who could ask for more? And he was man enough to change and stop drinking altogether and he was my big hero when we were out across the fields and the woods together.

The rest don't matter.

The village was at its lowest population ever when I was a young boy, maybe less than eight hundred people all around – there's over two thousand now. The school was small with not many children in it: only three boys and five girls in my class. But, to me, the whole purpose of school was to get me sitting up straight with my arms folded and my mouth shut. I believed they were just training me to be servile and do what I was told later on. I saw school as a place where I had to learn discipline and not much else, and where they hit me with a stick, or made me wear a dunce's hat, or tied me to a chair, or put me outside when it was snowing if I didn't conform. That wasn't for me. The teachers were part of the establishment Bob hated, so I hated them too. They were the same as the lords and judges and police and farmers and were good for nothing but to grind me down. I didn't see the point in learning what they were trying to teach me, so I didn't learn it.

'We're doing English today.'

'Not me.'

'You have to.'

'No, I don't.'

Every time they asked me a question, I answered with another question. They didn't know how to deal with that. If I'd hit them or kicked them, it would've been a different matter and they could've hit or kicked me back, or called the police. But I didn't – it was passive resistance. I wanted to do what I wanted to do, not what they wanted me to do, so they put me in a room on my own to stop this kind of anarchy from spreading to the other children.

Outside school I was always up to some mischief. Bob had a

pony and trap when I was young. He kept the horse in a field and after school I'd ride it bareback all round the place. I was a good horseman, even from a young age. I'd hack the horse round the village and across the cricket pitch, churning up the turf. The cricket club people were a bit toffee-nosed and they'd shout at me and wave their fists and threaten to call the police. But I'd just ride off and nobody could ever catch me.

I saw Bob drinking and fighting for the first eight or nine years of my life, but I never went down that road myself, even when I got older and grew to be a man. I could always take care of myself, mind you, but I was never gratuitously violent and I only ever used alcohol in moderation on social occasions. Drink was never my master, like it was with Bob. To me, heavy drinking like that's a criminal waste of time. All I was really interested in was dogs and ferrets and snares and lamps and guns – day and night. I never smoked neither and I was a fine fit runner and could outstrip any keeper I ever came across. But, even though I was never like him in a lot of respects, when I was young I could feel my father in my blood and, in my ears, the sound of him pounding through my veins, trying to get out and evaporate and fall like red rain on a West Country field.

He wasn't always drinking and, when he was sober, Bob taught me everything he knew about poaching – how to stretch a rabbit's neck to kill it, fast and easy. How to squeeze the piss out and how rabbits go off quick, so you have to gut them straight away, and how to leg them to carry on a stick. He told me things that weren't in any textbooks, about beasts and birds and how to understand the wildlife and know them like they were kin, their names and ways and how they lived – all sorts of things. Like, the red-legged partridge is sometimes known as the French partridge, to distinguish it from the grey English partridge – and he showed me how they jug on the ground in a circle, with their heads pointed outwards and, when they're disturbed, they prefer to run rather than fly. He taught me how to catch them by laying corn round a spring-loaded clap net and I'd bike thirty-five miles and back for a bit of poaching. I'd go anywhere – private estates and wetlands and marshes and farms and woods, and wherever there was a bird to be bagged or a rabbit to be caught or a duck or a goose or a small deer.

In the beginning, it was just going round the hedges and flushing out quatting rabbits and catching them with a greyhound. I'd never go the same way twice, in case anyone was watching me. I always went a different way. The rabbits would be quatting in a form and the greyhound would flush them and run after them and it was good sport. Or I'd wander round and nick the traps the gamekeepers had set for vermin like stoats and weasels and squirrels and suchlike. I'd take the traps and fox wires and snares for my own use. I didn't have any money to buy that kind of gear, so I'd steal the keepers' instead.

I was coursing hare up by the quarry on Tortworth Estate one day. I had two bitches that were very good; they caught eighteen out of eighteen hares on the trot over ten days, without missing one. They were so clever, if a hare was in a form, they could pick it straight out of the quat. Anyway, I'm up by the downs, near the quarry, and I go into a field off the road. I have the dogs running loose and they put up a hare and catch it and bring it back. Then they put up another and catch it. Next thing, this Land Rover pulls up on the road and Lord Ducie sticks his fat head out the window but, because he's on his own, he doesn't get out of the motor.

'What are you doing on my land?'

'Minding my own business.'

'Give me those hares.'

'Piss off!'

'I'll get the police.'

'Do whatever you want.'

He drives away.

I decide it's time to leave, so I go up a farm track and hide the hares in a barn. I hang them up high, in case a fox comes round. About ten minutes later, I can see a police car going up and down the road, below at the field where I've been coursing the bitches. Up and down, up and down. They can't see me. I'm up on the brow of a hill under a tree watching them. They come up to where I left the field, but they don't get out because they don't want to get their boots dirty. Then they drive away, down towards the village, and disappear.

Ducie knows me, but the coppers never come round the house. They know there's nothing they can do unless they catch me red-handed or Ducie has a witness or they have the hares, so they don't bother. I go back later when it's dark and collect the kill. When I get home I go out to the kennels at the back of the house to see to the dogs. I'm getting them fresh water when I see this snarling and a flurry of tails. I drop the bucket and go running across. I try to get through the pack and manage to see a big threadbare cat curled up in a ball of blood-sticky fur. The dogs have torn a leg off and are savaging what's left in a milling mass. I get them yelping away as best I can and into their kennels. The mangled thing on the gore-soaked ground tries to crawl away, but can't.

I kill it with a brick.

Bob had an old Austin A35 that had to be bump-started to get it going. I remember when I was about twelve, we met up with some others on a Sunday morning. One of them was Benny, the village idiot – his name wasn't really Benny, but we called him that after the character in the television series, *Crossroads*. Benny had been on the rough cider the night before and, when Bob reversed the car down The Butty, which was a narrow lane, it stalled. We all had to get out and push the car to start it again, but Benny farted and shat himself after being on the rough cider. It was a silent fart and we didn't know until we were all back in the car and driving down towards Arlingham to do a bit of hunting. All of a sudden, the car was filled with a terrible smell and we had to have the windows down and our heads hanging out so's not to get sick.

When we got to where we were going, the animals could smell Benny a mile off and we couldn't get near none of them. Bob made the dirty bugger wash his bum in a stream before we set off back to the village and the other men threw his trousers and underpants away. But Benny needed more than just a bum-wash to put him right. Cider was the medicine he said kept him sane in a sick society and able to function in this grunting hog of a world. A lot of local men drank the heavy brews like that, and I wonder if they knew the price they'd eventually have to pay for drowning their livers in scrumpy and flirting with an early death.

Another time I'm out with a dog and I bag a few hares. I'm on my way home and the farmer comes upon me and he's not too happy. Now, I'm still just a boy, but I'm tough and Bob's hard on me sometimes and he teaches me to fight as well as run. So, one word leads to another and the farmer takes a swipe at me. But I duck under it and belt him in the belly. He grabs hold of me and throws me against a fence-post and follows up with his fist, but I'm out of the way quick and he smacks his knuckles against the wood. While he's howling, I send a left into his kidneys and a right into his gut again. He doubles over and I take off as fast as I can. I can hear him shouting after me.

'I'll get you, you bastard!'

'I know who my father is, do you?'

I got my first gun licence when I was about twelve. I had two shot-guns, a .410 and a 12-bore. You could walk down the street carrying a gun in those days and no one would take a blind bit of notice. Imagine what would happen if you did that now! Have the drones hovering overhead and a UN task force on its way, led by the Navy Seals. It was round the old bathing quarry on the Tortworth Estate where I shot my first rabbit. There was a burrow underneath some hazel bushes with always five or six or seven coneys out on an evening. It felt exciting – not a hundred yards from where Bob shot his first rabbit all those years before. But the best thing about it was, it was on the lands of Lord Moreton, Earl Ducie's son. When the earl was alive, his son was called 'lord', and when the earl died, his son inherited the title and was the new Earl of Ducie. And the land and its animals were handed down from father to son, with no con-sideration at all given to the impoverished peasantry.

Anyway, as you know by now, I was brought up anti-authority. I hated anyone in uniform, or who spoke with a plummy accent, or who had a title – farmers and joe-cockys and gamekeeper bullies and all that lot. I believed, like Bob, that I had a right to the plentiful game that abounded in the English coun-tryside back then; it belonged to everyone, not just the privileged few. So it was even sweeter to think I was taking something from the lords and earls as well as helping to feed the family.

One of the greatest pleasures in my young life was running away from them and telling them to 'piss off'. I even used to go onto the Earl of Ducie's estate and hide in cover and watch him and his keepers shooting rabbits. They'd shoot the coneys and hang them up in a tree and move on. As soon as they were out of sight, I'd nick the rabbits and be off. I would've loved to have stayed and seen their faces when they came back and found the rabbits gone, but that would've been too risky – they might have taken a shot or two at me.

Once I had my guns I rarely went anywhere without them. After the first coney up at the local quarry, I found this orchard where I knew there'd be some more rabbits. I crept through the hedge and shot a couple of them. Then I put the gun down and went to collect them when the bedroom window goes up and this big fat face peers out wearing one of those old-fashioned nightcaps.

'Drop them rabbits!'

I put my fingers up at the man and shouted back at him.

'Piss off!'

Then I grabbed the gun and ran back through the hedge and away. I was to learn later, going through life, how to be invisible – not to be seen if at all possible – that a poacher must be like a ghost; you know he's been there but you can never see him. But a lot of the fun of it when I was young was being able to run off and knowing none of the buggers could catch me. I was fit and fast and I loved the laughing sport of it.

I'd pushbike out and around the streams in April, searching for duck nests and taking the ducklings with a homemade landing net. I'd box them up and take them home and put them in pens. Then I'd fatten them up and sell them. We had a big flock of ducks in our garden at home – two hundred Aylesburys. We'd drive them down to the fields to graze and waddle in the pond-water and the neighbours were always complaining about the quacking as we passed along the way. But we didn't care; it wasn't much to moan about, compared to every day some new story about the total lack of morals among the rich and powerful. So why take it all out on our ducks?

As well as the ducklings, I'd go stealing pheasant eggs in summer and put them under broody bantam hens. A broody hen will sit on anything, even a smooth stone. They'd hatch out the pheasant eggs and then I'd bring them on and we either ate them or sold them to local people or game dealers. You could get £2.50 for a pheasant back then and you could sell as many as you could catch or rear, and more besides. Of course, the estate managers didn't like me stealing their eggs and I could get into big trouble if I got caught. They came after me once and I made it onto a public highway where they couldn't touch me, but the keeper knew I had the eggs in my pocket.

'Alright, Tovey, you've outsmarted us.'

Then he smacked the pocket with his hand and smashed the eggs, rather than give me the satisfaction of having them. He went on his way, smirking, and I said, under my breath –

'Next time, I'll take twice as many.'

I'd take the red-legged partridge with a spring-loaded clap net, like Bob taught me to, and I'd fish and go lamping the pheasants at night. Now, there's two kinds of lamping, so don't get confused: for pheasants you just need a small torch to shine up in the trees, and a gun; for rabbits and hares, you need a lamp with a strong beam that mesmerises them for greyhounds to chase and catch them. It was a life of wildness, of ferrets and fenn traps and guns and greyhounds and foxes and pheasants – and cotton-ball clouds scudding on a summer sky and the sleeting rain blowing horizontal into my face in the wind-wailing winter. It was new life in spring and old life in autumn and I was always keeping clear of the world around me, that was trying all the time to catch me or con me in one way or another. Like, when this farmer called Jack Fleming used to get me setting traps for rats in his cow barns. I caught loads of vermin for him but he was a mean bugger and never wanted to pay me. He'd go missing when it was time to shell out and I'd have to traipse round looking for him.

Anyway, there weren't always collared doves in this part of the world, but when they came in, I started going round the lanes shooting them. It was illegal to shoot them, even though it was legal to shoot pigeons, but they were lovely to eat and I couldn't resist them. This farmer Jack Fleming only reported me to the police because he owed me money for catching the rats for him and, I suppose, he thought if I got sent away to reform school, he wouldn't have to pay me. Local copper Harris came over and told me to stop shooting the doves, but I could tell he wasn't all that bothered about it and only did it because of the complaint.

Fleming was known for being a nosy hedge-mumper, sneaking round the lanes to see what people were up to and not minding his own business. So I carried on shooting and eating the doves and nothing was ever done about it. I never got my money from Fleming either and he died and left everything to Frenchay Hospital in Bristol. He had no wife nor children and he left nothing to his extended family – or to me. The miserly bugger! I hope he died roaring.

Now, heritage and history fade fast in the brainwashed minds of the masses, with the middle-classes living in their comfort and conceit and the others either side of them on the social ladder misled as well, convinced by popular opinion that hunting and poaching are cruel. But I'd try to make a clean kill whenever I went out, although it wasn't always possible. Once, when I was young and out in the winter time, I shot a pheasant and it dropped onto a frozen pond. It was flopping about on the ice like a drunken penguin, but there was no way I was going to go out there and push my luck too far, stretched as it usually was like the thin ice on this thawing pond, ready to crack at any moment and plunge me eyeballs-deep into all sorts of trouble. I was just about to shoot it again and put it out of its misery when it slid over to the edge of the pond and I was able to pick it up and bite into its brain to kill it immediately – like Bob showed me how. How cruel's that? Like throwing live lobsters into boiling water? Or a gavage stuck down a duck's gullet to produce paté? I suppose it's all a matter of perspective, ain't it?

So you can see I was a bit of a wild boy when I was growing up. I'd go through the village shooting the streetlights out sometimes, and I went round and shot all the balloons they hung up for the Queen's Silver Jubilee. And I'd nick the railway detonators from the huts. Railway detonators are coin-sized devices that make a loud bang as a warning signal to train drivers. They're used for a number of reasons – in dense fog, when signals are difficult to see, or if there's been an accident, or if there's engineering works ahead, or to alert crews working on the rails. They were invented in the 1800s by an Englishman called Edward Cowper. They had lead straps either side, to fix them to the railway lines and hold them in place, and they had gunpowder inside. Anyway, I'd pinch them from the huts when no one was looking and fix them to people's windows and door-handles and letterboxes, then I'd shoot them from about twenty yards away. BANG! They could break a windowpane or shatter a letterbox and the people in the houses would run out, thinking the IRA had invaded south Gloucestershire. Then they'd call the local coppers and I'd be chased round the village, but I was like a shadow and they never could catch me.

I got through primary school by the skin of my teeth, but I was eventually expelled from the first secondary school I went to and I got expelled from the second school after thirteen days. I went to a third in Thornbury, which was about ten miles away from where we lived, and they got fed up with me not attending lessons. But, instead of expelling me, they just sent me out to help the caretaker, mowing and cutting hedges and doing maintenance work in a school for the mentally handicapped, which was next door. That wasn't too bad, because I was out and about most of the time and I got on alright with the daft kids – they were unfortunate and I felt so sorry for them, never to have the freedom of the fields, like me. But I eventually got expelled from there too, for swearing at someone.

They couldn't get no good of me at any of those schools and it was agreed that it would be best for everybody if I stayed at home, but a teacher would be sent out to tutor me. That didn't work either. A woman came out on a Monday morning and the first thing she said to me was, 'I've come to teach you.'

'You can piss off!'

She gave up in despair after ten seconds flat. Finally they summoned me before the Council's Educational Welfare Board in Bristol. I went down there with Bob to see what the authorities were going to do with me. I was thirteen now and we sat at a big long table with eight other people. One of them started.

'The boy's got to—'

'The boy has a name!'

'Sorry, Mr Tovey. Brian's got to . . .'

. . . do this and do that and do the other. Bob listened patiently until the man was finished, then he spoke back.

'If someone told you to climb up the suspension bridge and jump off, you'd have the right to refuse, wouldn't you?'

'Of course.'

'Well, Brian's got the right to refuse to go to school.'

'No, he hasn't.'

Another one spoke up.

'The law says you have to send your child to school, Mr Tovey.'

'The law also says I can educate him myself.'

This caused a flurry of mumbling and grumbling and whispering and flapping. Rules were consulted and options aired and opinions expressed and, in the end, it was agreed that I could be self-taught, but someone would have to come and check on me every Monday to make sure I was studying and not getting into mischief. They sent an ex-policeman round to keep tabs on me, but he just had a cup of tea and a bit of cake or toast and a chat about what we'd been poaching, then went away again. He was just going through the motions and wasn't really bothered, because he knew it would get him nowhere.

This went on for a few years, until I was sixteen. But the only thing I self-educated myself in was poaching – rabbiting and lamping and ferreting and shooting and coursing. I push-biked round the countryside within a radius of thirty-five miles, with the .410 in the leg of some old army trousers, sewn up and tied to the crossbar of the bike with laces. When I wasn't poaching, I earned some extra pocket money doing seasonal work on the farms – potato- and stone-picking and hay-baling and a bit of labouring on the building sites for £3 a day.

And so, up and into my teenage years, I gallivanted round the countryside looking for game and having a good old time. Over the fields and hills, with the grass under my feet and the wild wind blowing the cobwebs of the street away and the whole world smiling. The smell of the meadows and the marshes and the woodland marjoram and the air around me as fresh as spring water. The keepers and lords and earls and teachers and coppers all tut-tutting and saying how I'd end up bad some day. But I didn't care: Finger wet, finger dry, cut my throat before I die.

And houses are alright, the didicoy said, but they have them terrible walls!

Brian with coursing dogs, circa 1987

7

Bob – The Enemy

I was doing a bit of hod-carrying on a building site in Yate when I met Cora. I was thirty-three by then and she was in her early thirties too. Her mother didn't like me much and wouldn't have me in the house, so I'd have to sit outside in the car while I was waiting for her. I can't say as I blame her mother, considering the state I used to get into back then – drinking in The New Inn and The Beaufort and The White Horse and The Railway and The Gate and every other pub for miles around besides. I'd drink anything: Cheltenham & Hereford beer or rough cider from the local factory at 4d a pint – stuff called 'stun 'em' and 'splash pan' and I could down twelve large whiskies one after the other without hardly drawing breath.

Cora's mother used to call Cora her 'little bit of trouble' and kicked up a fuss when she started going out with a bad lot like me, but that didn't stop Cora. I don't know what she seen in me – maybe it was the way some women is drawn to men who's mad, bad and dangerous to know – but, whatever it was, I'm glad she did, because she saved my life.

One day, her father Joe came out. I could see him approaching the gate and I thought he was going to try to clobber me or run me off or something.

'D'you want to come in for a cup of tea?'

'I dunno. I bin sat out here this bloody long . . .'

Then I thought, I better accept the offer, and I went in for the cuppa. There weren't much talking and the atmosphere was a bit strained and I was glad when Cora was finally ready and I could get out of there. We was going out for about a year when she fell pregnant with my son Robert, so we got married and she wore my mother's wedding ring and moved in with me and my two other children, Brian and June, who were eight and six at the time. Then Robert was born in 1973. After Cora's father died, I used to take her mother a pheasant or a rabbit and she started to take to me a bit better, but for some reason she never came to visit us in our house.

I'm still drinking heavy at the time, and fighting with them who gets too chopsy with me. Eventually, I gets barred out of every pub in the local area and I have to walk over to Charfield to get a drink. But Cora bears with me and she becomes mother to all my three children. And once she even comes out poaching with me. She's dressed in britches, with a coat and a bobble hat pulled down over her hair. I have my little Austin car and we go up onto the Earl of Ducie's estate. I shoot some pheasants and the dog catches a rabbit and we have a lot of fun. On the way back to the car, we're come upon by a land agent. I warn him away.

'Stay where you are.'

He thinks Cora's a man because of the low light and the way she's dressed and there's two poachers for him to deal with, so he stands back. When we gets to the car, old Ducie's there with the boot up, looking for poached game.

'Put that boot down!'

'Or what?'

'Or he'll belt you.'

I point to Cora when I say that. Just like the agent, Ducie thinks Cora's another male poacher and he don't like the odds of two-to-one, so he moves away while we get into the car and drive off home.

Well done to Cora!

But the drinking was getting the better of me and was making me ill. It was affecting my liver and kidneys and every other organ in my body. I'd never admit to no one I had a problem and, if I'd gone on the way I was going, I'd have been six foot under long before my time. And I'd have missed out on the best part of my life, seeing my boys grow up into the good men they are today and having the company of the woman I loves for so many happy years.

I got stopped in my tracks one day, when I was labouring on a building site in Charfield for a few bob to buy something or other. It was shortly after I married Cora and I'd had a big drinking session the night before and I felt terrible. This was unusual, because I had a big drinking session most nights and I was always alright the next day. But it was different this time. I lasted as long as I could on the site, but I was disorientated and, in the end, a mate had to take me home. But I kept on drinking, though not nearly as much. It was another two years or so before I gave it up completely – when I was nearly dead and we had no money in the house, because I drank it all.

It got to the stage where a few pints would put me in bed for a week with the shakes – not even the strength to sit up. I knew then if I didn't stop I'd soon be dead. I told Cora to pull back the carpet in the living room and lay newspapers on the bare brown tiles, then put a mattress on top of the newspapers and make a bed for me there. I knew what I had to do – what I had to go through to save my life. I lay there shaking and shivering and not knowing where I was and the sweat from my body soaked through the mattress and the newspapers underneath and turned the floor tiles white. I was in a terrible state altogether, with delirium tremens and the horrors and the shakes and barrel fever or anything else you likes to call it.

I was sick for a full year and couldn't leave the house and could easily have died, if I hadn't had Cora to take care of me. When I recovered I saw an advert in the local newspaper for Alcoholics Anonymous. Cora rang the number and a priest came round to see me. The next day he took me to an AA meeting. I was frightened to go, because I was still shaking and very weak, but I went, and admitted I was an alcoholic, and I've never had a drink since. It wasn't difficult to give up the boozing in the end, because I was so sick, and I never had a longing for alcohol in all the years since then. I owes it to my family to stay sober because without them I never would have made it, and I got no illusions about what would happen to me if I took a drink again now. I used to drive blokes round to the AA meetings after I seen the light, but only one of them stopped drinking for good.

That was me!

Drink loosens the tongue, and the most dangerous thing a man has is his tongue. It can get him into all sorts of trouble. It's best to keep quiet and stay out of arguments and just try to enjoy life. I love my wife and family above all else – the only thing that will make me angry these days is if there's a threat to them. I'm not very big, but there's some people who've found out the hard way not to underestimate me. I ain't proud of the things I did while I was hard-drinking. But what's done is done and can't ever be taken back and it's a sinful shame when I think back on how I used to be. But when I was sober, I built up the bond I has now between me and my family and that bond was strong enough to hold us together in the hard drunken times.

I ain't had a drink since 1974 and that's over forty years ago.

Giving up the drink was the best thing that ever happened to me. Life in the Tovey household gets calmer then, because I'm not coming home pissed every night. I get fit again and I has three greyhounds hunting in a pack close to a brook called the Little Avon, below where we live. I cross the water and let the greyhounds loose. I'm walking up a steep hill and the dogs is working the hedge as we move along it. Suddenly, all three of them's gone in there and I can't see 'em no more. I goes through after them and can spot them away in the middle of the next field. They're chasing a small roe deer and they bring it down about a hundred yards from me. I'm running as fast as I can to get to them and I haul them away from the kill and tie 'em up. I has no vehicle with me and it's too far to carry all the way home. So I guts the deer and puts it up in a tree to keep it away from foxes and other predators. I throws the pluck to the dogs and they makes short work of it. Soon the area's clean and it looks like nothing's happened.

That night, after it gets dark, I comes back and takes the deer down from the tree and I'm carrying it back to the car, about half a mile away. I'm crossing an open field to the road when this keeper comes upon me. He's carrying a gun and he points it at me.

'You going to shoot me?'

'If I have to.'

'You ain't got the balls for that.'

I keeps walking towards the road. He knows once I get out there he's lost me. There's no mobile phones back then – he can go for help or call the coppers if he likes but, by the time he gets back, I'll be long gone. There's only one thing for it – if he can't shoot me, then he'll have to fight me and the winner takes the field. He throws down his gun and takes his jacket off and spars with the air. I throw down the deer and roll up my sleeves. I'm only a small man and this keeper's much bigger and he thinks he'll be able to get the better of me. But I've been fighting for seven years in the Navy and after that in pubs and on street corners and I'm no pushover.

We circle round, sizing each other up in the gloaming. He's the first to lunge, but I easily sidestep his right cross and land one on his jaw as he lumbers past. This makes him angry, and an angry fighter will always lose the bout. You got to stay calm and collected and wait for the right opening. He comes after me like a mad bull and I picks him off with stingers to the solar plexus and the kidneys and the small of the back, then dart out of danger before he can connect with a killing fist. I'm telling myself to keep out from him when, suddenly, he lands a lucky one on me. It's a big swinging swipe and it sends me staggering back, but I don't go over. He sees I'm dazed and senses blood and comes after me. Another brutal right to the side of my face sends me to the ground. He's standing over me and I wait for his boot to go in and finish the job. But this keeper must've learned the Marquis of Queensbury rules or something, because he don't try to do me on the ground – he stands back and waits to see if I'm going to get up. Big mistake. By the time I'm back on my feet, my head's cleared and I circle him like a snapping hound after an enraged bear. My fists is fast, flying into his sides and stomach and the big grunty begins to break down. He drops his guard to protect his hurting body and I launches a both-feet-in-the-air blow to his chin. He stands for a second like a statue, then he falls over like a felled tree onto his face. I picks up the deer and goes on my way.

It'll be the last time that keeper lets a poacher back up off the ground.

When I gets home, I hangs the deer in the lean-to and skins it. Then I joints it up and keeps some for the family. The rest I distributes around the village like always, selling to them who can afford it and giving away to them who can't. That's what my house is like, all the time – full of wild meat in the freezers and there's always something for them that likes a bit of game for their dinner and for them in need of a feed. Even so, like I said before, I still keeps myself to myself because I ain't never been one for the complicated issue, and was always only after the simplest of lives. But you gets caught up sometimes in things you can't control and can be blown along like smoke, no matter how hard you tries to avoid it.

I kept a lot of dogs at one time, along with a flock of geese and the two hundred Aylesbury ducks and fifty cockerels – twenty-five in the front garden and twenty-five in the back. We had big gardens and no money, but we had plenty of food. The toffee-noses in the village never liked the noise, thinking it lowered the value of their houses. And sometimes they was as bad as the lords and earls. But we wasn't next to or near any close neighbours and I didn't give a damn even if we was. I lived my own way and let others live their way. I never complained about nobody in the village and I couldn't explain why they would want to complain about me when I herded my fowls down the road to the fields where they grazed and grew fat. The council came out a couple of times and I said to them, 'Tell the Duke of Beaufort to get rid of his pack of hounds and I'll get rid of my dogs.'

'What?'

'Tell him to get rid of his pheasants and I'll get rid of my fowls.'

They had no answer to that. In the end they sent me a letter giving me permission to keep my menagerie and I retained my rights as a freeman of England.

Now, the Codrington family were slave-traders in the West Indies for hundreds of years and they made their money from slaves and sugar. From the middle of the eighteenth century, they preferred to live on their estates in Gloucestershire and left the management of the plantations to overseers. They were notorious authoritarians and, in 1786, Granville Sharp, a long-standing opponent of the slave trade, even wrote to the Archbishop of Canterbury about their ancestors. But we didn't worry much about their reputation and we poached their estate along with all the others, taking dozens of pheasants from them. There was always a big shoot up there and me and my boys went lamping one night near Christmas. We'd been rabbiting there before and seen how many pheasants they had, so we thought we'd take some off their hands. We got dropped off by a mate of mine and arranged with him to come back for us at a certain time. We shot eighty-one pheasants and had 'em all sacked up and got back to the meeting point forty minutes early.

The bloke who dropped us was late picking us up, because he

was scared of the Codringtons. He'd heard about their ruthless reputation and was probably afraid of being flogged with a horse-whip, even though they only did that to their slaves – when they was allowed to have slaves. We waited and waited and it was getting dangerous, because we could have been come upon at any minute. We heard the keepers patrolling and we hid ourselves and the guns and pheasants. In the meantime, our lift arrived and we was nowhere to be seen. He started calling for us: 'Bob! Brian! Robert!'

The keepers heard him and nabbed him and took him away, but they left the motor with the keys in it behind. We jumped in and took off as quick as we could.

He spent the night in the local police cells and went back for his car in the morning, but it was gone and he had to walk all the way to the village and arrived weeping and wailing. He was relieved when he found out we had the motor and he never got charged with anything. I said, 'That'll teach you to be on time.'

But he never dropped us off nowhere again. We lamped two hundred and forty pheasants from Codrington that Christmas, and another hundred and sixty from Tortworth, and sold 'em to butchers and postmen and villagers and even to the police. Everyone loves a pheasant at Christmas time. As far as I knows, the last of the Codringtons drives a taxi now and lives in a small cottage somewhere. James Dyson, who invented the bagless vacuum cleaners, bought the big estate.

Speaking of the Codringtons, I remember ferreting in Old Sodbury, which is near their land, with my two sons, Brian and Robert. Robert used to come out with us sometimes when he was younger, but now he likes to do things nice and legal like – he ain't what you might call a true poacher, like me and Brian. He also works now, at a regular job, so he don't do it full time, like us. He conforms to society more than us but that don't make him no less in my eyes. He's a strong man and he stays close to his family and never complains about anything we does and he don't compromise with the shysters and shadowmen.

Anyway, we're on a bank overlooking a church, with a bridle path at the bottom. We're after live rabbits to use for droppers and we'll sell 'em to people who wants to do a bit of drop-coursing for £5 apiece. We has eleven in hessian sacks when a couple of saddle-bumpers come along on hunting horses – a man and a woman. He shouts at us with a plummy accent.

'What are you doing?'

'Ferreting.'

'Ferreting?'

He says that like he don't know what it means.

'Aye! Can you be quiet!'

'I'm going to ride round my land and, when I come back, you'd better be gone.'

'Do whatever you want.'

We carry on and take no notice of the ponce. They ride round again and we can see a police car coming along the road, down near the church. Then another police car pulls up, then another, and another, and another, and another. Six police cars altogether park in a line down on the road, with the saddle-bumpers pointing up the bank towards us. I'm thinking we better do something here, so I let the rabbits go and we get the ferrets back out of the burrow and gather up the nets and sacks. The coppers climb up to the top of the bank and one of them speaks to me.

'We've had reports of someone ferreting.'

The rabbits is gone, so there ain't no evidence there, but we still has a couple of ferrets in a sack and the nets. More coppers come up, and one of them's a big mouthy clobhead – a bully, the type that would punch you in the bollocks in a police cell when he's backed up by his mates. He snarls at us.

'What you lot doing?'

'Piss off!'

Brian snarls back at him, then runs off with the ferrets and the nets. One of the coppers tries to stop him, but Robert puts his foot out and trips the twerp and he goes rolling down the bank.

'Oh, sorry.'

Now there's no evidence at all. But a police van's turned up, with a dog and handlers. The big copper grins all over his horrible chops.

'This is a bad dog. He'll catch that bastard and chew him up.'

I just grin back at him.

'Bet you a fiver he don't.'

Brian has a good head start and he runs and runs, with the dog and handlers after him – through a wood and across a main road and into a field with a load of sheep and cattle, in and out of 'em to lose the scent, and down into the valley. He runs for about five miles without stopping, carrying nets and sacks and ferrets.

Meanwhile, back at the bank, all the evidence is gone and some of the coppers is having a chummy chat with me and Robert. The local police know us well and one of them asks if he can come round and see our dogs, because we has about thirty of them at this time. 'Course, he's only pretending to be interested and all friendly, like, and he really wants to nose around and see what he can report to his sergeant.

'As long as you ain't in uniform.'

The dog couldn't catch Brian and the handlers brought it back and they let me and Robert go home. Brian always carried change for a phone box, in case he got come upon and chased for miles. So he went into the first public box he came to and called me and told me where he was. I went over and picked him and the ferrets up. We'd lost the rabbits, but we'd won the bet.

The mouthy copper never did pay me the fiver.

Bob with 'Wickwar Sharky', who won the Quainton Plate in 1985-6 season, Oxfordshire Coursing Club

8

Bob – Hare Coursing

Coursing a dog after a hare or a rabbit is a sport that's been around for hundreds of years in the countryside. Let me explain. There's spot coursing, which is a dog after a rabbit for a kill. Like, if I'm out poaching across the fields with my dog, I might not get a run all day. So, to keep the greyhound interested, I do a bit of spot coursing, especially around Christmas time when people would have a holiday and some time on their hands. That meant catching maybe forty or fifty rabbits with ferrets and keeping 'em alive. Then I'd go to a nice big field with my dogs and maybe a group of others would come with me. I'd drop a rabbit out of a sack on a spot and give it about fifty yards start before letting one of the dogs after it. The rabbit's out of its familiar runs and don't know where to go, so it's at a disadvantage and gets caught nearly every time.

This gives the dogs a kill and bloods 'em and they stays interested when I'm out hunting with 'em. It may sound cruel to them who knows no better – and I've seen some cruel bastards who'd burn a rabbit's eye out with a cigarette, or tie their back legs up to give their shit dogs a better chance – but I never engaged in cruelty of any kind and I has no truck with them who does. The rabbit's killed quickly, much quicker than it would be by that evil disease myxomatosis, introduced to cull the coneys by so-called 'humane' people.

But the rabbits are just a warm-up for the real thing: hare coursing. Hare coursing's banned now, of course, but there was a time when it was widespread. There was two kinds: being just out for a run and a bit of sport across the fields, and competition coursing, for trophies and prize money. Competition coursing started off as park coursing, which got banned eighty-odd years ago. A park course was held in a special field where hares was caught and kept in an enclosure. They were trained to run down the field to an escape at the other end. Two greyhounds would be slipped after each hare and the one that scored the most points before the hare escaped or got caught was the winner of the course. A lot of horse racing tracks started off as coursing parks for greyhounds – Haydock Park and Kempton Park and Sandown Park and others too, and you can still see where the dog courses was run in them places, if you looks closely enough.

Lord Lonsdale, who donated the original boxing belts and who was also known as The Yellow Earl, because he liked to wear that colour, had his own park course at Barleythorpe Hall in the East Midlands. They had an enclosure with a five-foot wall round it where the hares would be kept after being netted . They'd be local hares and put into the enclosure a couple of days before the course, which would be held on a nice long flat field. There was a chute in the wall that would be lifted and a hare driven out and they had their course – all nice and easy. The earl had first-class railway carriages to keep his dogs in and he was a man who had enormous wealth from the exploitation of the Cumberland coalminers and he devoted hisself to the outdoor life. But the likes of poachers never would have got a look in at something like that back then. We was classed as low-life, scurrilous characters – and you've seen how poachers is depicted in books and stories down through the years: sly scoundrels, slipping darkly along the lanes and in and out of crouched corners – evil outlaws, not to be trusted, who would skin a man as quick as an animal. Even though, in reality, we was nothing of the kind.

In any case, park coursing wasn't a proper countryside pastime like open coursing, which replaced it when it got banned. Open coursing didn't have penned hares and the animals had to be driven in onto the course. It needed a lot of ordinary people: beaters, flankers, slippers, judges, spectators and dog-owners. Beaters would take their flasks and their sandwiches and you were out in the clean air with the fields under your feet. Open coursing wasn't as exclusive as park coursing neither, even though the dogs that got run always belonged to the toffs, but it was a day out for everyone. Except for the hares, some people might say, but most of the hares escaped and many more died of disease caused by intensive farming methods and by shooting than was ever killed by coursing dogs. You might get as few as two hundred hares killed in a whole year's coursing – you'll get that many killed on the roads in a month. There was no cruelty involved, despite what people who never knew nothing about the sport might say.

Gradually all British coursing became open meetings, where hares native to the ground and knew where they were going were driven onto the course. The course was always in the shape of a horseshoe and beaters would drive the hares forward and flankers would keep 'em in. A slipper would have a brace of dogs on a double slip-lead behind a shy and, when a hare went by close to it, he'd give it a 150-yard lead, then slip the dogs. The dogs had to be clearly sighted on one hare or the slipper wouldn't let 'em go. Or if too much mud was accumulating on the hares' feet, so they couldn't run properly, the course was stopped. A judge on a horse would keep up with the course and award points to a dog every time he turned the hare – either white collar or red collar, to tell them apart. Four points was awarded for the first turn – one for the turn and three for speed, then one point for each turn after that and one point for a kill. The course would continue until the hare was either caught and killed by the dogs or it escaped. The dog with the most points at that stage won the course and went on to the next round.

But the sport was never about catching or killing the hare; it was about the working ability of the dogs. Some greyhounds would run clever to try to catch the hare, one in front to turn it back to the dog behind. But the hare's even cannier and could usually avoid these tricks and outsmart the dogs. A good strong hare could outrun two greyhounds any day and the ones who got killed were usually sick or old and would've died soon anyway – and much more slowly. Like I said, it was a great day out and attracted all sorts.

I even remember one time having my fortune told at a hare course by an old duckerer, as the Gypsies calls their crystal-gazers. He told me to sit while he looked at the palms of my hands. I tells him I don't believe in this stuff and he laughs at me.

'We all wants to believe, mister, even if we say we don't. We wants to see what's in the stars.'

I know Gypsies is superstitious, with their four-leaf clovers and rabbits' feet and horseshoes and their old sayings – like never argue in the morning and the hawthorn blow's for bad luck and better never to have been born, than cut your hair on a Sunday morn.

He asks for all the details about when and where I was born and he says them newspapers is all liars, they gives everyone born under a star sign the same horoscope. But Gypsy horoscopes needs dates and times and even places of birth. He says newspapers know nothing about astrology.

'Astrology, mister, was invented by three wise men, two shepherds and a Gypsy chal.'

And he knows things about my father being a butcher and my mother dying young and me being an only child and he says I'll live to be seventy-seven and never be filthy rich, but will sometimes be happy and frequently content. Which is all a man can reasonably ask for, ain't it? He tells me everyone has a good spirit and a bad spirit and life's only a dream and it really begins when you die – when your spirit leaves your body. And some people, like me, dreams in black and white and others in colour, and it's them who dreams in colour that's the prophets and the peacemakers. We talk afterwards and the old fortune-teller says he don't know his exact age, but it's in the region of ninety-nine, and his birth certificate's on a tree, somewhere in Spain. His words drift back to the old days, when he'd be away on the tramp as soon as the blossom came and the thrush began to sing. And how he buried his grandmother outside Budapest with her pipe and an ounce of baccy to see her on her way – and how, when she was young, the yawn of her voice in song had a culture all its own.

'I thinks about it, mister . . . at fresh of the morning and at balance of the day, I thinks about it.'

That was twenty-five years ago, when I was Brian's age now – and I'm still alive. I wonder if the old duckerer is. Anyways, before hare coursing got banned, people used to say to me, 'Why don't you muzzle the dogs and that would make hare coursing more humane.' In the first place, like I said, not many hares was caught by the dogs and them that were got killed quickly. If the dogs was wearing muzzles, they couldn't get a bite on the hare to kill it quickly, but the muzzle would crush it in their attempts to do so – the hare would be lying there with a broken back and its guts coming out of its earholes, and it would still be alive – is that more humane? It's just one example of people talking through their arses about something they knows nothing about. But, even with the open coursing, it was really a sport of the well-to-do, just like fox-hunting. Coursing clubs would turn down ordinary men who tried to join, calling them low-class or poachers or thieves or suchlike. When I first started going to hare coursing meetings under National Coursing Club rules, people wouldn't talk to me or my sons, even though we was long-netting for them. They tolerated us because we could get them the hares they wanted, but they wouldn't let us join their 'we're-better-than-you' clubs.

The Waterloo Cup was held at Great Altcar, near Liverpool, and this was the blue riband event in the coursing calendar. A three-day meeting with a sixty-four-dog stake and a purse run-off for first-round losers and a plate run-off for second-round losers. Over a hundred courses altogether. You needed a lot of hares for that because it's not just one hare for one course; you has to take into consideration the ones that gets out the flanks and doubles back and don't go through the course, and the ones the slipper thinks ain't right, and so on. For every hare that's actually coursed, there might be ten or twenty that gets driven, but not coursed. With television cameras there and sports writers and all sorts of gentry, it would have been an embarrassment if they ran out of hares halfway through – they'd look like right mugs altogether. Now, the Waterloo Cup wasn't supposed to use netted hares, unless they was local or had been relocated the season before – that's because newly relocated hares wouldn't have had time to settle into their new surrounding and would run all over the place and knacker the dogs that was unlucky enough to course one of 'em. But that's not the way it worked.

They couldn't keep a population of hares the size they wanted and they needed a couple of thousand hares to be put down every year beforehand, so they'd be sure to have enough for the whole competition. We netted hares at Newmarket for the meeting and them hares were taken to Great Altcar and we'd feed 'em on crushed oats and carrots and let 'em out as near as two nights before the Waterloo Cup was run. Sometimes we'd even go up there in Transit vans the night before, when there was nobody about, to avoid saboteurs who'd try to disrupt the event and because coursing laws stated that netted hares had to be released into the area six months before. Like I said, hares that weren't native didn't know where to go – if a dog got a big strong one, it'd go round and round and try to get back through the beaters and it'd take the dogs with it, so your chance of getting through to the next round was gone because your dog would be proper fagged out, if you see what I mean. Unlike a greyhound that got on a native hare and had a quick run, up the field and a few turns and out, like on a park course. It was a matter of luck if you got a good local hare that would give your dog a short chase or if you got a hare that was brought in from somewhere else.

Understand?

You also needed to be nominated to run a dog in the Waterloo Cup by one of the sixty-four nominators, who were all bloody freemasons and the like. We got a dog called 'Solo Concorde' in once because we netted the hares for them, but it had to go in under someone else's name, someone who was associated with the club, because they didn't want it known that the likes of us was allowed to run a dog in such an elite competition as the Waterloo Cup. And, even after getting the dog in, we wasn't treated fairly. You see, the slipper can favour one dog over the other – if he's got lord so-and-so's dog up agin' mine, he can twist my dog round so the lord's can get an advantage and be first to turn the hare and get four points. Or a short slip will favour a dog with early pace and a long slip will favour a bigger dog that takes a while to get into its stride.

Our dog was up agin' an Irish bitch in the first course and she was the third favourite to win the competition. But the course was flagged 'undecided' because the judge deemed that the Irish dog was unsighted and didn't see the hare. It was a Newmarket hare that ran and ran and ran for a mile and a half, back through the beaters, and our dog's tongue was round his bollocks and Brian had to get him out of a ditch. The Irish bitch was buggered too, but the masons was probably glad about that, her being third favourite for the cup, and they wouldn't want her winning any more than our dog. Being undecided, the course had to be re-run, and our dog won it the second time out. But he was knackered, and in the next course – agin' a dog that'd had one twenty-second run after a local hare and was fresh – he had no chance and was out! There was all sorts of dirty tricks to lessen an ordinary man's chances of winning anything – that's if he could get his dog in in the first place.

In the end I got fed up with the discrimination so I organised my own course – the Yeovil and Sherborne Coursing Club. I was secretary and Brian was a steward. We'd get permission from landowners to hold a meet on suitable ground and the course would be inspected to make sure it was safe and that the hares would get fair play. There's a lot of work involved in open coursing; you got to get the beats and the right conditions for slipping and keep dogs from fighting; it takes a long time. It's an all-day sport. The meet would start at about 9:00 a.m. and the first brace of dogs would be in the slips by 9:30 a.m. I released a lot of hares where we'd be coursing the following season, giving them time to settle into their new surroundings, so there was always plenty for the meets and they was easy to run out. We usually held eight-dog stakes, with four pairs of greyhounds. The winner of the first pair met the winner of the second pair in the semi-final and the two winners of those met in the final. That meant a dog had three runs in the day. Pickers-up would go out onto the field to retrieve the dogs after a course and, if the hare was caught, it was their duty to make sure the animal was dead.

Then it got banned in 2005 and that was the end of a way of life for many people in the countryside. There's nothing left of it now. A trainer friend of mine died recently and he left me a bronze hare – that's the only trophy I kept from the coursing days. All the silver cups from Yeovil and Sherborne were sold off at auction and the money divided among the few members left. Because it wasn't about cups and trophies, it was about being out with the dog – being equal partner with the dog – sensing its excitement, blood up, adrenaline flowing, quarry in sight. Whether it was dog agin' hare or dog agin' dog that was the joy of it, the sport of it, the meaning of what it was all about. If you don't understand that, you don't understand dogs. And even if it hadn't been made illegal there ain't enough people in the countryside left who knows what they're doing now, enough to be used as good beaters and flankers no more.

I has mixed feelings about hare coursing being banned. In one way, it provided a livelihood for many country people, not just us poachers and hare-netters, and it was a sight to behold – a little six- or seven-pound hare outsmarting two eighty-pound dogs, for the most part. In another way, when hares was brought in and not given enough time to settle in the area, two eighty-pound grey-hounds chasing a six- or seven-pound hare that don't know where it's going ain't really my idea of sport. One greyhound after a local hare or rabbit is fair and brilliant to watch for a man like me – just like one dog after a fox. I'm not saying it was right to ban hare coursing but, in the end, too many hares were being netted and put down too late – a week before the meeting or even the night before, like we was instructed to do by them who'd hired us.

One way or the other, we really got no say in whether this is banned or that's banned. They tell us we live in a democracy and they give us the impression we has a say but, in reality, we got no say in nothing. The decisions are already made. Half a million people marched through London protesting agin' the banning of hunting with dogs, but nobody took any notice of them. Everything has to be politically correct these days, and that correctness is put upon the many by the few who shouts the loudest. There was a time when you could go to the pub and stand your gun in the corner while you was having a pint. If you did that now the pub would be surrounded by an armed-response unit and somebody would get shot, not by your shotgun, but by some trigger-happy policeman.

As far as coursing's concerned, I don't give a damn about any ban. If I wants to go across a field and get a run after a hare, I'll do it! As for the banning of competition coursing, I can take it with a pinch of salt because there's nothing I can do about it – and it makes our drag track more popular.

But park coursing's still economic in Ireland where, like I explained, hares is kept in pens and trained to run up a field and use the escape at the end of it. They don't have the same class system over there and ordinary men can get a run for their dogs and the coursing's fairer. It's a big industry in Ireland and the government there is afraid to ban it. But English coursers like us can't afford to run our dogs over there – all the expense of getting across, only to get stitched up by the Irish, like they was often stitched up over here. And open coursing was always a better sport, even if it was controlled by the bloody freemasons!

It's gone now and it'll never be coming back. And I'm still out there, when I can be, running my dogs – in spite of all the laws.

Slipping greyhounds at Yeovil & Sherborne cousing meet, 1998

9

Brian – The Law

I read somewhere recently that several senior police officers are being questioned in connection with corruption in the force. Hard to believe! And the tabloids tell us there's a sharp increase in serious crime and all the prisons are full to overflowing, and they can't fit no more in. We'll have to build special camps to keep them corralled, penned in like the pheasants on the shooting estates. Or else send them over to one of the Central Asian 'Stans for rehabilitation, where they still use the old methods. And that's not accounting for the psychos at large on the city streets and in the government, and begging babies and multicultural misfits and and all sorts of unrecognisable others, leading to further strife on top of the established turmoil. Murders and molestations after dark – pimps and procurers and perverts of the very worst kind. You'd think the cops and courts would have enough to deal with, wouldn't you, without bothering with the likes of me and Bob?

I'm poaching over on Tortworth one night when I'm about fifteen. I leave my pushbike well hidden and make my way up to

some woods. I shoot a dozen or so rabbits on the way and gut
them and leg them and hang them in some nut bushes to collect
on the way back. The wood's small and there's a full moon and
it's easy to see the pheasants up in the trees. I start shooting them
with my bolt-action .410 shotgun and I stash them in the postbag I have over my left shoulder. I've already shot thirteen and
the bag's full and heavy. I shoot the fourteenth and it drops down
out of sight. I unbolt the gun and put another cartridge in before
going to retrieve the bird, then I hear some rustling in the bushes.
Maybe the bird ain't dead, I think, so I turn my torch on and
shine it in the direction of the sound. But it's not the pheasant;
there's a black Labrador standing there with the dead bird in its
mouth. I growl at it: 'You bugger, you got my pheasant!'

I put the gun up to shoot the dog, then I hear a shout:

'Stop where you are!'

It's the Earl of Ducie and his son, Lord Moreton.

'Bollocks!'

I turn to run – straight into a big thorn bush. I'm all scratched
to buggery round my face and arms and I can hear them coming
into the wood. It's not a very big wood and I get back out of the
bush and run round the side – not the way I came in, but onto
a ploughed field. I came in across meadows, but I'm forced now
to try and get away across the ploughed earth, carrying a gun
and thirteen pheasants in a bag down one side and wearing hob-
nailed boots. I switch the gun to my left hand for balance.
Luckily it's not real boggy plough and I run as fast as I can,
trying to get to the road. Ducie drives a Land Rover with no
lights down a track, trying to get in front of me, while Moreton
chases behind, but not gaining any ground.

I get to the road before the Land Rover, but I know I won't

be able to outrun it – and they can hear my boots clip-clopping on the tarmacked surface, so I have to find a hiding place soon. I come across the entrance to another field and see a cow trough, which is fairly full. I chuck the bag of pheasants under the trough and climb into the cold muddy water with the gun. I know if they come into the field, the dog'll sniff out the birds and I'll be caught, but it's my only option right now. The Land Rover pulls up at the gateway and Ducie looks out across the field, but can't see me nowhere. He waits for Moreton, who's coming on foot, to catch up. The dog's inside the motor.

'Where did the bastard go?'

'Down that way.'

Moreton gets into the Land Rover and they drive off down the road. I climb back out of the cow trough, dripping wet, and retrieve the pheasants. Then I go back to the woods because my pushbike's hidden in a ditch close to the road where I went in.

As I'm getting the pushbike out of its hiding place, a vehicle pulls up, lights blazing. I think it's the ponce-faces come back again.

'Are you alright?'

'Piss off!'

I jump onto the bike and pedal away for all I'm worth. A bit down the road I look back to see if they're following, but it ain't the earl and his son who's pulled up, it's an old bloke and a woman. They thought I'd been run off the road and only stopped to see if I needed help. And I smile and think to myself, maybe human nature has something to be said for it after all. I got pneumonia a few months later. I couldn't breathe and collapsed and passed out. My lungs filled up with fluid and there was no air getting into them. That's why pneumonia's called 'old man's friend', your lungs fill up and you die in your sleep. I was taken to hospital and given strong antibiotics and I was laid up for three weeks. I'm not saying the water trough gave me the pneumonia, but it might have.

There's a big stream near Damery, which is about halfway between Bristol and Gloucester and, two days later, I'm up there on my pushbike again on the way to Michaelwood, because I know there's a lot of game there. I'm above the stream now and I shoot two mallard ducks with the one shot. I retrieve them from the stream myself because the water's not that deep, maybe knee-high, and I hide them in a hedge to be collected on the way back, just like I did with the rabbits before. I get back on the bike and carry on another two miles to where Michaelwood's on the left and Furze Ground Wood's on the other side. Then I hide the bike and go off to shoot pheasants. Unbeknown to me, the keeper's driving round and sees a bit of the pushbike, because I never hid it well enough.

I come out of the wood with ten pheasants in my postman's bag, put the gun in its sleeve and tie it to the crossbar. I'm cycling down the lane when this Ford Escort van forces me off the road and into the ditch. I know it's keepers, so I get my gun out of the sleeve and run across the field with it and the pheasants, towards a barn. The police have already been called and I see them driving up to the barn, so I hide the gun and the birds. I got the coppers in front of me and the keepers behind, so I'm blocked off and I get nabbed.

Three coppers grab hold of me.

'What you up to?'

'Out for a run.'

'In Wellingtons?'

'Cross-country run.'

They have no sense of humour and the keepers' dog finds the gun and pheasants. I get taken to Dursley police station and they tell me to take my boots off before they lock me up. When I do, four cartridges fall out of one of my socks.

'You always take shotgun cartridges out for a run?'

'I stick them up my bum for a sprint finish.'

'How many more you got?'

Another two fall out of my other sock.

They give me a thorough search after that and lock me up to wait for my father because I'm still a juvenile. When they interview me, I tell them I was out shooting pigeons where I had permission and I was cycling around, knocking on farmers' doors to see if I could shoot some rabbits. I deny I shot the pheasants.

'I found them in the lane; must have been hit by a car.'

'All ten of them?'

'A lot of careless drivers in these parts . . .'

They let me go in the end, but bring me back a couple of days later and charge me with poaching, armed trespass and something else that I can't remember now. I go to see a solicitor, but can't get legal aid and, what I don't know at this stage, the same solicitor acts as the prosecutor in the magistrate's court and he doesn't tell me when I'm giving him the full story. As far as I'm concerned, it's a clear conflict of interests, but he never lets on and, when I go to court, there's the bugger prosecuting me – or else it was his twin bloody brother.

'I found the pheasants.'

'Why did you run, then?'

'Van forced me off the road. I thought they were criminals, going to abduct me.'

'The gun was with the birds and cartridges fell out of your socks.'

'Can you prove that gun or those cartridges killed the pheasants?'

'No.'

The armed trespass charge is adjourned *sine die*, but they find me guilty of poaching and I ask if this means I'm now a criminal.

'A petty criminal, MrTovey.'

So I says by that do they mean my crime was insignificant and, if so, will my sentence also be small? I'm fined £60 and £3.75 costs and the restitution of the pheasants. Nothing petty about that! They're all laughing behind their hands in the court and I think it's at the funny side of the solicitor I went to see being the prosecutor – as if I'm thick and don't know I should've appealed. Which I don't at that age. But I had no one to advise or defend me, so I had to take it on the chin. I was only young then and knew nothing about the law, so I promised myself I'd learn as much as I could about it as I moved along in life, so this kind of thing wouldn't happen to me again.

And I did – how the British conscientious classes are easily outraged over the rights of dumb animals, but collude in the real injustices of the world by watching subliminal shite on the television; and how social revenge can have a strange effect on the minds of some buggers and can turn perfectly respectable morons into salivating sadists – and how bumholes appearing as prosecution witnesses are full of their own sense of self-righteousness and couldn't care less about the principles of probity and fair play. Most of all, I learned that the best way to avoid all this bollocks was to not get caught.

Despite my new knowledge, I get jailed three times altogether for poaching and pinching. The first time comes in 1982, when I'm about eighteen, after I poach a fallow buck on the Berkeley Estate. I cycle out to the deer park where a lot of deer escape and there's always loads of them about. I go out there in the evening, with about half an hour of light remaining in the day – enough to stalk round the perimeter of the park and get a shot. Some fallow deer are coming out and I'm using a 12-bore with BB lead shot. I come up on this big albino buck and shoot him in the heart at twenty yards. I get up quickly and cut his throat and bleed him out and gut him, then I drag him behind some big fallen oak trees in the wood, so if anyone's out looking and hears the shot, they won't be able to see the dead deer.

Now, there's no way I can carry a big fallow buck like that home on my bicycle, so I get to a public phone box and call my mate, who has a car, and I ask him to come out and pick the deer up. While I'm waiting, a misty fog blows in from the River Severn. It comes in real fast and I can't see more than a few inches in front of me, it's that dense. My mate comes and we can't find the kill. We search around all over the place, but we're getting nowhere and we won't be able to see anyone coming upon us. We drive back home and I get old Jack, our spaniel, into the back of the car and take him out to find the deer before it's eaten by scavengers. We park up, come across the fields in the dark dense fog, and head into the oak trees that are hundreds of years old. The dog finds the deer straight away, within seconds – he was a great old dog, Jack – and I put the buck on my shoulders and carry him to the car.

There's a big tin shed on the playing fields in our village and I take the deer over there and hang it, cut its head off and skin it. Next day I joint it up and make £70 on the meat.

So I go up to Gloucester with my seventy quid and buy a new, powerful Weihrauch German air rifle, that's just on the limit of being legal, and I'm eager to try it out as soon as I can. Bob has an old Triumph car at the time and we leave it in a pub car park and make our way out onto the Tortworth Estate, where I shoot eight pheasants. I hide the birds and the gun close to the road, so's not to be come upon with them while we go back for the car. But some bum-licker has rung up Lord Moreton to say they've seen us out poaching in the woods – maybe seen the torch or something, or maybe it's just some nosy nobody who can't mind their own business and wants to suck up to the lord. When we drive back up the road to make the pickup, Moreton's there with my new gun and his dog's sniffed out the pheasants.

'That's my gun . . . and our birds!'

'They're my birds, you poached them.'

'Give me my gun back, you bugger!'

'I'm confiscating it.'

'Give me my gun!'

'No!'

He pulls an iron bar out of his jacket and waves it at me. So I pick up a brick and throw it at him. It hits him on the head and he falls to the ground, shouting at Bob in his posh accent:

'Mr Tovey, help me.'

I pick up my gun and the pheasants. Bob doesn't go near him.

'Would you help me if I was on the ground?'

He starts screaming for his keeper.

'Keepah! Keepah! Help me!'

This giant comes lumbering out of the night towards us.

'I'm coming, your grace!'

When he gets close enough, Bob sticks his foot out and trips him up and he goes over on top of his grace. We throw the birds into the car and make off, while they're trying to pick themselves up off the ground.

When we get home, we hide the pheasants, but the coppers ain't long in coming round and I'm arrested and taken to the station five miles away, where I'm searched, and they take my wellingtons and socks away – but this time there's no cartridges to be found. They question me about assaulting Lord Moreton, but I deny everything, saying it must have been someone else who hit him with the brick.

'Like who?'

'I don't know. Maybe a Gypsy or someone like that.'

'And why would he hit the lord?'

'The bugger was waving an iron bar about.'

They lock me up, but release me later that night.

'Can I have my boots and socks back?'

'No, we need them for forensic examination.'

Now, that's just pure maliciousness, because they haven't got enough evidence to hold me, and I have to walk the five miles home in my bare feet. I get charged with ABH, assault with a brick, night poaching and taking game without a licence. They don't take any fingerprints or photographs and I get legal aid to hire a solicitor to defend me. I'm taken to the magistrate's court and I plead not guilty. Moreton identifies me and, without any other evidence or witnesses, it's Moreton's word against mine. They believe him and I get convicted and sentenced to Usk Detention Centre in Wales for three months.

But that's not the end of it.

A couple of days previous, I'm up on Tortworth Lake feeding in some Canada geese with bread. As soon as one of them comes close enough, I grab it by the neck. But the park keeper's hiding up by the boat house and he shouts out:

'Stop!'

I do a runner and he comes after me on a pushbike. I gain ground and get up a big bank, but the only way forward is through an open prison called Leyhill. I climb over the chain-link fence at the back and keep going. The prison was an old American army hospital in the war and the prisoners are housed in Nissen huts. They're all out on head-count parade and I have to run through them. They don't know what's happening as I barge between the ranks with a goose over my back. The screws are speechless. Someone shouts, 'Oi, where you going?'

I shout back.

'I'm a gamekeeper . . . chasing poachers.'

Then I run away through the prison fields and over a wall and onto a road, before they can gather their wits and come after me. After about a mile I stop to catch my breath. I wait to see if anyone's chasing, but no one is.

A Canada goose is as tough as a farrier's crotch and hardly worth all the running. But I sell it for £3, which is better than nothing. A couple of days later, the coppers come round.

'Were you up by Tortworth Lake on Sunday?'

'I can't recall.'

'Would you come to Sodbury police station?'

'What for?'

'You know what for.'

I'm questioned about the goose, which I deny all knowledge of, as usual.

'The park keeper saw you.'

'Did he?'

I'm charged with stealing a Canada goose to the value of £15 and let go.

But now, in court, they add this offence to the one of hitting Moreton with the brick and the park keeper's there to give evidence against me. The old magistrate thinks he's a right witty bugger.

'And what happened to this goose?'

'We don't know, your worship.'

'Let's hope it's not on Sarum Plain, to be driven cackling home to Camelot.'

Hee haw, hee haw, hee haw – they all laugh like demented donkeys at this quote from *King Lear*, even though none of them probably knows what he's talking about. I certainly don't at the time. Neither do I laugh when he adds another three months to my sentence and I'm banned from using a firearm, even an air rifle, for five years.

By now I've learned enough about the law to know you always gets stitched up in magistrates' court, because they're all the same class of people who run the show and they think they're superior to the ordinary man because they were born with a silver spoon up their bum and went to college and suchlike. So I appeal on length of sentence and conviction for the goose and, five weeks later, I'm in Bristol Crown Court, waiting in this codified corridor with an assortment of fallen angels – shoulder-rubbing with the pickpockets and pushers, shoplifters and shysters and indecent exposers in public places.

'Next case?'

'Tovey, your honour.'

'A foreigner?'

'A poacher.'

'I see. Certainly looks the type.'

The conviction for the goose stands, but I get three months knocked off the sentence. I've already done two months on remand, so I've only got one month to go. This is the time of Willie Whitelaw's 'short, sharp shock' policy for young offenders and I'm put to making concrete blocks in Usk. But it don't bother me too much, apart from being confined and not being able to ramble. I'm fit as a butcher's dog and the tough regime inside the detention centre's no problem for me.

I get released in September and I'm back out poaching the very next day.

May twelfth is traditionally known as Brancher's Day, when rook fledglings start to stretch their wings in preparation for leaving the nests. Rooks are wary and sharp-sighted birds and this is the most effective way of culling them to protect the songbird population. People get together at rookeries with guns and shoot all the young rooks as they walk along the tree branches – that's why it's called Brancher's Day. Rooks are also seen as pests to farmers because they destroy their crops – although I always thought they helped the farmer by keeping slugs and insects down, but what do I know about farming? I always saw the rook as a social and merry bird who keeps an intelligent eye on what's happening around his territory. But this is tradition and rook pie was a popular dish back then, even if it's rarely eaten now. Anyway, I'm out around Primrose Vale on Brancher's Day, shooting the rooks. I'm walking back across a farmer's land and I see this bloke coming along the field, shouting at me. I have a 12-bore and, like I said, after being in the detention centre, I'm automatically banned from carrying any kind of firearm for five years. I have a balaclava on and I pull it down over my face so he can't identify me.

'What are you doing?'

'Exactly as I want to do.'

I walk away, not looking for no trouble, but he comes up behind me and is about to punch me in the back of the head. I turn round quick, like, and hit him with the barrels of the gun and walk away again. He doesn't try to follow me a second time.

Four days later a police car pulls me up in the lanes.

'Come with us.'

'What for?'

'We need to question you about an assault.'

I go with them because I've got no choice. I don't know how I was identified and I deny everything, but I'm put on remand in Gloucester Prison while they come and search the house for the gun. There's six licensed guns in our house at the time and they can't identify the one involved in the assault. But I'm still charged with ABH and possessing a gun within five years of release from a detention centre. I'm kept on remand and I can't get hold of the prosecution statements until I'm taken to Crown Court in Bristol. I try to get a witness to give me an alibi, but I'm not able to. Had I been on the outside, I might have been able to sort something, but it's too difficult from the inside.

The judge I get has a reputation for his heavy sentences and those going up before him in front of me are coming away with the likes of ten years. I'm thinking I'm going to get a stiff one for hitting someone with a 12-bore shotgun, especially with my previous being taken into account. I've already pleaded guilty, as advised by my barrister, because that might get me a reduced sentence – so there's no trial as such, just the judge's summing up and that. Anyway, he's waffling on from behind his bench about how measures will soon be in place to enable the forces of law and order to identify us criminals from space, while we're innocently going about our daily business. And I'm not paying much attention, until he says –

'Actually, I know your village very well. My father was vicar there for a time.'

It only turns out that his father was the old vicar I used to push round in his wheelchair when I was a young lad. I don't know if the judge recognises my name and remembers that time, but he gives me a year, which is very light, considering. I've already been on remand for four and a half months and I'm sent to Bristol Prison and given a job painting cells. Three and a half months later, I'm free again.

Within two days of being released, I'm back out poaching.

Out poaching on Tortworth Estate, 1990s

10

Bob – Lamping and Other Stories

I think Brian already told you there's two kinds of lamping. The first kind involves being out at night with a small handheld torch and a gun to shoot pheasants roosting in the trees, and we've said a lot about that. The second kind's going out at night with a fairly powerful, solid-beam lamp and a greyhound in search of rabbits and hares. For me, this is a great way to see a sighthound in action. It takes patience and skill and you has to know what you're doing – so does the dog. The first thing I does is go out during the day and trek the area I'm going to lamp that night. I'll know where the quarry's likely to be and I'll remember fences and barbed wire and other things that might damage the dog. The greyhound will be running at full pelt in the black dark, except for the beam from the lamp, so I don't want it taking its head off on a wire or breaking its legs in a hole.

The best time to lamp is on dark, windy nights with plenty of cloud and as little moon as possible. I make sure I'm downwind of the rabbits or hares and that'll deaden the sound, as well as the smell, of me and the dog approaching. I takes the time to position myself and the greyhound where I wants to be, from the reconnaissance earlier in the day. Then I scan the field with the lamp to find the coneys quatting in the forms. A lot of people use lurchers for lamping, but I always prefer the greyhound. It's by far the best dog going and it has to be a fast hound that'll be quiet and do as I tells it. I've lamped with a brace of dogs as well as with a single dog, it makes no matter to me – though two dogs can sometimes get tangled up in each other and have a tug-o-war with the kill afterwards, where a single dog will be single-minded and bring me back the rabbit or hare in one piece. The greyhound must be trained to come back as soon as I calls it, after it makes the catch and, if the quarry ain't dead by then, I'll kill it myself in seconds.

I keeps a tight grip on the greyhound until I'm ready to slip him – until I sees the ruby glint of a rabbit's eyes. If the lamp comes across anything else, like a deer or a fox or a badger, or even a cat, I might hold the dog back – or I might not. Once I see the rabbit or hare, I'll keep the lamp beam on it until I'm sure the dog sees it too. As soon as he spots it, he'll perk up and try to pull away. I lets him go and he's off like a bullet out of a gun and it's a sight to behold. It's like being back when the prehistoric people moved through their dark world at the beginning of time. I feel what they must have felt back then, in the night – under the never ending black sky. It gives an edge to my senses and I knows I'm alive and alert.

Adrenaline rushes through my veins and through the dog's, and the short hairs stand on the back of my neck and it feels like I'm part of the greyhound, running with him. I'm no longer myself, so I ain't able to explain myself. And there ain't nothing to explain – no sense nor sentiment in the primitive night. To be able to explain it would be like being able to explain the meaning of everything. And who can do that? I just forget who I am – what I am – and every step becomes its own little lifetime as I runs through the dark field. Birth and life and death. And again. And again. Until it's over and the dog brings me back the kill.

If I hunts the same area a few times over, the rabbits can get lamp shy – they gets crafty after a while and run through the hedge. Soon as you shines the light on 'em, before you can shoot 'em or put a dog on 'em, they'll bolt, and that's when some people say to use a red filter lens to confuse 'em. But I don't, because it don't shine a long way, so I just leave the fields be for a while and go lamping somewhere else.

But not everyone has the choices that I do – to go where they wants and hunt where they wants – so they got to improvise. I suppose I'm a bit like that fella in Australia I heard about once, who staked a claim to a remote bit of some red desert and declared independence from the rest of the country. He made his own money and printed his own postage stamps and paid no taxes and was completely in charge of his own little acre of land, without interference from any authority. I ain't got the same exemption from the law, but I knows how he must've felt, to rise every morning to a brand new sun and to walk at night with the darkness as your friend and to feel at one with the free birds and all the wild things around you – and I stretch out my arms and say 'Halle-bloody-lujah!'

Slimbridge, on the Severn Estuary, is a wetland area of marshes where Siberian wildfowl spend the winter. It's full of geese and ducks and curlews and all sorts of other birds and it belonged to the Berkeley Estate before it became a wildfowl sanctuary. The

Dumbles is an area of the foreshore with gulleys going through it out into the sea and geese fly over it in the morning and sometimes feed there. The toffs used to shoot geese from the foreshore before it became a wildlife trust and a sanctuary for game birds, and they used to have a decoy down there – not a decoy you'd use to lure in geese over a stubble field – a wetland netted decoy.

Let me explain: a wetland decoy has a big wide circular mouth, made of sticks. It's covered in nets and it gradually gets narrower and narrower as it goes in, for about seventy or eighty yards. Wildfowl will swim happily in the mouth because there's nothing to threaten or obstruct them. A specially trained dog flits in and out of the decoy, attracting the wildfowl and taking them further and further in. The birds only get brief glimpses of the dog and they follow it because they're curious. The dog charms them to follow it in, just like a stoat will charm a rabbit, and they'll go deeper and deeper, following and following. All the time, the decoy's getting narrower and narrower and they go into a funnel at the end which can be shut off. Then the hunters get in front of the mouth of the decoy and the ducks has no place to go – so they move in there and kills 'em. The Berkley Estate decoyers caught thousands of ducks and geese over the winters for the castle and those connected with it.

But people like me was never welcome there.

Then Slimbridge was taken over by the Wildfowl Trust and now the castle crowd have a shoot once a year down there – but, as a rule, there's no shooting allowed. In Scotland, anyone can shoot from foreshores when the tide's out, but in England you have to belong to a club, because they've paid for the rights to shoot from what was, and still should be, free fowling ground.

Gloucester Wildfowl Club has the shooting rights to the fore-shore near Slimbridge between low and mean high tide and you got to do a course in bird identification to become a member. I've been shooting birds for longer than any of them and I don't need no identification course to know what I'm shooting. All fore-shores is Crown property between low and high tides and anyone can go fishing there without a licence – but these clubs have exclusive shooting rights from the councils so ordinary people like me, who want to shoot a duck or a goose for dinner, have had that right taken away from them – without even being asked!

But it never bothered me whether I was welcome or not, and the Dumbles was always one of my favourite hunting haunts. I'd go over there, hit and run, sneaking in through the dykes and gulleys and reed beds, get a few shots away, bag 'em up and get out. We liked to go down there at Christmas time and, one year, Brian went over on his bike when it was dark. He walked along the canal then slipped down into a dyke, where he couldn't be seen by anyone in the bird towers, watching with their binocu-lars. He waited for the morning flight off the estuary and shot ten geese, but they was too heavy to carry home on his pushbike, so he made it back to the towpath, hid the birds, then walked into the village and found a phone. He rang me up and I drove over there and picked him and the geese up. Ten shots from a 12-bore makes a lot of noise but, on that occasion, no one came out and he got away with it.

On another Christmas Day, I sneaked out on the foreshore to do some shooting and this time I brought a dog. He was the old springer called Jack, who found the albino deer for Brian, if you remember, but he was nearing the end of his usefulness. I shot a few geese and one of them fell into the nearby Sharpness to

Gloucester Canal. By the time I got over there, old Jack had gone in after the goose but couldn't get back out, because the water level was about two foot lower than the edge of the canal. The dog wouldn't let go of the kill and he was paddling to keep hisself afloat and was nearly dead with the cold by the time I pulled him out. Once he was out of the water, the spaniel got the life back into him and dried hisself out in the long grass. But it just goes to show, a good dog won't give up what it's retrieved, no matter what. Jack was twelve years old when I shot him, because he was ill and dying. He'd done enough work to shame a bulldozer and retrieved tons of game in his dog's life. But when it's time to go it's time to go. No use hanging about trying to prolong this life – better to move on into the adventure of the next.

And it's things like that what makes life such a sweetness – the excitement of poaching, the not knowing what might happen next, the whistling gladness of it all. When the family was growing up, I had to poach to feed them. And I was very successful at it – pheasants and partridge and rabbits and fish and deer and anything I could get. I remember once I went down to Bristol with a bit of scrap metal and made about fifteen quid. On the way back, I spotted a cock pheasant behind a barn, so I went home and got my gun and came back and shot it. It was close to one of the big estates and, as I was making my way back to the car, the estate agent came through a hedge with a threatening scowl on his ugly mug. I knew he was going to blame me for shooting the pheasant on the estate, which I didn't, it was just outside it. He was a big bugger and I wasn't going to give him the chance to come at me, so I raised my gun and shouted at him.

'Stay where you are!'

He backed off, into the hedge he'd come out of. But when I

got to the car, the earl who owned the estate was there with the boot open. I didn't take too kindly to that.

'What d'you think you're doing?'

'Looking for game.'

'And did you find any?'

'No.'

'My car's on a public highway; you've no right to be meddling with it.'

But they thought they could get away with anything, and most of the time they could, because of the undue deference shown to them by the forelock-pulling public – and the police. He knew me and I knew him. He came towards me with a walk that once might have been used to follow funerals.

'What's in your bag, Mr Tovey?'

'None of your business.'

I knew his reputation, but he also knew mine and, without his agent to help him, he didn't fancy having a set-to. So I was able to drive off without interference.

About a week later, I got a message from the same earl asking if I'd go see him. I went to the estate office and knocked on the door. He opened it. He was all nice and polite, not his usual arrogant self at all.

'How are you, Mr Tovey?'

'I'm fine. How're you?'

'Let me get straight to the point . . . if I give you all the rabbiting on the estate, will you leave the game alone?'

I think I told you already, a rabbit is called a coney and it ain't considered game – it's classed as vermin by the people who attend pheasant and partridge shoots. I looked him square in his inbred eye.

'I give you my word.'

He started to smile, thinking he had me in his pocket.

'You do?'

'That I'll shoot pheasants on your land whenever I want to.'

The expression on his face was worth twenty pounds, as I turned and walked out. We was never going to be friends, but now we'd be worse enemies than ever.

I didn't care.

And I was true to my word and took pheasants from his land every chance I got. You see, I didn't consider them to be *his* pheasants. They was wild birds and there for the taking by anyone who had the skill to do it. I had that skill – the skill to know where pheasants are and how to get 'em. The skill to entice a bird to where you wants it. Like, I know pheasants love daddy-longlegs, or crane flies as they're called. Pheasants will follow 'em anywhere. The daddy-longlegs is impossible to control and they'll fly wherever they wants to, all over the place. But they sometimes eats the root hairs from vegetables, like carrots or parsnips or sugar-beets, and if you goes to the trouble of laying a trail of root hairs, you might get a good few of 'em to follow that trail – and the pheasants will follow the daddy-longlegs, away from the private estates and onto land where you can trap and shoot 'em. If you can't be bothered with luring the daddy-longlegs, just lay a trail of corn – but the birds prefer the flying insects and, while they're about in September and October, they'll ignore the corn and most other kinds of bait.

The folding .410 shotgun was always my choice, as you know, along with a good torch and a postman's bag to put the birds in. I'd get enough for my family and a lot more to sell or give away. I used to be able to get £2 for a pheasant and £3 for a partridge and £2 for a mallard. But them days is all but disappeared, because people don't want to eat game no more – the women can't cook 'em properly these days. They don't know how good a hen pheasant is to eat and think it's cruel to kill animals when there's plenty of meat in the supermarkets. But the beef and lamb and veal and pork had to be killed too – and it weren't reared in the wild like the animals I killed. They say abattoirs kill the animals humanely and maybe they does, but it's on an industrial scale and the animals know what's happening – they can smell the blood and hear the calls of distress and, if you look in their eyes, they're all wide and panicking. I kills game quickly, like with partridge – I'd use a drag-net that would take two men to work. It would be about twenty-five yards long and four yards deep. We'd drag it over stubble or clover and, when we came to a covey of partridge, they'd fly up and hit the mesh. We'd drop the front of the net and gently get 'em out. Then I'd bite their heads to crush the brain and they'd die instantly.

Another way to get pheasants is to peg out a fighting cock on a length of baler twine in a field, at the end of January or beginning of February, when cock pheasants is pairing up with the hens. A cock pheasant could have up to four hens and the fighting cock will crow and draw them in, because they'll think they're being challenged by another bird entering their territory. 'Course, a cock pheasant ain't no match for a fighting cock – be like an ordinary bloke taking on a prizefighter – so no damage will come to my bird and I just shoot the pheasants when they comes in to challenge it. Actually, sometimes you don't even need to shoot 'em. When he gets into a bundle with the fighting cock, the pheasant don't pay no heed to what's going on around him and you can just get right up to him and wring his neck or hit him with a nut stick. Same thing if two cock pheasants is fighting each other – they'll be so intent on scrapping, they won't notice you approaching them. But, if the gamekeepers hear the fighting cock crowing, they'll come along and kill it, so I don't leave it pegged out for too long.

I've never gone to jail for poaching like Brian has. Oh, I got pulled all the time, but never put away. I've been pulled dozens of times over the years. You can't go a lifetime of poaching without getting come upon a few times. If getting pulled now and then is going to frighten you, then don't do it. But you got to keep your wits about you and let the buggers know you're not afraid of them and you know your rights, few and all as they may be. I remember once coming down by Little Wood with the greyhounds – up comes a keeper.

'What you doing?'

'Out for a walk.'

'No footpath here.'

'There's one through the wood, right by the side of your release pen.'

Nothing he could do, and he knew it. There's rights of way all over the countryside and, if you're on one, the lackeys can't do nothing to you. But they'll test you out to see if you'll back down. If you does that, then they has you.

Just like on the Severn foreshore – there's hares on the land round there and I can get a good flat run. If I'm come upon, I can get onto the foreshore between low and high tide and there's nothing they can do about it – although they'd like to. A lot of the time they got binoculars and they watch from towers and they'll come after me in Land Rovers. But I knows the lie of the land and can give 'em the slip, because no one knows terrain like a poacher. But you're bound to get a lot of pull-ins, especially if you're out poaching thousands and thousands of times.

If you're a poacher, every grass and grumbler's after you – from the lords and ladies to the farmers and estate workers and police and vicars and Uncle Tom-bloody-Cobley and all. Everybody! They're driving along the roads and they see a light in the woods and, instead of carrying on and minding their own business, they can't leave it alone. They has to ring someone.

'Oh, I seen a light in such and such a place.'

I was on my way to do some lamping one night, but didn't have anything but a rabbit skin in the motor. This copper stopped me for no other reason than to be a nuisance.

'What have you got in there?'

'Nothing.'

'Get out of the vehicle.'

I gets out and he starts searching around on the floor, to see if he can find something. He cops hold of the skin that's underneath the seat and he nearly shits hisself.

'Jesus! What's that?'

It's just a skin I uses for geeing the dogs up, but I don't tell him that.

'It's a scalp.'

'A what?'

'A scalp . . . you know, I bought it off a redskin when I was over in Arizona.'

I takes the skin out of the motor and shakes it at him.

'I don't know what the procedure is for this . . . '

'D'you want it as evidence?'

I throw it towards him and he jumps back, afraid to pick it up.

'I'll let you go with a caution.'

'What kind of caution?'

'Eh, just a caution.'

He buggers off and I picks up the skin and puts it back in the motor and goes on my way, laughing. But there was always that kind of harassment – being stopped for nothing at all. Some local coppers like PC Harris, men who knew me, were alright sometimes. But mostly they was a bunch of bastards that loved licking up to the lords.

I started this chapter about lamping and I'll finish it with a lamping story. I remember going out one night with a Welsh friend of mine – I had a greyhound and he had a lurcher. We made a few kills and were about to go home when the dogs put up a fox. They chased it and caught it and my mate said he'd take it back to Wales with him. That was alright with me, because I didn't want it. You can't eat a fox, so what good is it? It's like Oscar Wilde once said about the foxhunting fraternity: '*the unspeakable in full pursuit of the uneatable*' – and that just about summed up the bum-bouncers and their prey. Anyway, he put the fox in a bag and drove me back to my house. When we got back there, he tipped the bag up and the fox grabbed hold of his hand and wouldn't let go. It was only playing at being dead and that's how clever the fox is; if he'd waited and tipped the bag up outside the car, the fox would've run off and escaped. He was screaming and the dogs were going mad in the back and I had to run in and get my .410 shotgun and shoot it. He was leaping about all over the place and he was lucky I didn't blow a few of his fingers off along with the fox.

And they say a hot-cross bun baked on a Good Friday is great for the gout!

11

Bob – Long-Netting

I've been long-netting for as far back as I can remember. When I was a lad, I used to set out the nets and pegs in a field, then walk round with a box of matches, shaking the box and making a slight noise, driving rabbits into the nets. I'd catch about fifty at a time and kill 'em and, like everything else, we'd either eat 'em or sell 'em in my father's butcher shop. It was a way of making a living for us country people who had little else to sustain us in the hard days after the war. People who was being rationed used to say 'the farmers has plenty of food' – and they had, so had the landowners. But they wanted to keep it all to themselves and not share it out with people who had no land to call their own. So I went out and took some of that food from them – especially the wild stuff that wasn't theirs to begin with, the rabbits and game birds and fish and fowls and the odd deer, there and here – in the nets as well as other ways. But most of the long-netting I done through my life was for hares, not other wildlife, and for that you needs a special kind of skill.

Let me explain it a bit, so you'll know what I'm talking about.

Long-netting ain't for the lazy man; it's a strenuous activity and a job for a group of people working together as a team. Over the past few years, we've only used nets that range in length from a hundred to a hundred and fifty yards – maybe a total length of two to three hundred yards altogether, because there's very few good men to set out and gather in these days. They're mostly either dead or too old. We used to set up nets that could total up to five or six hundred yards in length and use thirty or more beaters and ten or more netters . . . but you don't know how it works, do you? I ain't explained it. OK, I set the nets in a field, about fifteen to twenty yards in front of a hedge, or in a tramline made by a tractor. The boxes are laid out ready, and those of us who knows how to handle hares wait quietly in the hedge while the animals are driven through by the beaters. They run into the nets and get tangled up and the netters take 'em out and box 'em up.

The boxes are made so there's four compartments to each one, just the right size for a hare so's they can't hurt themselves. You has to be gentle with hares when you're handling them. If you hold them the wrong way, they'll die. The right way to hold them is just in front of their hind legs, by the loose skin on their backs. Once they're safely in the boxes, they can be transported to where they're needed and released. Now, you'd think a wild animal like a hare would go mad in a little box, but they don't. They feels safe in there and you can tickle 'em on the head and they'll settle down nicely. We've netted thousands of hares and very rarely had one die in the boxes – the one or two that did was weak and would've soon died anyway.

Size of mesh is the difference between hare nets and rabbit nets. The mesh is bigger in hare nets so the animal gets its head through, but not its body, and gets tangled up. Rabbits will get their bodies through hare mesh and escape. With rabbit nets, the mesh is too small for a hare to get its head through, so it don't get tangled and can get away. I set the nets tight where there's plenty of hares so they're easy to get out of the mesh. I don't want 'em too tangled up so it's taking a long time to free 'em and there's other hares coming through fast and you're running here and there and the hares in the nets are screaming out a warning to the others, who'll turn away and run off in another direction. If there ain't many hares about, I set the nets baggier so the animals get well tangled, because I wants to catch every one of 'em and I don't want none getting away.

You got to be fit and active, because continuously short-sprinting from the hedge to the net takes it out of you and it's worse than jogging for ten or twenty miles. You need to know what you're doing and there ain't many left now who does. Once it's out of the nets, I hold the hare where its back legs comes up to drive its body in running – there's a piece of elastic skin there and that's where I lift 'em, supporting the weight with my other hand or arm, so I don't harm or hurt 'em. Hold 'em by the legs and they'll kick out and break, or by the ears and they'll squirm and maybe snap their necks. The boxes we use is specially made – the same size as a form where hares quat in the wild. Like I said, once the hares is in the boxes, I just tickle their heads and that quietens 'em down. Afterwards I gather in the nets and move on to the next field. The hardest part of it is the setting out and gathering in. Long nets is heavy, even when setting them out dry – and they're even heavier if they gets wet and you're gathering in – maybe half a hundredweight in a 150-yard net, hanging from a stick on your arm, and you needs to be strong enough to hold 'em.

Everything's sacked up afterwards so the nets don't get damaged or dirty and we move on. On a single day, we'd net hares over a large area, not just in one field – we might re-set the nets half a dozen times and that's a lot of work. And there's a lot of things to worry about as well – the weather and wind speed and hedges and gates and all sorts of other considerations. I has about a thousand yards of long nets altogether but the trouble these days is, you can't get hare nets no more – nobody makes 'em. So once the ones I use now are gone, that'll be the last of it.

I told you in an earlier chapter that we netted hares for the Waterloo Cup and other coursing meetings and you're probably asking yourself by now why I still do this – why I still goes long-netting for hares, even though coursing's banned. It's because people wants 'em. They wants 'em and I supplies 'em. If someone rings the Game & Wildlife Conservation Trust looking for hares, they get given my number, because me and my boys is the only people long-netting in the country now. There's fewer hares about nowadays because of 'lead poisoning', and by that I means shooting, but we can still find plenty if we wants to.

Sometimes we only catch a few and other times we can catch a few hundred. We relocate 'em to different parts of the country, from where they're not wanted to where they are wanted. Like, we takes 'em from airport runways and farms, and sends 'em to the likes of gamekeeper colleges and university research stations and game reserves and over to Ireland, where hare coursing's still legal. We takes 'em from military airfields and release 'em on army and navy bases, that used to keep beagle packs in the days before the hunting ban, but still likes to see a few hares running. Army and navy bases is fenced in, so the hares become isolated and smaller and they needs fresh blood.

They can't shoot 'em on the airfields for fear of damaging the planes with a stray bullet or buckshot, and that's where we comes in. It's a kind of countryside recycling: taking hares from where there's plenty and they're not wanted, because they're doing too much damage and going to be shot, to where they are wanted. Places where the population has dropped off or where farmers and landowners likes to have hares on their land, just to see 'em boxing and gadding about in the mad March mornings or in the evenings when the sun's starting to sink behind the hills.

We've netted hares all over – even on the shooting estates in February when the pheasant season's over, so's not to disturb the birds. The hoorays never had no problem with us being on their lands then, because we was doing them a favour. We also relocated some good strong hares from Salisbury Plain to Castlemartin tank range in Wales – before the war there was plenty of hares around that area and after the war there was none. People couldn't understand why – but it don't take a genius to figure that out, does it? They wanted a population of hares again, so we obliged 'em.

The best time to release hares for breeding stock is in early spring. If you net 'em in springtime when they're in young, you get two or three animals for every one you net and they stay around. But if you don't relocate them far enough away from where you netted 'em, they can go back, because they got good homing instincts.

Anyway, this pest controller fella gets in touch and asks us to come up to Broughton Airfield in Chester. The airfield was overpopulated with hares and it was dangerous having them running round all over the place with planes coming in. It's always difficult on an airfield, because we got nowhere to hide.

We can set the nets up and the hares are coming forward, but where do we hide? If they see us they won't come to the nets. There was some red boxes on this airfield for fire hoses or something and we set up our camouflage scrim around them and hid down behind it. The beaters drove the hares forward and we had a successful day in the end. The local newspaper was there reporting and taking pictures, because it was a conservation thing and the hares was being released somewhere else, where they was wanted. We relocated them to this lord's estate at Rhyl in North Wales, which is near the sea. The hares were released into a wood but, being used to the warm runway, seven of 'em came back out and just sat on the tarmac road, thinking they was still at the airport.

They wouldn't move, no matter what we did, and we was worried they'd get run over by cars or lorries. In the end, the lord had to go get one of his retrievers and the dog soon drove them back to where they was supposed to be.

We've also sent hares to the Middle East for falconry. We was asked to get half a dozen hares for some Arab Abdullah who intended to use 'em to populate an island in the Gulf. So we did. We was instructed to put 'em in a pheasant release pen on land that I won't name and the gamekeeper was supposed to look after 'em. But the stupid bugger never fed 'em and, after a buzzard had a couple, the rest died. So we netted and boxed up some more and, this time, instead of trusting some idiot to take care of 'em, we was instructed to take 'em to a service station in Chieveley, where we was met by this Arab sheikh and his two bodyguards in a big black Mercedes. The bodyguards were huge blokes and they were armed. But, when we opened the van and showed them the hares in the boxes, they stood well back and one of them asked, 'Are these creatures dangerous?'

Me and Brian nearly fell on the floor laughing – great big blokes with their guns, frightened of a few hares. The sheikh was standing there eating a McDonald's and drinking Coca-Cola and he wanted me and Brian to go over to Bahrain or Qatar or some other Gulf state and set up a population on an island. But things weren't too stable in the region at the time and we didn't want to get stuck in some war. Besides, our van was full of red diesel and we couldn't be driving it all the way over there and hoping not to get a pull from some Emirates plod. The hares got sent out there in diplomatic bags in the end, rather than have them go through quarantine, and we never did get our boxes back.

We've netted hares for Gypsies as well. Not like the old Gypsies of years ago, the ones I went out with on that night I told you about, or who told me my fortune. These days a lot of them go coursing in four-wheel drives and they're very threatening to anyone who comes upon 'em. They has money and they sometimes pay for permission to use land, then they protect that land from others and even from poachers like us. But most Gypsies has gone to bricks now, so they ain't real Travellers no more. They course with lurchers, running their four-wheel drives across the land and chucking the dogs out after the hares to give 'em a run.

It ain't proper; it's cowboy stuff and there's no real sport in it and they bets a lot of money on their dogs. But they do a lot of damage too, going through gates and fences and a lot of them is tough gruntys, so you don't want to tangle with 'em. But the landowner gets protected from other gangs and they've always been straight with us and paid us for the hares we netted for them. They don't know how to do it for themselves because they've lost a lot of the old skills and can't catch hares with anything other than a dog these days. But I got no problem with Gypsies and they got no problem with me. We live and let live, even though we has a different understanding of the countryside and the animals in it.

We used to go to gamekeepers' colleges – many of the students was city kids who didn't have a clue about country ways. They had to learn how to beat for the shooting season, and beating hares is just like beating partridge or pheasant. We'd take 'em out and show 'em how to beat to a set point, which would be the guns in a game-bird shoot. We netted for Eton College and we did a five-year study with Oxford University – we caught the hares and relocated them, they tagged 'em and used tracking collars to see where they wandered and how territorial they was and we helped many a researcher get their doctorates that way. We netted hares for J. Arthur Rank, of flour and films fame, who liked to course round Druid's Lodge in Wiltshire. Although it was classed as an open course, the field was hemmed in with sheep hurdles and chestnut fencing, with panels lifted out every hundred yards or so to give the hares a chance to escape. And Rank had a Rolls-Royce with a turret built onto it and his man in the car used to have to pedal like a good 'un to turn the turret round so old J. Arthur could get a good view of the course in any direction.

I've also long-netted for the Queen Mother when she was alive. The area round Stockton on the Salisbury Plain's a bleak place in winter and it breeds hardy hares – good strong 'uns. We've netted 'em there and taken 'em to Windsor Great Park for

Major Barrington-Browne and the Eton Beagles, before the hunting ban. We've netted hares from Land's End to Lockerbie and put down good breeding stock in many places, all in the name of conservation.

Although coursing's banned in the UK now, it still goes on in Ireland, where they often run short of hares. We netted thousands for those events and we used to send fifty or sixty at a time over there in the back of trucks carrying oil drums. They had canvas sides and tops and the drivers used to put the hare boxes in the middle and surround 'em with the oil drums. Irish hares are redder and smaller than the English ones and those we sent over didn't suit the park coursing there too well, so we stopped doing it. For all I knows, any that escaped the dogs might have bred with the indigenous hares and improved their size and strength. Or maybe they didn't inter-mate and just died out. But I've heard stories of bigger, lighter-coloured hares being seen in the Irish countryside. If that's true, it's all down to me. And I can see the Irish out there, looking for their little ginger hares in springtime, with the trees budding as the sap starts to rise, and the birds coming back from their winter holidays. The air warming up and summer waiting in the wings – and they comes across one of my big jacks and they stops and stares at it in wonder, and a sudden shiver runs down their spines.

Sometimes you get things running into the nets that you don't really want, like muntjac. Roe deer and muntjac come forward with the hares, in front of the beat, and we try to let 'em out the flanks before they gets to the nets. If they do come into the nets, they can smash 'em, break a top line or take forty or fifty yards of net down and you'll get hares coming through and getting away because that section of the net is broken. They can be a real nuisance. The nets will stop some, but it depends on the size. If they gets caught in there, it's a bugger getting them out, especially if it's a buck and the net's all tangled round the antlers.

You're in the middle of a drive, with hares coming through, and you has to get the deer out and the nets back up as quick as you can and everything's frantic all around you. That's where the skill and experience and stamina comes in. If you ain't got it, then don't go long-netting.

The muntjac's a wild deer from China that was introduced to this country in 1812 by John Reeves, the assistant inspector for tea with the British East India Company. They escaped from Woburn Abbey Estate in 1925 and bred fast and they're now established in the countryside all over the UK and Ireland. The males have short antlers, but they fight for territory with their tusks – sharp canine teeth that can do a lot of damage. Bigger muntjac can sometimes be very aggressive and we've caught plenty of them in our long nets when we've been out for the hares. Like I said, they can break a net or take it down, so we try to get 'em out the flanks before they can do too much damage. If they do get into the nets, we try to get 'em out quickly and either let 'em go or put 'em in a cage, if we've got one with us, because they're sought after for some of the smaller parks and worth a bit of money. If they're too tangled up and we can't do that, we'll break their necks to stop 'em struggling and joint up the meat later. But you got to be careful with 'em and not get yourself hurt.

Talking of muntjac, I've got a friend called Ernie, a Scotsman who worked on the power stations in China during the early 1980s. When he came back, he brought me a Chinese communist hat with ear flaps and a red star and a hammer and sickle badge on it. I wears it when I'm poaching and the ya-yas hate it when they comes upon me and I've outsmarted 'em and I'm wearing this Chinese communist hat. They does be spitting nails!

I had to go long-netting on the Isle of Sheppey round about 1992 and there was a military base there. They didn't like the hat and took it seriously and asked me if I was a communist. You know what these soldiers are like – brainwashed to move and shit and think as one and can't cope with anything out of the ordinary. I was worried in case they started shooting. But they didn't and we got the all clear.

We didn't know the area and, if you ain't been somewhere before, you has to use your own judgement as to how the hares will run. We set up 500 yards of long nets in this huge sixty-acre field and were waiting for the beat when we sees these two big greyhounds chasing a hare off in the distance. The hare has a good fifteen yards on the dogs and is beating 'em easy. But he runs straight into our nets and the dogs kill him. It just wasn't that hare's lucky day.

Anyway, one day later in my life, I'm out for a stroll with Ernie. We wasn't hunting or poaching, just enjoying the countryside. I likes to be quiet when I'm out, just like my father taught me, but Ernie was keeping on gabbing and he was getting on my nerves. We came upon a tree that had fallen down and was leaning at an angle agin' another tree. There was some movement underneath it, so I decided to take a look to get away from Ernie's chatter. I moved away some of the undergrowth and, to my surprise, there's this big buck muntjac, lying down, hiding from us. Being the poacher I am, I start trying to get him out by kicking at him with my foot. The next thing, he charges at me and I'm telling you, as well as his sharp-pointed antlers, he has a pair of tusks like the fangs of a tiger. I'm completely unarmed, so I grab hold of a stick and break it across his back, but it does no damage and the muntjac keeps after me, trying to gore me with the antlers and sink its tusks into my leg. I shouts at Ernie.

'Do something!'

'What can I do?'

'Get him away from me!'

'Then he'll come after me. You should've left him alone, Bob.'

Anyway, Ernie starts to throw stuff at him, stones and sticks – but he keeps chasing me around, until I climbs a tree and I'm out of his reach. Then he turns and goes after Ernie, who runs off out of sight with the muntjac after him.

I didn't see him again for a few days and, when I did, he was walking with a limp.

'I'm never going nowhere with you again, Bob Tovey.'

'Why's that?'

'That bloody deer . . .'

'You should've left him alone, Ernie.'

Now, I'd caught plenty of muntjac in the long nets. We had six one time – we killed three by breaking their necks and let the other three go. But this buck was the biggest I'd ever seen, and me and Ernie was getting on in years then, not as strong as we once were. If I'd been younger, I'd probably have killed him. But, on this occasion, the muntjac nearly killed me and gave Ernie the chase of his life.

That story has nothing to do with the long-netting and I was just trying to explain why you got to be careful with the muntjac.

And talking about Ernie reminds me of another Scotsman, Ian Galbraith, who was a policeman and part-time gamekeeper up in Inveraray, a town in Argyll, on the western shore of Loch Fyne. Galbraith phoned me in 1998 and asked me if I could come up and move hares from one part of the estate to another, where they was trying to build up a population.

'Where will we stay?'

'You can stay in the police cells.'

'Is that right?'

'They're rarely used and comfortable enough.'

'Alright.'

I organised for about six or seven of us to go up there and everything was going to plan and Galbraith was on the phone regularly and looking forward to seeing me. Then everything went quiet and I never heard no more from him. I rang the police station where he worked and spoke to the sergeant.

'Forget all about it!'

'But, we're all set to come up there.'

'Forget all about it!'

He wouldn't say no more than that. Sometime later, the story broke in the newspapers about how Galbraith's wife had shot him dead with his own hunting rifle, while he was in bed, after being to the pub. She tried to claim it was a break-in and she'd been raped, then she changed her story and said he was a monster who abused her for years. She was found guilty of murder and sentenced to life, but released on parole in 2003.

And so, you see, no matter what plans you makes, you never can tell what's going to happen – and, although some believes in fate and fortune, this world ain't really so rectangular after all!

Then the same pest controller who we long-netted for up in Chester contacts me again and asks me to come to RAF Mildenhall, which is an American airbase in Suffolk. When we gets there, we find this bloke driving round in his Land Rover, setting off Harris hawks and goshawks and peregrine falcons, to scare away the pigeons and seagulls, so they don't get sucked into the engines of the fighter and bomber planes. They was bombing Iraq at the time and the pilots said the hares was interfering with their concentration on take-off and landing. We went there and sized the place up and security was very tight, but a price was agreed and we were all set to do it. But then it got cancelled. I don't know why – maybe they checked our criminal records and found we had some previous and didn't like that. Or maybe they didn't like my communist hat and thought I was a threat to national security. Who knows? And to this day I don't know either if the hares are still there or not.

Anyway, to finish this chapter, hares are delicate creatures when it comes to their immunity and they can get syphilis and other infections too, and we got to be careful when we're relocating 'em so's not to spread disease around the whole country. If I nets diseased hares, I kills 'em and burns the carcasses. Us Toveys has long been the number one hare netters in Britain. We don't do it for money, just expenses and a bit on top. The beaters and helpers gets paid £40 a day and we gets a couple of hundred quid. We do it because it's part of our way of life. We enjoys it. But the bad winter of 1981/82 in our local area crooked the hares round there and they never recovered after that. And shooting and disease and roadkills and the protection of natural predators has reduced the population further. One day, they'll probably be gone altogether and that'll be a real shame – because the hare is, in my opinion, one of the finest animals to ever grace the English countryside. We kept a book of how many hares we netted over the past forty odd years. The last entry in that book is 2012 – 10March: fifty live hares at Ballington.

Nothing after that.

Not many wants the hares so much no more.

Bob, hare-netting at the Pentons, Weyhill, near Andover, October 1998, filming for Chris Chapman's 'On Assignment' programme

12

Brian – Poacher vs Landowner

I hear the Saudis have beheaded around seventy people over the past year, and not a word about it on the television or in the newspapers. I'm glad me and Bob never went near the place with our long nets – probably be made into shish kebabs by now. Apart from that, the news is of the need to manufacture more bombs for the blowing to bits of women and children and the making of the rich even more obscene than they already are. But it's always been like that – them who has ain't never satisfied and always want more – and more and more. Everything we hear is just the static of want; want this and want that – want, want, want. All the time's spent wanting and not really living – listening to the want static. And what they want is only good while they ain't got it. As soon as they get it, it loses its value and they want something else.

I've known a few gamekeepers in my time and maybe one or two have even been alright. But most were bullies who thought they were hard cases, with the law behind them. I've never been afraid of any of them, mind, but discretion is the better part of valour and it was always best to keep away from them if I could. To me, a gamekeeper's like a prison screw or a copper or a prosecutor, and I don't know how anyone goes and does a job like that. Self-righteous buggers who never look inside themselves to see their own little flaws and failures as they pass subjective judgements on those who, in their ignorant and misguided minds, they consider to be wrongdoers. And them all up for every fiddle and fraud they can get away with in the name of their shifty professions. Let him who is without – eh! Anyway, I've tried to avoid them for the most part and let them get on with their dubious jobs – long as they let me get on with mine.

I suppose you could say, if it wasn't for the rich landowners there'd be no game at all, because the farmers would have exterminated every wild thing that threatened their livestock or their crops. That might be fair comment, but it's just the arrogance of it all – the sanctimonious elitism of it – that gets me. The dukes and earls thinking they own everything and treating people, especially poachers, like dogs – and it's them I like to get at more than anyone, the aristocrats and self-appointed controllers of the countryside. It's the sheer belligerence of those people I hate – types who believe they have rights that were given to them by nobody but themselves.

When I was young, I used to deliberately run my dogs up on Earl Ducie and Lord Moreton's estate farm, knowing full well they'd come out and chase me and I'd do a runner to a footpath and be able to tell them to 'piss off' when I got onto public land. Once on a right-of-way or bridle path, I could stop running because I was safe.

'Keep off my land!'

'Wasn't on your land.'

'I saw you.'

'Did you take a photograph?'

'I know you, Tovey.'

'You don't know me at all.'

Even if they did see me, I could deny it. They knew it was me, but they couldn't prove it. Although, if they got me into a magistrate's court, with the help of the police and the prosecution service, my word would never be taken before theirs.

The Earl of Ducie was waiting for me round the lanes once, after I'd been coursing the dogs by the farm. Old Ducie would always come out after me personally – with others, of course, and rarely on his own. It was like he got some perverted pleasure out of chasing people like me, who he considered to be vermin – less than a rabbit or a fox or a rat, and he'd have shot me dead if it were back in the olden times when he could've got away with it.

'Two lovely dogs you got there.'

'Yes, they've caught dozens of your hares.'

'I don't want you on my land again.'

'I got thirty or forty years on you. I'll be poaching your pheasants after you're dead.'

He is, and I am.

Back when foxhunting was legal, I came across a skulk of foxes that were worrying the ducks we kept in our big garden. I shot two of them and took them over to Beaufort Hunt Kennels at Badminton. Back then, the hunt fraternity thought as much of their foxes as they did their pheasants – it was all part of their hunting pageantry and elite heritage. So I thought I'd get on their highly bred nerves a bit. The gamekeepers up there were renowned for their heavy drinking and, as I approached, one of them came out of the clubhouse drunk and fell against the wall. All the better, I thought, they won't be alert. I went across and hung one of the dead foxes on the wire kennel fence to drive the hounds mad, but the buggers in the clubhouse were so pissed they took no notice. So I went back over there, opened the door and threw the other dead fox in. There was uproar. They were falling over each other trying to get out to see who it was and, when they did, they could hear the dogs going mad at the other dead fox. I was dressed darkly, with a scarf over my face, so they couldn't identify me. But I deliberately let them see me so they'd give chase – which they did. They staggered down the lanes after me, brandishing pickaxe handles, but I was fit and sober and knew where I was going, even in the dark, and they were never going to catch me.

Next morning, I got a phone call from my brother, Robert.

'Someone was up the Beaufort Hunt last night with dead foxes.'

'Was there?'

'Yeah, they reckon it was them anti-hunt people. Coppers swarming all over the place.'

I started laughing.

'Was it you?'

I said nothing.

'It was you, wasn't it?'

I was always up for a prank like that, even as I got older. It was a trial of tenacity – a battle of wills – to see if I could out-smart them. They had all the resources of money and privilege and the law behind them; I had only my nerve and my skill as a poacher. When the foxhunting ban was coming into force, the saddle-bumpers wanted our support to try and stop it – the ban, that is – forgetting that they wouldn't spit on the likes of us before then. We just stood back; it wasn't our fight.

I went up onto Princess Anne's Gatcombe Park Estate with the greyhounds, for a run after a hare. Because it was Princess Anne's place, I knew security would be tighter than anywhere else. But, as I said, I liked testing my gamesmanship to be able to get away and it wasn't long before a Land Rover was headed towards me. Now, the people in the Land Rover might be game-keepers, or they might be MI5, but I'm not waiting around to find out. I do a runner into a small copse and hide in there. The Land Rover drives round looking for me, round and round every-where, but they can't find me. They hang about for ages before giving up the search, then they take an exit onto a little lane. When they're gone, I use the same lane to make my escape and I'm chuckling to myself that I was able to avoid them so easily.

It's getting on in the evening, almost dark, and I can hear pheasants jugging in the kale fields, which is a nice cover crop for game birds, just like buckwheat or mustard. If there's no trees, pheasants will roost on the ground, especially in kale, and there's a scarcity of trees in this area of the estate, where the kale fields are. So, I decide to come back and drag-net for them.

Bob's already briefly mentioned drag-netting for partridge, and we have a drag-net that's twenty-five yards wide and four yards deep. There's a line coming off each of the front corners and, with a man either side, it gets dragged along over stubble and grass and short kale. The front of the net, where it's being pulled along, needs to be kept about four feet off the ground – so you go forward, pulling against each other lightly, to keep it up. The mouth of the net's taken over the pheasants and the part that's coming behind, dragging on the ground, puts the birds up and they get caught. All you do at the front is drop the mouth of the net down and you got them underneath. I've dragged the fields below Hollyberry Wood on the Tortworth Estate up and down in the dark in October time, when the young birds are jugging on the ground. With drag-netting, you're not using any lights or guns or anything else to give yourself away. All you need's a little bit of moon overhead.

Gatcombe Park ain't the kind of place where you can go in a motor and park it up somewhere. If you do, the registration will be taken and you'll get traced and have to answer questions about what you were doing there and all that rigmarole. I let things settle down at Gatcombe for a week or two, then I get this woman to drop me and Bob off up there with the drag-net. It's late in the evening and we wait till it gets dark, then drag-net over the kale fields where the birds are roosting. We drag two fields and get twenty-two birds and I go round, hitting them with a priest, which is a short club that can be kept in the pocket, with lead inside it for weight. We bag up the birds and the net and are heading back to where we've arranged to be picked up by the woman driver.

'That was easy enough.'

'I thought security would be tighter, but when I came up with the dogs, I was easily able to give them the slip.'

Next thing, the Land Rover's coming towards us. This time, it has a powerful searchlight on the top and they're scanning the fields for us – we must've been seen on CCTV or something. The light beam catches us and stays on us.

'We better make a run for it.'

'Into that copse where I hid from them before.'

But the beam follows us and now they know where we're hiding, even if they can't see us. We're carrying twenty-two pheasants and a heavy drag-net, which we can't run far with, so we decide to hang the lot up in a tree. I climb up and Bob hands the two postbags up to me and, after that, the bag with the drag-net. I hang the lot from a high branch with plenty of cover round it, so they won't easily be seen from the ground. Then I jump back down. By now, the Land Rover's at the edge of the copse and the light's searching through the trees for us. A loudspeaker blares out:

'Come out!'

We crouch down and keep quiet.

'This is the police. Come out!'

We stay where we are.

Next thing, I can hear something moving towards us from the other side of the copse. I think they've sent in keepers from that side to flush us out into the searchlight and the hands of who-ever's shining it. This is becoming more of a test than I bargained for. It's time to make a move. Now, I'm as fast and sure-footed over rough night-time terrain as any animal, but Bob's getting on a bit and won't be able to outrun a Land Rover with a searchlight. I signal to him that I'm going to make a break for it and draw them after me. He points to the tree. I leg him up into the lower branches and I know he'll collect the net and post-bags and make his way back to the rendezvous point when the coast's clear.

I break cover and run straight into the searchlight, to make sure they see me.

'There he goes!'

'Get after him!'

I dodge and weave like a hare being turned by dogs, as I scarper across the open fields. The Land Rover might be faster than me, but it can't turn and manoeuvre as quickly and I manage to keep ahead of it, darting in and out of the light beam so they'll keep following me, away from the copse and Bob. I look back and see some others with torches emerging from the trees and there's orders being shouted that carry across on the night air.

'Stop, or we'll shoot!'

I take no notice. A shotgun ain't going to have my range and, anyway, none of them keepers can shoot straight. I hear a bang and something whistles over my head, obviously meant as a warning. But it's not buckshot, it's a bullet. This is serious – I'm being hunted and I'm a sitting duck out here if one of them has a night-sight on a high-powered rifle.

There's a stone wall up ahead and I vault it easily and keep running. The Land Rover can't follow, but the searchlight can and I need some cover quickly. Another bang and another bullet whistles close – closer than the first. The next one'll hit me for sure. I see a hazel wood to my right and I run straight in and keep going. The next thing I know, I've fallen into Gatcombe Water and the flow's carrying me along towards the sewage works.

I swim as hard as I can and get washed into a shallow stream that runs close to Avening Road and the B4014. Once I'm out on the road I'm safe, except that I'm soaked to the skin and it might be hard to explain that away. I trudge on for a few miles, keeping close to the hedges where I can hide if any vehicles come along – and I finally find a small roadside service station with a public telephone.

'Can I make a call?'

'Of course. What happened to you?'

'Got caught in a shower.'

'It hasn't been raining.'

'No?'

'No.'

'They throw all sorts of stuff out of aeroplanes these days.'

I call home, hoping Bob will be there and not sitting in some police cell. He is and I tell him where I am and he comes out to get me.

'They didn't see you up the tree, then.'

'No.'

'The birds?'

'I got them, and the net.'

I don't tell Bob about the bullets and he turns to me as we're driving along.

'They weren't no gamekeepers.'

'Who weren't?'

'Them who came through the copse.'

'Who were they?'

'Dunno, but they weren't keepers.'

'What would you have said if they'd seen you?'

'That I was doing a bit of bird-watching.'

We laughed about that many times afterwards, but never did find out who it was chased me through Gatcombe Park.

We used to put crow-scarers in the woods. They're like bangers. We set them up and 'BANG!' – they go off every few minutes on a timing fuse. 'BANG!' We put them in woods on an estate we're poaching. If the keeper's out and about on a night and he hears 'BANG!' – then a few minutes later, 'BANG!' – he thinks there's somebody poaching in such-and-such a thicket. But we'll be in another wood maybe a couple of miles away. We scatter the crow-scarers in twos and threes in different areas around the wood, several nights in succession, to draw a lot of attention. The keepers think there's poachers coming there regular, like, for their pheasants. They'll never know it's just crow-scarers because there's nothing left after they go off – just a bit of cardboard that drops down to the ground. So the keepers are out there waiting and waiting, maybe for a week, with nothing to show for their trouble. All the other woods are left unguarded and we're there, taking the birds.

Once we've got what we came for, we can skip safely home in the spectre-light from the moon, hearing the night cries of this wild west country. And, as we walk across the purring land, I sometimes think it would be good to be able to fly like the birds above – shit down on top of the heads of all the hypocrites and soar over the rest of the poor fools, scuttling in their never ending struggle to be free – just like me.

I'm out ferreting on Tortworth Estate one day and approaching a rabbit burrow in a little rocky area that I'm going to start at. Then I hear this cawing noise. The further I go, the louder it gets.

'What the hell is that?'

I come over the brow of a hill and, down about twenty yards away is a big crow-catcher. The keeper's obviously doing some vermin control and this thing's appeared overnight. It's about twelve feet long and eight feet wide and six feet deep – a wooden framework with a door, covered in chicken wire. There's funnels leading into it, wide on the outside and narrow on the inside, just like with the pheasant traps. They're mostly on the top but the silly bugger's only gone and put a few on the bottom as well. He's chucked a load of bread in there and the crows and jackdaws are going in through the funnels to get it, but can't get back out again. There's about a dozen jackys and a couple of crows in there, all creating a hell of a racket. But, because he's put some funnels down low, what's happened is the noise of the other birds feeding has attracted pheasants and they've gone in as well and can't get back out. I can see at least four of them in there now. It's a poacher's payday!

I carry on ferreting and get about a dozen rabbits, gut them and leg them and put them in the bag. Then I go back to the crow-catcher and see there's another couple of pheasants in there now, making six in all. I open the door, which is just on a latch, and go in. The jackys and crows are all flying round my head and pecking at me while I try to corner the pheasants and wring their necks. Then I take them out and have them as well as the rabbits. The keeper will come at some time and kill the other birds that I've left in there, and never know I've been by.

I go back to the crow-catcher and raid it every day and, over the course of a couple of months, I get a total of sixty-two pheasants from it. Easy as pigeon pie. Thanks, mister gamekeeper. Until one day. The easiest way the keeper can get to the crow-catcher is to come up this field to a stile, twenty yards from the pen. He can't drive to it so he has to come on foot. Anyway, I'm in there one day and just coming out with a brace of pheasants when I hear this shout:

'Oi, you, what you doing there?'

Here's the keeper coming over the stile and it's lucky I'm coming out and not in the middle of the cawing jackys and crows, or I might not have heard him. I run and he gives chase and I leave the door of the crow-catcher open, so the birds are all flying out into his face as he passes. That gives me a good head start on him and he chases me for about three hundred yards and then gives up. I hide the pheasants in a wood and come out round the side and across the fields back home.

Later that night I return to get the pheasants and the crow-catcher's gone. I do a bit of poaching while I'm out and I'm on my way home in the early hours, just when it's getting light. I'm coming up through the churchyard when I see these three heads peeping out – two behind one of the big tombs and another behind the church wall. Now, I'm thinking whoever it is might be getting ready to jump out and mug me for my pheasants. There's a standoff for a few minutes, with them watching me and me watching them. I get fed up with that and discharge my gun into the air. Well, you've never seen blokes run so fast in your life. Turned out later that they were three black fellas who'd come up from Bristol and broke into a shop in Wotton, but I didn't know that at the time. They got chased and did a runner across the fields and ended up in the village churchyard and, while I thought they were going to jump me, they thought I was the local law, out searching for them with a shotgun. I never heard anything more about them and I don't know where they ended up – probably down in the next county of Wiltshire.

But to finish off about us poachers versus the landowners – there's enough violence in this world, without adding to it over a few rabbits and pheasants, ain't there? What with left and right and black and white and all the in-betweens and ups and downs and ditherers. There's children working their lives away in the slums and side-streets for the making of cheap rags and other rubbish, so we can say we're civilised and we have this and we have that – and the air around us loud with the pleas of the abused and tormented and tortured, and the moon wearing ear-muffs so's not to hear the screams. Some people have enough problems with the polluters and politicians and their shadowmen superiors lurking behind every lie, without the smoke-screen of getting all psychotic over the catching and killing of a wild animal or two.

Which is in our nature to do.

You agree, don't you?

Brian, Bob and Cora, Lower Woods, Wickwar, circa 2004

13

Brian — Prison

One time I had a small lorry that was registered in the name of a dead man. I used that truck to go nicking Cotswold roofing tiles from cow barns and churches and old buildings on the big estates – tiles that were rare, hundreds of years old. They were worth money and I knew every old barn and building where they were to be found. I had a mate called 'Cider Chris'; he put an ad in the paper advertising the tiles and he got a hundred replies. 'Course, he didn't have any tiles to supply at that point; we had to go out and nick them.

Three of us were doing it over a period of about two years alto-gether – so long that there was hardly a roof left on an old building anywhere in south Gloucestershire. So many Cotswold tiles had gone missing that police and landowners were marking what was left with a special dye that would only show up under ultraviolet light. They were on such a lookout for anyone suspicious out of a night in a van or truck that they were pulling all sorts of people over – painters and plumbers and fly-tippers and bail-skippers. But not us, we were keeping out of their clutches.

It was our opinion that these old tiles would otherwise have blown off the crumbling buildings in a big wind and got broken. They were valued by weight and we were getting £300 a square – up to £1,500 a time. We sold them to reclamation yards, who sold them on for repairs to listed buildings and to rich people who wanted their houses to look like old-time castles. The tiles weathered over hundreds of years to get that unique colour and the new ones weren't the same, so there was only a limited amount of them to be had. It was supply and demand – anything rare is worth money.

The lorry was legal to carry one-and-a-quarter tons and, every time we went out, we loaded six ton of tiles onto it. So you can see, there was always too much weight and it was difficult to drive. On this last night, we stripped down tiles from an old abandoned church that was in a hollow dip and we could hear the Duke of Beaufort's dogs barking in the distance. It's autumn time and raining hard and I have to drive along steep windy lanes to keep away from the main roads. I can't get any speed up to climb this particular hill and the truck starts slipping. The only other way home is to go back and use the main A38. As I come to the end of the lane, a police car goes by. He carries on and I turn onto the A road and head in the other direction. But the patrol car spots us and thinks we looks dodgy, because it turns round and comes right up behind me and follows me for about two miles. I assume he's putting the plate through the records and finding out the truck's registered to a dead man.

There's no way I can outrun him with the weight I'm carrying, so I turn off into a lane – and the patrol car follows at about thirty yards. One of the men I'm with is called Roger and the other's Cider Chris. Roger's so frightened of the dark, his girlfriend has to walk him home of a night – and we call Chris 'Cider Chris' because he's an alcoholic who later dies of sclerosis of the liver. There's a farm track down the end of the lane.

'When we get to the track, I'm slowing down.'

'What then, Brian?'

'We jump out and make a run for it across the fields.'

'It's dark out there.'

'Don't worry, stick with me and you won't get lost.'

It's about two in the morning and very dark – I mean countryside black. Just as I start to slow down, Cider Chris jumps out one side of the van and runs into a field. He gallops for about fifty yards and then collapses. Roger jumps out the other side and I know the coppers have seen both of them. I get out carefully, so I won't be seen, and use the shadow of the truck to hide me from the lights of the cop car until I get into the darkness. Roger's panicking and I know he'll give us away if we don't get moving. I tell him to follow close to me, but I don't need to, because he's practically hanging on to my leg and shivering like a plucked chicken in a gale. Other police have arrived now and they have a dog with them, so Cider Chris is a lost cause. The dog finds him hiding in a hedge and they take him away.

We have a five-mile trek to get to Wotton-under-Edge, where Roger lives and, while the police are dealing with Chris, we get a good head start on them and they never catch up with us. When we finally arrive there, Roger's traumatised from the dark and says he's going straight home. I'd rather hang around till the heat's off, just in case, so I bypass the roads and stay out in a wood until morning, then I go back to my village. But, for some reason, the police are hiding close to Roger's house and they nab him as soon as he shows himself and they take him in for questioning. He has tile dust on him and they have fingerprints and other evidence. So they've got the two men they saw escaping from the vehicle in the lane and the lorry ain't registered in my name.

I should've been in the clear, shouldn't I?

Unfortunately they found a rough-drawn map in the footwell of the truck, and that incriminated me. You see, the reclamation yard where we sold the tiles was having its weighbridge repaired and they sent us to a quarry to get weighed in. They drew a rough map of where the quarry was, I memorised it and told Chris to throw the map away while we were driving along. There was a hole in the footwell and, when he screwed it up and chucked it, the piece of paper didn't go out, but went down the hole and got stuck there. The police found the map and the quarry, which made a record of every vehicle that used its weighbridge, including mine. They got a description of three men who were in that truck – and one of those descriptions fitted me.

As well as that, I'd been pulled previously in the vehicle, just after I bought it, so, even though it wasn't registered to me I was still linked to it. They brought me in and questioned me and I denied everything. They couldn't pin me to the tiles, because they only saw two men jumping out of the truck, but they still charged me.

Roger had already admitted to the charge, because they had him bang to rights. I said I gave him the truck to put a new exhaust on it for me and I wasn't driving it that night – he backed that story up. Cider Chris had to go to a special pre-trial hearing, to see if he was fit to plead. He claimed he was crazy, due to alcoholic dementia. He said he didn't know where he was most of the time and he drank a gallon of rough cider every morning and he believed it was still 1964.

It took the court twenty-two months to decide whether Cider Chris really had alcoholic dementia or if he was trying to pull a flanker and I was on bail for that length of time. In the end, they gave him the benefit of the doubt and he was found unfit to plead and the charges against him were dropped. That left me and Roger. They panicked Roger by turning the lights off in his cell and making sinister noises outside the door, and told him he'd get three years if he didn't admit to sixteen other charges of stealing roofing tiles, to a total of £100,000 – so he did. They had no hard evidence against me, just a vague description from the quarry and my link to the truck, but nothing to place me at the scene on the night in question. So they changed the charge to one of conspiracy – conspiring to steal roofing tiles with two unnamed persons, even though Cider Chris had walked away from it scot-free.

I got myself a barrister and went along to Bristol Crown Court. The judge was another one who liked to hand out harsh sentences and who looked the sort who'd be out hunting with the Duke of Beaufort and all the other broad-bummed buggers I was stealing tiles off. I asked the barrister what I could get if I was found guilty.

'On a bad day, four years.'

'Shit!'

'On a good day, on appeal, no less than three years.'

If you get a three-year sentence or over you get banned for life from having a shotgun licence – I couldn't risk that.

'I want to plead guilty to something.'

'I advise against that. You have a good chance of being found not guilty.'

'Not good enough.'

The barrister didn't want me to, but he agreed that the prosecution might go for a guilty plea on a lesser charge, rather than risk an expensive trial where it was fifty-fifty if they'd get a result or not. So it was agreed that I'd plead guilty to 'knowingly allowing my vehicle to be used for the theft of three loads of roofing tiles to the value of £3,000 by two unnamed persons'.

The judge sentenced me to two years, reduced to twenty-one months on account of my guilty plea. Roger got three years, reduced to two because of the length of time it had taken them to decide whether Cider Chris was demented or not. So, when you think about it, I came off worse than anyone else and I don't know if that was because my name was Brian Tovey. Probably was. But I didn't get a lifetime shotgun ban, and that was more important to me than doing twenty-one months in jail.

They sent me to Gloucester Prison first, but after a few months, I got moved to Leyhill. Now Leyhill, if you remember, was the open prison where I'd run across the parade ground with the goose over my back. It was right in the middle of my poaching territory and I knew every field and wood and stream and lane for miles in any direction. By the time I got sent there, the Nissen huts were gone and replaced with accommodation blocks and the regime was fairly lacksadaisy. I'd been in tougher places.

The layout of Leyhill was something like this: you had fifty-five hectares of land, with the chain-link fence at the back that I climbed over with the goose, which led to a lane and then up a bank and away to Tortworth Lake and beyond. There were gates in the fence that you could squeeze under if you were slightly built. The interior had numerous buildings, including a sports hall and a theatre and accommodation blocks like A and B and so on.

There was farmland that the prisoners worked on, and gardens and a wooded area close to the theatre, and open fields away to the sides and an administration block at the front with a low wall that led to a road. We were mostly unsupervised and, as long as we were back in the accommodation blocks before they locked them up at night, we could do more-or-less what we liked. They took a head count in the morning out on the parade ground and you had to be there for that. Otherwise it was a bit of a holiday camp for me and I was able to creep out of the prison whenever I liked and come back before lock-up.

It wasn't long before I was sneaking things back and forth for the other inmates. They'd pay me to take out letters and the like and bring back cans of beer and bottles of spirits. No one else knew the lie of the land like I did, and if they went out they might get lost in the dark and not be able to make their way back in time for lock-up. If that happened, they'd be deemed to have escaped – although technically you can't escape from an open prison, just abscond – and they'd get time added on and be transferred to a tougher nick. But I was able to make my way up through the woods and away across the fields and streams and I knew every inch of the land in light or dark.

I arranged for this woman I knew to pick me up in her car and I'd go deliver what I had to and buy the stuff to bring back and still have time for a bit of fun, if you know what I mean. Well, it wasn't long before some of the others wanted to come with me. I didn't want to get slowed down by people tagging along and falling into thorn bushes and making a load of noise, but they offered to pay me well, so I agreed. I started taking them out for the evening – those who lived locally could arrange to see their wives and families, the others could go get a burger or a pizza or I'd take them to The Cross Hands pub for a few beers. Nobody said anything to us because the prison clobber was decent enough, nice shirts and good quality jeans, and we didn't look out of place. It was alright, just as long as we got back before they locked the accommodation blocks up.

One night I planned to go out with this big bloke called Noah – he was six foot eight and built to match. There was something on in the theatre and, instead of going there, we were ready to sneak away through the woods. But then it started snowing and that made for a change of plan and a cancellation of the excursion.

'They'll see our footprints, Noah. Only ours will be leading to the woods, the rest'll be going into the theatre.'

'I don't care, I want to go!'

You didn't argue with Noah when he said he wanted to do something. So we went – up through the trees and out towards Tortworth Lake and the road where the woman with the car was waiting. On the way, we were nearly come upon by a keeper on a quad bike with his lights off. He was looking for poachers, not prisoners, but I didn't want us to get too shitted up by having to make a run for it, so we hid down until he drove off. As luck would have it, I saw him before he saw us and we continued on and had a nice evening out.

When we're coming back, I see two screws as we're approaching the wood – this time we're not so lucky and they see us as well. We can't come back the conventional way, so we has to run round the back of the prison and squeeze under the gates, but Noah's so big he gets stuck. The alarm's sounding now and it won't be long before they lock the whole place up. I can hear the screws coming and calling,

'They ran round this way!'

I'm pulling at Noah and, just before the screws come in sight of us, he manages to get through and I'm thinking it might have been easier to go over the fence rather than under the gates. We make our way quickly up to A Block, but the place is locked and we can't get in. There's a window into the kitchen but that's locked too, so Noah head-butts it and smashes the glass. Well, I'm through the smashed window like a ferret down a rabbit burrow, but big Noah gets stuck again. I pick up a metal tray and hit him on the head and knock him back out into the yard. The next thing, he grabs hold of the window frame and rips the whole thing out of the wall and gets himself through. Nobody hears the bashing and crashing over the noise of the alarm siren and we make our way swiftly and stealthily to our rooms without anyone seeing us.

Next morning they did a head count and noticed the cuts and bruises on Noah's forehead. He got shipped out, along with another bloke who had nothing to do with that night and was crying like a baby at the thought of being transferred to a tough closed prison for the rest of his sentence. I said nothing.

Then Cider Chris decided to get a torch and my crossbow from Bob and meet me one dark evening in November. Maybe he felt guilty about getting off scot-free and me and Roger doing the time, or maybe he just wanted to make a bit of cider money. Anyway, he brought the bow and we went lamping up along Tortworth Lake, all the way to the boat house. I got twenty-six pheasants over a period of three nights and Chris took them back with him to sell. But, on the third night, he was drunk-driving home and he hit a nine-year-old girl who ran out from between some parked cars. He was arrested, but refused to blow into a breathalyser. He tried his old trick of alcohol dementia, but it didn't work this time and he got five months in a category C prison.

Another night, I'm taking out two kitbags of jeans and prison shirts to sell, which I nicked from the laundry. The shirts are decent, like I said, and I can get £20 a pair for the jeans. I intend to sell one of the kitbags as well and fill the other with booze to bring back. I've arranged for the woman in the car to meet me and everything's set up. Then this bloke comes over to me.

'I hear you're going out tonight.'

'That's right.'

'Can you take out some packages for me?'

'Risky, with the kitbags.'

I explain to him that if I'm come upon I'll be dropping the kitbags and making a run for it. His name will be on the packages and they'll find them and he'll be shipped out. He says he'll take the chance and he pays me £10. Well, as sod's law would have it, when I get up by the sports hall and start going across the fields, I hear a shout behind me.

'Stop!'

I turn and see two screws coming after me fast. I drop the kitbags and run through the prison houses to a barn where I've arranged to meet the woman with the car. I know the alarm will go off soon and they'll lock the place up and I have to get back in before that happens.

'Quick, get me round to the back of the prison.'

She drives me past the main entrance and round to the lane at the back and I squeeze under the gates again. But the accommodation blocks are already locked. Then I notice a group of blokes outside the library, which is also locked. They knock on the door and a screw emerges.

'Can't you people hear the alarm? Get back to your block, there's been a breakout.'

They start traipsing back to the accommodation blocks and I file in behind them, hands in pockets. The screws unlock the door and let us in. Next morning there's a head count and the bloke who sent the packages gets shipped out – and another innocent bloke as well.

It was like 'Carry On Up The Clink'.

But it couldn't last forever and one night I'm in town to get some tobacco when I'm come upon by a group of screws from Leyhill who're out on a stag night or something. They recognise the prison clobber and I'm off down the street like a bitch on heat being chased by seven sheepdogs. Shouts of 'Stop where you are!' come from behind me, as I duck down this alleyway where a crowd of weird-looking winos are loitering – up to no good for sure. I zig-zag through them, with a bump in the solar plexus for an old woman with a moustache, sending her sprawling.

'Stop that man!'

'He tried to molest me!'

Now the down-and-outs are after me as well as the screws. Maniac on the loose, mugging methylated spirit drinkers! I round the corner and see a church across the way.

'There he goes!'

'Where?'

'Into the church. I saw him run into the church!'

The hunt's in full cry now, with all the hounds slobbering and me as the fugitive fox. The screws are out in front, being of fitter frame than the winos. There's a late service for all the faithful in progress as the chase bursts into the place of holy worship – all howling and baying for blood. But they're instantly subdued by the menacing voice of the vicar, as he bellows out over our sacrilegious heads, 'This is a house of God!' – in no uncertain terms. There is some religion left in the world, for those who know where to find it.

I duck out a side door in the confusion, but the screws have telephoned the prison and it's locked up by the time I get back. So, next day, I'm shipped out to a category C prison on Dartmoor called Channings Wood.

But I only had a few months left to serve and then I was free as a bird again.

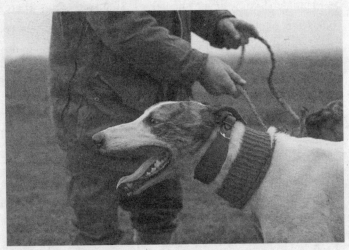

Two coursing dogs, after a run

© CHRIS CHAPMAN

14

Brian – Poaching Tricks

There's a lot of rainbow trout in the streams around our village and up towards Kingswood. Sometimes I'd shoot them in the shallows with a .22 air rifle – smaller fish, maybe two or three pound in weight. In even shallower water, on a night with a lamp, I'd use the .410 to get bigger fish – maybe three- or four-pounders or more. I'd travel miles to get them, mostly on private farms, but also at Damery, where there's lovely clear water, and on the Berkeley Estate. They don't like me poaching their fish because they have fishing clubs paying them for the privilege. But how can a fish that swims up and down a stream belong to someone who owns the land either side of that stream? It's like saying, 'I own that water while it's flowing through my land.' How bloody presumptuous is that? I could catch a couple of hundred rainbow and brown trout over a short period of time, and it makes no difference to me what side of the river bank I'm on – the right side or the wrong side.

But I don't do so much trout fishing these days, apart from what I need for the family. People don't want them now –

wild-caught fish, they prefer their fish filleted and from a supermarket, with the head off, or battered and deep fried. They're no good to me if they're more than I need to eat and I can't sell them. Why kill them in the first place if I can't do either?

But it's nice sometimes to be on the bank of a river, where you can hide awhile from the brute swagger of the world – with the moon pulling its reflection over the water and the scent of the earth rising up and the air dew-fresh around you. You can let your mind off its level-headed leash for a scamper – until the fish bite and you call it back into concentration.

There ain't many brown trout about now, but plenty of rainbows, and if you don't want to hang about, another way to poach fish is to kill a rabbit, slit its guts a bit and fix it to a branch overhanging the water. In the spring and summer, when it's warm, it don't take long for the blow to hatch on the carcass and the maggots drop into the water. The maggots draw in the trout and they come there constantly for a regular supply of food. Once they're used to feeding there, I take the rabbit away and replace it with night lines baited with maggots or worms. In shallow water I use single-hook night lines – a length of fishing line attached to a six-inch peg driven into the ground at the side of the stream. The flow of the water will take the lines in to the side, where the fish are lurking. In deeper water I use a line with five or six hooks on and a stone or brick tied to the end as an anchor. All the hooks are at different depths and I catch loads of trout that way.

Other times I use a funnel trap – a net of about eight or nine feet in length with a round ring at one end, a foot or two in diameter. About a yard from the end there's another smaller funnel hole. I set it in the stream; the trout go in the large hole and swim down through the smaller hole, but can't get back out again. They all get caught in the last yard or so of netting – it's a bit like the pheasant funnel trap, only with a net and for fish. I left one behind one evening when I had to do a runner. I was on a 250-acre farm up near the Sherbourne Estate, where the farmer was hiring out fishing rights to clubs and individuals to use a stretch of the River Leach that ran through his land.

Now, these so-called legitimate fishermen are only too happy to be unofficial wardens of the river when it comes to poachers like me – they have to pay a fee for what they catch. I don't. Anyway, this particular evening I've been doing the rabbit trick on a remote stretch of water where none of the fair-weather fishermen were coming, because they tried it and didn't get no trout there. After a week of eating the maggots that were falling from my rabbit carcass, the fish were queuing up to feed there and it was time for me to take the rotting coney down and throw in some night lines.

It's starting to get dark and I'm just setting up the lines, watching the river run away, as if it knows something I don't. Chuckling to itself as it flows, with little cross-currents and bits of broken water and backwashes and whirlpools – when I'm approached by four of these fellas carrying rods and reels and baskets and landing nets and little stool things to sit on. The fish've stopped biting in their favourite spots because I'm luring them away, and they're looking for a fresh place to park their fat bums.

'What are you doing?'

'Same as you, fishing.'

'Have you got a permit?'

'Don't need a permit.'

'He's a poacher . . . look at that dead rabbit!'

All four of them make a move on me and I stand my ground, to see which will be the bravest. The one who asked for my permit's in front of the others, and I throw the stinking rabbit at him and it hits him across the mush. He starts to heave, like he's going to throw up. The one behind him rushes at me and I side-step him and he goes into the river, which is only waist-high. The other two back off, but there's no use setting night lines here now, because they'll only go for the farmer and he'll call the police and all my work with the rabbit's gone to waste and the fish've had a free feed.

But I'm not going to go away empty-handed, so I move upstream about half a mile to set up the funnel net I'm carrying in my bag. It's not dark yet and, after a while, I can hear the sound of angry voices coming from round a bend in the river-bank that's shielded by young sally trees.

'Shit!'

They come into sight before I can get the net out of the water and packed away in my bag. It's the four fishermen, one of them dripping wet, with a couple of young farmhands and the farmer himself on a horse, brandishing a big stick. But no police. They're probably thinking the seven of them can deal with this themselves and give me a good hiding, which they won't be able to do if the coppers are about.

'There he is!'

They come at me and I have to leave the net where it is and do a runner. The fishermen and farmhands can't catch me, but I know I'm not going to be able to outrun the horse.

After about a hundred yards, it's almost upon me and I feel a whack of the farmer's stick across my shoulders. I keep running and the horse comes alongside me and the farmer turns it in on me and I'm forced by its flanks down the bank and into the water. I wade across and come up onto the other bank and I think the bugger will be satisfied with giving me a swimming lesson and go back laughing to his fee-paying friends and tell them how he dealt with the dirty poacher. But he doesn't. The horse is already in the water and coming after me. This bloke wants blood.

I weigh up my options and decide that running on ain't going to be good. He'll only catch me up again and, considering the mood he's in, he'll probably ride the horse over me – trample me into the ground for my mischief-making. The bank on this side of the river's steep and he's at his most vulnerable coming up it. The horse is neighing and struggling on the muddy slope and the farmer's hitting the animal with his stick to drive him up. There's a load of teazles growing along the bank, so I pluck one and stick it up the horse's nose. The animal's already agitated and now it rears up and sends the farmer tumbling off its back and into the river.

The others have caught up now and are on the opposite side. The farmhands go into the water to fish their master out and the anglers are throwing stones at me. The farmer's furious.

'Get after him!'

Without the weight of the shit-kicker on its back, the horse is able to come up the bank on my side of the river and I grab hold of its bridle. They're all wading across now, all seven of them. The horse is still skittish, but the skill I learned as a boy, riding my father's horse over the cricket pitch, comes into its own and I get the animal under control and swing myself up into the saddle and gallop away across the open land and into the safety of some coverts.

It's dark by now and I know they'll never catch me, so I dismount the horse and turn it round and whack it on the quarters, to send it cantering back towards the river. I mean, I don't want to be hung for a horse thief as well as a fish filcherer, and I've lost my funnel net into the bargain. But these things happen from time to time and the world's an uneven place, with many ups and downs. And certainly ain't round!

Speaking of nets, I was doing a bit of beating for a keeper up Great Shefford way, who wanted to net some hares. While I was there, I noticed they had a lot of partridge on a shoot next to the long fields we were working, so I thought I'd have some of them. Partridge will fly, then drop down and run. So I got to know the direction they favoured to run in and set up a 200-yard long net at the end of the field. I set it very baggy, very loose at the bottom, then I drove the field down towards the long net. The partridge quickly got tangled up in the baggy nets and I caught fifteen of them live and put them in boxes. I released them on land where I had permission to hunt and brought them on.

It's just a different way of catching partridge, other than with a clap net that we mentioned before. It's just a different poaching trick – I'm not saying someone reading this book's going to run out and start long-netting partridge but, if you are reading, it means you're interested – for one reason or another. And everyone should have something in their life – something out of the ordinary. Otherwise it's gone quicker than a quail's heartbeat and you wish you had it all over again so you could do something different.

I've lamped for partridge too, as well as long- and drag- and clap-netted them – on a night with a .410. You can lamp anything, really, not just pheasant and partridge and rabbits and hares – woodcock will come up the beam at times too. I caught forty-five woodcock of a night out lamping. Or you can catch them in mist-nets – a fine-mesh net I put at different heights on poles. Mist-nets are used by the scientific community for catching birds and bats for banding and other research projects. They're made of nylon and suspended between two poles, like a big volleyball net. When they're set up properly they're invisible and the mesh size can vary according to what you're trying to catch. Of an evening, just before it gets dark, woodcock will come out of the trees and start flying around. If you're prepared to wait for a few hours, you can get them in the mist-nets. They don't fly high, just over the hedges, so you got to set the nets just right. Or, if you're impatient and you're quiet enough, you can get a shot at them instead.

Woodcock are lovely to eat. Beautiful – nearly as nice as collared dove. And it's one of the best things in life to be able to hunt and cook your own food, to rely on your skill and not the supermarkets. It's almost enough to make me want to send an anonymous donation to the Society for Retired and Starving Gamekeepers – provided they sign a statement admitting to their sins against civil liberties.

Bob's already told you about the different ways to lamp. Now, when I'm out lamping for rabbits or hares, I walk the dogs up the outside of the beam. Greyhounds get very clever; they go up the edge of the lamp beam and in, taking hares and rabbits straight out of the quat. And Bob taught me how to get them to retrieve as well. Greyhounds ain't natural retrievers, like spaniels; they got to be taught. But once I take the rabbit or hare off of them when I'm training them, I give them a biscuit as a reward. After a while, they get used to me having the kill and not them – they know it's not theirs. This and all the other skills is what I mean in Chapter Six about learning all I needed to know without a formal education. If I'd gone to school, proper like, I might have ended up as something else – maybe an opinion-pollster, or a pickled-onion packer, or a private pension peddler, instead of being a self-proclaimed authority on the greyhound and the gun.

Skills like long-netting pheasant in woods where there's plenty of them about. I make a little ride, cutting a place where I can run the net through. It's got to be done clever, not like cutting a hundred yards of bushes out of a wood that's going to be obvious and draw the attention of keepers and the like. Just clear an area at the end of winter or early spring and keep it clean, but not too obvious, so that when I set my long net up, it's not going to get tangled with branches and stuff. I set the net up nice and baggy, early in the season – end of September or maybe October, when there's lots of pheasants feeding together in one place, and they're tamer. Then I get back out and beat it up with sticks and collect all the birds that get tangled in the net. But it's not so easy once they get wild and wary.

Sometimes I long-net hares at night. I know the fields and where they like running and how they want to escape. I set up my nets and drive them and I get some – a few but not many. During the day, I can get lots – I got beaters driving them to the nets and flankers to keep them in. Of a night it's different. I haven't got much control. It's dark and they can see where they're going, but I can't see them to drive them towards the net, and a lot of them get away out the flanks. I only do it in the dark if I haven't got permission – if I'm poaching. I've even set long nets in the rides for deer – in the woods. Then I beat them out and I can catch one or two roe that way.

There's other tricks too – a crossbow's a handy thing if you're poaching near the pens, early in the season when the pheasants are tamish – before they've been shot at a lot and beaten out of the woods. Once they've been constantly driven over guns, they start getting wise to it all and won't be so easy to take. You hide and, when they come out to get a feed, you can get them with the crossbow. It's quiet and won't alert the keepers, so close to the pens. You can take the bow part off and put it in one pocket and the stock part in another pocket. You can use bolts that are pointed and go through the bird, or square-headed ones that don't. My crossbow has a hundred and seventy-five pound bowstring pull and I need a goatsfoot to cock it. But the downside of the crossbow is, you can lose a lot of bolts and sometimes that's not economical, because the bolts can cost you more than you'd get for the pheasant these days. Still, diversity, they say, is the spice of life and otherwise I might just have to build myself a raft out of empty soup cans and float away to the Fijian Islands.

I've used snares too, in case you're asking. I'll set up a feed bin near some thick blackberry bushes and the birds come through in a nice lot of cover to feed on the corn in the bin. I set up an H-frame made out of nut sticks, with single-strand wire snares dangling off the cross bar, between the bushes and the bin. You need nice straight nut sticks, quite thick, so they don't bend. The frame's got to be set at the right height so the pheasants go under it – the birds have to stoop down to get beneath the cross bar of the H-frame to get to the feed, and they're caught by the neck in the snares.

Depending on the length and strength of the H-frame, you can set up half a dozen or even a dozen snares from the one cross bar, to up your chances of getting a few birds. But you're not going to catch enough to get fat on with this method; you're only going to get one or two every time – and that's if there's a lot of pheasants about in the first place.

There's many snaring methods used for poaching. When keepers release pheasants, there could be thousands of them in some woods. They'll be roosting everywhere. They can't all roost up in the big trees, there's not enough room, so some have to roost lower. You find, going through the woods, that there's opportunities for snaring them at different heights. Or you can make a two-inch hole in the ground, going down a few inches, with corn in it and a snare set round it, or hooks with raisins on, and lots of other ways as well. All these methods will catch you a few pheasants, if that's all you want. But I'll lamp hundreds over a few nights with a little torch and a .410. No matter how many tricks you learn, lamping on a night is by far the most effective way – it's hit-and-run. You see the pheasant roosting, there's no keepers about, you're in – BANG! BANG! BANG! – you got yourself a few dozen and you're gone.

At the risk of repeating myself, the thing about traps and snares is this: you'll catch pheasants, or whatever you're after, but you'll also catch things you don't want to catch, like blackbirds and magpies and vermin like rats and squirrels, especially in hard weather when it's cold. Then there's the keepers – keepers will even put a pheasant in a trap, then lie in wait for you to come and get it. So you got to be careful on the approach – first scan the surrounding area from a safe distance. If there's one watching, you'll soon spot him. Then chuck a big stone at him so he breaks cover and gives himself away. It's a game of cat-and-mouse with the keepers. I know where they set their own traps – a layman wouldn't – so I go along and take them and I got my traps for free. But when you got a bit of land where you have permission, you can set nets and traps and snares up to draw game in, without having to worry about someone pouncing on you from behind when you're not looking.

Another way to trap pheasants is to make a cage with chicken wire, with a funnel leading in. The funnel's wide at the entrance, but gets narrower, just like the crow-catcher I told you about. The pheasant can get through it to eat the corn inside the cage, but can't squeeze back out through the narrow neck at the other end of the funnel. I make those cage traps out of battens and nut sticks. I put a lot of corn on the outside to begin with, until I have the birds coming every day. Then a little bit of corn on the outside and a lot on the inside. The pheasant pecks the corn on the outside and wants more – he goes in through the wide neck of the funnel, squeezes through the narrow neck, and can't get back out. I don't set these cage traps in the heart of the estate, where the keepers are watchful – I set them up on the edges, where the pheasants come when they've had enough of being shot at and rousted about by beaters and dogs. There's less chance of getting caught that way.

If I bring those pheasants onto land where I have permission and pen them in and feed them for a while, then they'll stay about. I start whistle-feeding these pheasants early in the season – whistle them in and feed them with corn. Once they start feeding, they'll keep coming. They associate the whistle with the corn – and they associate it with no danger and they'll feed and feed and feed away. When the weather's mild, there's plenty of food for them, insects and berries. But once it starts getting into the winter, if it's hard, the corn's got them. I had a red post office van once and, when I went down to the fields to feed them in, one cock bird in particular would run four hundred yards after the red van, because he knew he was going to get fed. He connected the red van with food. I never shot him because he was such a character and he drew the other birds in.

The corn I used for drawing in pheasants and ducks and other game, I nicked that off the estates. I took it in a backpack, maybe a hundredweight at a time. They put tons of it down in feed bins – they might have fifty or sixty forty-five gallon feed bins around the pens, where they released thousands of pheasants. They'd all be full to the brim. Well, I went round and took some out of each bin and filled up the backpack. I bagged up the feed when I got it home and we used it for ourselves during the season, to draw in birds to where we had permission to shoot. So, not only did I take their birds, but I used their own feed to draw in those birds. I had a half-ton of corn in store at one time and I was using it to feed my own fowls as well as drawing in wild birds – more even than I could use.

So, you see, there's many ways to catch wild game – or poach, if you want to call it that. Gypsies use catapults, with a metal or bone Y-frame and strong rubber bands for shooting ball bearings. I've used them too, when I was younger. You can get a few birds if they're on clear branches and you can get a clean shot. If they're in bushes or thick cover, the steel balls will ricochet and you've got no chance. It's the same with an air rifle. Both of these are nice and silent but, if it's too windy, it'll put your aim off. Like I said, a .410's the best. Don't matter where they're roosting – and you can line several birds up with one shot. I know the best places to set up and I've shot birds out of the same trees, the same bushes, for the past forty years. They keep coming there, and they always will.

It's all down to skill – and the tricks of the trade.

Bob, long-netting at the Pentons, near Andover, October 1998

© CHRIS CHAPMAN

15

Bob – Eccentric Characters

As well as the poaching, I used to do a bit of sheep-rustling too. I remember being up on Oxwick Farm one time, near a building called Cromwell's Barracks, where the Roundheads gathered before marching down and laying siege to Berkeley Castle during the Civil War. I was in a ditch, cutting a sheep's throat, and I had this idiot up a tree, keeping a lookout for the farmer. He fell asleep, this bloke, and he never seen the farmer coming and the next thing I know the shit-kicker's looking down into the ditch at me.

'What you doing?'

'Sheep run into some barbed wire, just trying to help her.'

'Is she alright?'

'I think so. I'll have her out of here in a minute.'

'Need any help?'

'No, I'll be alright.'

'Good man, come up to the house and I'll give you a drink.'

As soon as he was gone, I had the sheep on my shoulders and was away, leaving my snoring lookout up the tree.

Sally Grosvenor, the deceased Duchess of Westminster, was one of three illegitimate daughters of a woman called Muriel Perry. The girls were raised by a governess and rarely saw their mother, who served as a nurse in the Great War and who was supposed to have little interest in them. The only one who visited them was a man they called 'Uncle Bodger', who'd bring them presents – they had no other family or friends. Uncle Bodger's real name was Roger Ackerley and he confessed on his deathbed to being the girls' father. Sally and her twin sister ran away from home when they was eighteen and she married Gerald Grosvenor, who became the Duke of Westminster and the wealthiest man in Britain. They never had no children and, when the Duke died in 1967, Sally travelled round the world first, then moved back to the family home in Gloucestershire and lived in a big house with about thirty acres of land round it. She kept a breed of black sheep and I used to poach the land and my greyhounds would bring down some of her flock. A greyhound will kill a sheep by biting into its throat or the back of the neck – they're powerful dogs for any kind of hunting. I butchered the beasts and sold the meat and the hides and boiled up the heads and the bones for the dogs. She had no keepers up there, so it was easy enough to get away with.

I also used to steal her vegetables and she put a notice up in the window of the local post office asking – 'If the person who is stealing my sheep and vegetables comes to see me, I will give them some free of charge.' But I never did, because I didn't trust her not to call the law.

The Chief Constable for Avon and Somerset used to go up there for dinner parties and he'd bring a plod with him to stand guard at the bottom of the drive. There's no street lights anywhere near; it's pitch black and there's a bit of grass where the copper could keep back out of sight. He'd stand there on duty and you couldn't see the bugger, barring a car went by and you got the reflection of the headlights off his silver buttons. I was up there to get a few pheasants on one of the very rare occasions when I poached after having a drink – I didn't fancy going all the way in and there was some cockerels out clucking, so I got a bit of mortar out of the wall and chucked it down. They thought it was corn and I drew 'em over and shot 'em. I stuffed them in my pockets and went on my way. As I was coming back past the house, I suddenly sees this copper standing in front of me.

'What's this, then?'

He gave me such a start, I kicked him hard in the shin and ran off into the dark, where he couldn't see me to come after me.

After going past there a few times with the .410 folded and being taken by surprise by that copper in his hiding place, I decided I'd give him a fright, instead of the other way round. There used to be a big stuffed grizzly bear up on the Duchess's land and it was half-hidden in some trees. There's no way the copper would know it was there, but I did. Anyway, I goes up there one dark night and throws a stone at him. It hits him on the helmet and he starts to come after me. I let him keep sight of me until I disappear into the trees and he follows me in – then he comes upon the stuffed bear. I'm behind it and I lets out a deep growling sound. Well, this copper nearly shits his trousers and he's off out through the trees and away down the road. I don't know where the Chief Constable thought he'd gone when he came out after having his cigar and brandy, but he never got him back out there. The plod must've told all his mates there was a wild bear up on the Duchess's land because I never saw none of them on guard at the bottom of the drive no more.

The stuffed bear's gone now. It rotted away in the rain.

Anyway, I was in the lanes shooting pigeons one day when Duchess Sally came past on a horse.

'What are you doing?'

'Shooting pigeons.'

'Why?'

'They're eating my cabbages.'

She was having a problem with vermin on the estate and she had one of the Duke of Beaufort's keepers over there, because the old Duke was always visiting for one reason or another, maybe knocking her off or something, who knows. This keeper's name was Barratt and he was useless. He'd bring over a dead squirrel or a rabbit that they'd killed on the Duke's estate and go sit at the bottom of her big garden under a tree and let off a shot every now and then, so she'd think he was doing his job. He'd take her the dead rabbit or squirrel and she'd give him a couple of quid and he'd go and have a drink. I had a chat with her and she seemed quite friendly for a toff and, in the end, she asked me to go up there and sort out the vermin – which I did with my son Robert, who had a little Jack Russell terrier that went under the sheds and killed the rats, while my spaniel worked the hedges and I shot whatever came out.

I cleared all the land of vermin and she was as good as gold. She was nice and polite, for a ya-ya, and down to earth, and she'd send us out tea and biscuits. She even signed a book for Robert and dedicated it to him. He still has it – it's called 'Just Dogs'.

But she wasn't stupid, she knew what I was – it just suited her purpose to employ me. Anyway, I'm up there on my own one evening and there's some kind of wedding reception going on. The Duchess sends me out some sandwiches and her butler says I can come in for a drink if I wants. I tells him I don't drink no more but I'd like to have a look at the guests – just to be nosy and see who was there. He goes and asks her and comes back and tells me I can stand to the side of the main hall and, as long as I keep myself out of sight and don't interfere with the festivities, it'll be alright.

By the time I goes in for a gawk, the guests are all well intoxicated. The bridegroom's all done up in a silver suit and the bride's far too young and beautiful for him. They has this group of classical musicians up on a little stage and people is dancing round in a wide circle – all moving in harmony, in the same direction, like they all knows exactly what they're supposed to be doing.

Then this young fella in a blue silk suit butts in and upsets the synchronicity – bumbling his way through to a tray of champagne held by a waiter. He's obviously pissed, because his tie's undone and the tail of his shirt's hanging out of his trousers. The dance stops and, when the next one starts up, the drunk grabs hold of the bride and drags her out for an embarrassing display of stumbling around the floor. Everyone's glaring daggers at him and the bride's eyes are appealing for help. The groom eventually goes and rescues the girl and the atmosphere lightens again, with high-pitched voices and 'darling's and 'how delightful's. Before the next dance can begin, the blue-suit stands in the centre of the big hall and tries to lead everyone in a sing-song.

Regrets, I've had a few . . .

'Sit down!'

The groom shouts at him and the guests start coughing politely and turning their heads away to pretend this ain't happening and that makes the man more determined than ever. I'm just enjoying the spectacle of it and seeing the toffs in their element.

He continues with his Frank Sinatra impression, then he's up with an unsteady leap onto the little stage and grabbing hold of a microphone.

The band leader is trying to wrestle the microphone back from him, when someone's foot kicks over the cello-player's chair with a string-twanging crash and one of the fiddlers sticks his bow up the oboist's nose. By now security are on the scene and they grab the miscreant – but he's being awkward as a tup and not wanting to let go of the microphone.

I'm imagining this fella must be some previous lover of the bride who's been dumped for an older, richer man and is intent on disrupting the genteel reception and causing chaos.

A hefty pull by the bouncers sends the blue-suit flying off the stage and onto his arse, still clutching the microphone and entangling the flex round the flautist, sliding him off his stool and taking several other instruments along with him. Everything's in an uproar! And while they're unravelling the waltzes from the reels, the blue-suit howls out some more of the gin-sodden song before they drags him to the door.

A few minutes later, the Duchess's man comes to me again.

'The Duchess wonders if you might do her a favour.'

'What?'

Apparently, the drunk's the groom's younger brother and he's the prodigal son of the family, with a grudge agin' his father for leaving everything to the eldest. He's threatening to come back in and spoil the party, but they don't want to have him arrested and cause a scandal.

'The family has a house in Wotton-under-Edge.'

He presses an envelope into my hand that has inside it an address and a key – and two fifty-pound notes.

'Would you take him there . . . across the fields?'

I goes outside to find the blue-suit sitting on the gravelled driveway, slugging from a bottle of whisky. He holds the bottle out to me.

'I don't drink, and you've had enough.'

'How do you know?'

'I've been trained.'

I take the bottle from him and hand it back to the butler, then I lift him to his feet.

'Let's go.'

'Where?'

'Home.'

I has to half-drag him, because he's completely inebriated now and he's still singing as we go.

He takes out a packet of cigarettes, but can't find his lighter.

'Do you have a light?'

'No.'

It's a trek across the countryside to Wotton-under-Edge and it's about 2:00 a.m. when we gets there. The blue-suit's sobered up in the fresh air and the night-time chill, just as the Duchess knew he would, and he still has the cigarette dangling from his mouth. We're making our way along Old London Road, towards Westridge Wood and the address in the envelope, when this idiot goes and knocks on someone's door. A muddled old pensioner in pale striped pyjamas looks out at us from the low light in his hallway.

'Could you possibly oblige me with a light?'

'Are you mad?'

'Maybe.'

'It's two o'clock!'

A woman's voice calls down the stairs.

'Who's that at the door, dear?'

'Two escaped lunatics, love.'

'What about my light?'

'I don't smoke.'

'Surely you have a gas cooker or some such appliance?'

The old man slams the door, just as the blue flashing lights come racing down the road. Suddenly, we're surrounded by a swarm of policemen.

'And what have we here?'

'Couple of poachers, sarge.'

It's only the big fella who bet me the fiver his dog would catch Brian, and didn't.

'I know this one. Tovey, ain't it?'

'Aye, and you owe me a fiver.'

The blue-suit's starting to get uppity, as his class tend to when they're asked to be reasonable. But, after our trek through the brambles and bushes, his shoes are covered in shite and his shirt's torn and his face is scratched and his hair looks like an unruly rook's nest – and he stinks of whisky.

'I'll have you know that I'm no damn poacher!'

'Oh no, what are you then?'

'I'm the second Marquess of Evesham.'

The coppers are in convulsions of laughter and we're both arrested for causing a disturbance and dragged protesting to the station. And in the night I hears him howling and banging his cell door and, to take my mind off it, I lie back on the bunk and imagine I can see the stars above in the sky and feel the free wind across my face and I sleeps for a short while. In the morning, the Duchess comes and everything's sorted out and I'm free to go with no charges pressed – they even gives me back my two fifty-pound notes.

And they says that a little knowledge is a dangerous thing – but complete bloody ignorance is a crime!

That was one Duchess. Another was Mary von Teck, who became the Duchess of Beaufort when she married the Marquess of Worcester – who became the 10th Duke of Beaufort. She lived at Badminton House on the Beaufort Estate and died in 1987, aged 90. She was out riding one day when a Pyrenean Mountain Dog frightened her horse. Instead of getting all indignant about it like the gentry normally did, she said to the dog's owner, 'What a beautiful animal, would you sell it to me?'

The owner wouldn't sell at first, but she offered him enough money to buy six Pyrenean pups to take its place. She brought the dog back to the Beaufort Estate and had it shot. Then she got her men to hang the carcass up on a clothesline and she beat it with a stick every day for a fortnight. You or I would be locked up in a nuthouse for behaving like that but, if you were one of them, you were said to be 'eccentric' rather than insane.

They were a rum lot, all the aristos whose land we poached, and most of them thought they could do as they liked, until you

stood up to 'em. They all had histories and skeletons in their cup-
boards that they tried to keep out of sight. They were no better
than us and, in some cases, a lot worse. Take Lord Podge, for
instance, third son of the eighth Duke of Beaufort and a great
friend of the Duke of Clarence, eldest son of Edward VII.
When a house in London was raided by Scotland Yard in 1889
and a number of male prostitutes arrested, they named Lord
Podge as one of their clients. Don't forget, homosexuality was
illegal in them days and Podge faced a hard-labour prison sentence just like Oscar Wilde. But, if Podge was brought to trial,
the Duke of Clarence, Queen Victoria's grandson, would also be
implicated. So Podge conveniently disappeared to the French
Riviera. A warrant was issued for his arrest, but it was too late,
he was long gone. He never came back to England to face the
charges and spent the rest of his life in the South of France with
his male companions.

It was common belief that Podge was allowed to escape to
save the monarchy's blushes. The scandal was even debated in
the House of Commons and the government accused of criminal conspiracy. But there was never any inquiry or
investigation. Less than two years later, the Duke of Clarence
died, of pneumonia they said, leaving it clear for his younger
brother to become the next king.

And they had the gall to call us criminals!

But it ain't just the aristos who was eccentric, if that's what
you wants to call it.

There's a picture of me long-netting hares that was painted
by a famous wildlife and animal artist called Mick Cawston.
Cawston lived in a small cottage on a farm in Burnham-on-
Crouch in Essex. He loved to paint dogs – pointers and spaniels

and terriers and greyhounds – and he rang me up one day to ask if he could come along to our drag and do some sketching. At the time, we was running some whippet courses and he come along in his old battered jacket and long hair and torn jeans, looking like a bit of a tramp.

He took photos and drew sketches of the whippets and then painted pictures of them, and I'm sure he was able to sell them pictures to all the old women who'd pay a lot for oil paintings of their dogs. We got talking about hare-netting and, as it happened, we was going down to Sir James Scott's in Ropley, near Winchester, netting hares – Scott was an acquaintance of the artist and Cawston came along a few times to the long-netting. That's when he painted the picture of me. It was a miserable rainy day and he did a great job and the painting's hanging in my front room at home. He was recognised as one of the finest wildlife painters of all time and I found him to be alright. He was one of the boys and easy to get along with. He was a very talented bloke and there was no edge to him – like, he weren't up above no one else. But, under the surface, he was a haunted man who lacked belief in hisself and he suffered from deep depression. He stabbed hisself in the heart in 2006 and died at the age of forty-seven.

Nowadays we rents land off a man called Albert Chadwick. Albert's a big fella and he can lift a bale of hay with one hand. His family had two farms in the area – the Top Farm and the Bottom Farm. Then Albert's father died and left all his money to an animal sanctuary. From then on the family was struggling – they had fields of turnips and corn and wheat and barley they couldn't afford to have harvested. That was a benefit to us, because it used to attract the pheasants in the winter time and we'd just walk up there and shoot 'em. Over the years, things deteriorated into bankruptcy and Albert had to sell the farmhouse and the barns, one by one, to townie yoikes who converted them into their sterile 'living spaces'. Until, apart from the fallow land itself, he was down to one yard full of rubbish and he lived in a cow barn – an old milking shed that was converted into a makeshift bungalow. He got a bit violent with the builders who was doing the barn conversions – and who could blame him – and they called the police and he was locked away in Gloucester nuthouse for a while. And not for the first time either, as it happened.

Now, Albert had a twitch in his left eye that he couldn't control. And the story's told that he used to frequent a bar in Bristol called The Pound Of Flesh, where the barman wore pink chiffon shirts and Albert's eye would wink and blink all by itself and he never had no problem getting served, no matter how busy the bar was. Rumour had it that the odd free double brandy become involved, until one night the barman follows Albert into the gents' toilet to negotiate terms. Chadwick, not being too sophisticated in the subtleties of these circles, lays the bugger out on the piss-stained floor. He was barred after that.

As I was saying, we rents the shooting and sporting rights to Albert's land for £100 a year – and we rents the twenty-acre field where we holds the drag racing for £80 a month. We pays another farmer £50 a year for the shooting rights on his farm, which is beneficial to him because we keeps the land clear of vermin that would damage his crops and his poultry. It's always handy to have shooting rights. Like I said before, you can feed game onto land where you has permission and you can get back there quick if you gets come upon when out poaching. If you're coming home along a public highway, either walking or biking or in a car, and you gets stopped with game, you can just say, 'Oh, that pheasant? I caught that earlier on land where I have permission.'

For instance, I was long-netting one night over by Frampton-on-Severn with a 150-yard net. I was told there was a lot of rabbits there, so I set the net up but, as luck would have it, I only caught one. I put the gear back in the motor and drove off to try my luck again, up around Berkeley Castle. Unbeknown to me, one of the back lights wasn't working and I gets pulled by the police.

'You're Bob Tovey.'

'That's right.'

Immediately they seen it was me, they was suspicious and decided to search the car.

'Where did this rabbit come from?'

'Found it on the road.'

'Didn't poach it?'

'Don't do any poaching now.'

They told me to get the brake light fixed and let me go. Now, if I had a dozen or more rabbits in there, I couldn't say I found 'em all on the road, could I? That's why it's always handy to have permission.

'I caught 'em on Albert Chadwick's land, where I has permission.'

'Is that right?'

'It is, officer. Just on my way to the pub now, thank you.'

Anyway, Albert's another one of the many different and 'eccentric' characters I've come across on my way through the years.

Then there's the tale of the two Colonels – Colonel Peter Hawker was a young soldier in the Spanish Peninsular War, who served with distinction under Wellington. He was seriously wounded at the Battle of Talavera in 1809 and came home to live at Longparish, near Andover, in Hampshire. Hawker was famous for being a shooting man and he wrote a book called *Advice to Young Sportsmen*, about hunting and wildfowling, which was published in 1814. Now, we was down round Longparish netting for hares nearly two hundred years later and we met another Colonel – Colonel Ted Walsh, who was a keen photographer and who published books on sighthounds.

Ted wanted to come long-netting with us, so we brought him along several times and he took pictures – he also took pictures of my dogs running at the Cotswold Coursing Club, particularly one of a greyhound with its mouth open and the jaws ready to snap shut on a hare. Some of them pictures are in this book. This probably ain't much of a story, but it's just a coincidence that Hawker and Walsh were both colonels at Longparish a couple of hundred years apart.

Me and my sons have netted hares for the countryside television presenter, Johnny Kingdom, for his programme *Johnny's New Kingdom*. Johnny was a poacher hisself for a while, as well as being a lumberjack and a quarryman and a gravedigger, before becoming a television personality. He suffered from depression following an accident on a tractor – then someone gave him a video camera to take his mind off things and that changed his life. Johnny was a real showman and we got on very well with him. He knew nothing about netting hares, mind, but that's what he was with us to learn – and show to the public on his programme. He kept in touch with us for a long time afterwards, but not recently. I reckon he must be getting on a bit in years now and may be suffering from ill-health. I don't really know.

We also made two television programmes with photographer Chris Chapman for his *On Assignment* series – one about open coursing and long-netting and the other about poaching and drag racing. Chris's pictures is on display in London and New York and he's won many awards, including Photographer of the Year. I found him to be a very nice bloke altogether – well spoken and refined, but with a great sense of humour. He came out into the woods taking pictures of us poaching pheasants and came long-netting as well. He was really easy-going and we had a great laugh with him while we was filming. He also allowed us to use some of his pictures in this book – and on the cover.

Thanks, Chris!

About fifteen years or so ago, I was contacted by one of Hugh Fearnley-Whittingstall's researchers. She said they wanted to make a programme with Hugh going long-netting then cooking a hare on a barge and having a chat with me. I agreed and arranged with a gamekeeper I knew to do the long-netting, all legal like, on this lord's estate down in Corsham, Wiltshire. I met the woman there and she spoke to the gamekeeper, who told her it was alright, but not to bother the lord about it. She had a green light from me and a green light from the gamekeeper, but she still went and seen the lord. Of course the lord, for his own reasons, didn't want publicity or no one making television programmes on his land, so the whole thing fell through. The programme got made, but it was all staged. All you see on the television is fifty yards of long net with a rabbit in it. They didn't know how to catch a hare and it was all bullshit.

And I never got to meet Hugh Fearnley-Whittingstall!

16

Brian – Greyhounds

I make no apologies for my way of life and won't compromise with townies who frown with the privilege of political correctness on my activities. Country people have moved to the towns to get work and the majority of people living in the countryside now are town and city people who've got no knowledge of animals or the hunting of animals, whether for food or for sport. People are detached from nature now – nature's alien to them and they don't understand it. They're removed from having to kill to eat; someone else does it for them, hidden away in abattoirs and factory farms and slaughterhouses. People will eat the meat they buy in a supermarket, but they don't want to think about it being slaughtered and bled and gutted, but it is – it's just not them doing it.

Death's camouflaged from them and they pretend it don't exist. But death's as natural as birth, as natural as eating or sleeping or breathing, but they believe it's something to be avoided – unnatural. They're the ones who're unnatural. Dishonest. But they'll be the people who shout loudest against hunting and killing. Then they go hunting at the supermarket, where their kill is nicely cut and packaged for them. Their lifestyle of work, work, work, to pay for all the stuff they don't really need don't allow them time to come into contact with the real world – the natural world.

But I'm always willing to listen to their point of view.

Bob's always been mad on greyhounds and he passed his preference for the breed over lurchers, or any other sighthound, down to me. He used to cut notches on the kennels when he was young, for the amount of hares or rabbits each dog had killed, and I've had my own dogs that could match any in the land when it came to hunting and wild coursing. I've been a registered dog trainer for many years now and I've run greyhounds on all the tracks around the country, like Nottingham and Reading and other places besides. But a lot of dog tracks are closing down and I concentrate on the drag coursing and the lamping and the bringing on of dogs from a young age. Greyhounds are elegant dogs and they've always been a part of my life – we've always had them and still do. My grandfather had them, my father had them and I have them.

But a greyhound's only worth keeping if it can be used for hunting and racing. They're quiet dogs, clean and good-natured, and they'll run themselves into the ground after a hare. Like, Bob had a dog once that ran itself to death – it got right up behind this hare, but the animal kept jinking in front of its nose and the dog couldn't pick it up. It's no use trying to call a greyhound off a chase; they just keep on going no matter how you call them. In the end, this dog had to stop because he cramped up. His muscles were hard and solid and he couldn't walk. Bob was miles from anywhere, so he started to carry it. After about fifteen minutes, the dog wanted to get down and it was able to stagger about. By the time Bob got back to his van, the greyhound was a bit better, but completely exhausted and unable to stand for long.

He got the dog home about an hour later and put it in its kennel with a bucket of clean water. It had a drink and Bob gave it two raw eggs and some milk. It lay down on its bed and seemed contented enough. Bob asked me to look in on it later in the evening and the greyhound was alright. But, in the morning, it was dead. We were both sorry this happened – he was a good dog and we liked him a lot. Bob did all he could, there was nothing else he could have done – and no use taking him to a vet, because a vet wouldn't have been able to do anything either, except charge a fortune for an overnight stay. And the dog would still have been dead in the morning.

As far as I'm concerned, the greatest finder, shifter and killer of ground game is the greyhound. Greyhounds are gentle animals, quiet and polite – until something moves. But they're like high-performance athletes once they're in pursuit and they can get injured easily. I was out once with a dog for a bit of sport – just the greyhound and no gun – and a hare got up. I slipped the dog and he started off. All of a sudden there was a noise like two stones banging together and he went down in the field. When I caught up to him, I saw that his front leg was broke in half. I had to go to a nearby farm and get the farmer to come shoot him for me. It was the humane thing to do, rather than let the animal suffer. 'Course, you'll always get some people to say otherwise – smug so-called celebrities who think more of their pampered cats and dogs than they do of the poor and pitiful. Running round making themselves even richer flogging cologne or cosmetics that's been tested on animals born in laboratories and never seen an open field – and never will. But if we shoot something to eat because we prefer that to buying it off the supermarket shelves, they'll send round the *Sunday Slanderer* to pursue us for the full and sordid story and, if it ain't incriminating enough, they'll beat it till it fits their formula.

OK, if you keep dogs, you're responsible for their well-being. When I get home from being out, either poaching or racing, no matter how wet or cold I am, I always see to the dogs first. I give them warm food and fresh paper for bedding. I always use paper, it's warmer and cleaner than straw and straw can house fleas and ticks. To me, the dog's an essential part of life and must be cared for – but it ain't a pet and I never had a dog indoors; they were all kept in kennels and the kennels were cleaned every day and plenty of fresh paper put down for bedding. Greyhounds have sensitive stomachs and don't need a lot of rich food – cereal mixed with the meat is usually good for them and chewing bones will keep their teeth clean and healthy. Exercise on a hard surface keeps their nails short and their toes up taut and not splayed out and their coats are easy to keep clean. Some greyhounds smile – it can give people who're not used to them a bit of a start because their teeth show and they look like they're getting aggressive. I've had a few smilers over the years; it's harmless and can be a bit of a laugh.

Bob kept a few lurchers once, but not for long. I don't rate them like I do the greyhound. Some people prefer them, but not me. And things are a lot different now than in the days when we had dozens of dogs and hundreds of ducks and other fowls about the place. We don't keep ferrets now, either, but we do keep a good springer spaniel or two. They're always hard workers and very gentle in the mouth so's not to damage the game they retrieve. They pair up well with the greyhounds to flush game for the faster dogs to chase, or I use them to work the hedges and I shoot whatever comes out and they retrieve it.

Spaniels get very clever and, early in the season, when pheasants have just been released from the pens and they're still half daft and the blackberry bushes are thick, the birds can't get out very quick and a good spaniel will go in and catch a dozen or two. The shooting fraternity calls it 'pegging' because a bird caught by a dog like that hasn't gone over guns and is classed as a loss. But it's a good way of poaching – if you got the dog to do it.

I've even hunted deer with dogs – greyhounds, that is, up on the Duke of Beaufort's land. I put the dogs on a deer in daylight – they're a lot faster than the deer and they'll bring down a fallow or a roe the same way as they would a sheep: by the windpipe or the back of the neck. Once the deer's brought to ground, I'll run up and cut its throat and bleed it out. There's no dog in the world can beat a good greyhound and they're stronger than they look. I've hunted deer with a single dog and with a pack – I was up in the woods with a tiny little bitch once and she brought down a fair-sized fallow on her own. Even without a gun, it's great to be out there with a dog or two – darkness dropping from a star-filled sky and a soft mist washing away all the bitterness and bollocks. You can take your own time on the outskirts of a bustling world, where there's no stopping for anything. Loiter outside the mainstream of society with the greyhound stepping into your stride beside you. Man and dog. Together.

Like I think I said already, I'm licensed for training dogs with the Greyhound Board of Great Britain now, so I don't shoot them any more, unless one breaks its leg or something down the fields and it's the most humane thing to do, like as happened that time I told you about when the farmer shot my injured dog. I became a licensed trainer in the late 1990s, attached to Reading Greyhound Stadium, which closed down in 2008. I was successful there and I had a very good strike rate and percentage of wins for a trainer. Now I operate as unattached, not with any track, but running my dogs anywhere I like. The thing is, greyhound tracks are closing down all the time because they're becoming increasingly less profitable and the land they're on's worth more being put to other uses – like supermarkets or second-hand clothes shops. But to me greyhound racing's a good sport, in the absence of anything else. Let me put it this way, I love to see a good dog after a good hare and that's my first love – out across the fields and the greyhound pitting its wits against the hare and the hare outwitting the dog most times – or even the catching of one every now and again to eat. Then there was competition coursing, which was run by a clique of cheats and the chosen few and, after that, there's track racing, where the ordinary man will get a fairer shake.

But not always.

For instance, if your dog's a bang railer – which means he likes to run on the rail round the track – then he should be drawn in an inside trap. Other dogs are wide runners and should be in the outside traps. A 'grader' is someone who sits in an office and grades the dogs, knows all the dogs and how they prefer to run. But bookies don't like people winning, because they lose money. They'll complain to the racing manager if someone's having it off them too many times. That's when graders can be influenced to put railers in outside traps and vice versa – a dog will come across the others at full speed and greyhounds get injured that way. Another dangerous aspect is the shape of the tracks, with tight bends either end of long straights. But most tracks are located in inner cities where land is valuable and it would cost too much to realign the bends and make them nice and sweeping – they'd be much better as straight runs, like our drag track, but that's not going to happen.

As well as that, in summer the sand on the track can get dry and very loose. Groundsmen water it to try to keep it firm and what you get is a certain depth of firm sand, with loose sand underneath. A dog's running and its paws are digging in for purchase – his foot goes through the firm sand and into the loose sand and he slips and breaks a hock. The tracks need watering right down, but this don't get done because of laziness or carelessness due to people being paid a minimum wage to do the job and their hearts ain't really in it. I don't call it cruelty; I call it a preoccupation with profit over outlay and the welfare of the dogs. No one wants to see a greyhound getting hurt and it could be avoided if the money was there. But there's less and less investment in track racing and, eventually, I can see it dying out altogether through lack of interest by future generations.

At one time there were thousands of dogs about and they weren't kept track of like they are now and, over the years, before I was a trainer, I must have shot close on a thousand of them. And I know you'll ask, how can anyone who thinks so highly of his hounds do something like that? You see, some greyhound trainers are no good and they blame the dogs – but it's them who ain't up to scratch, not the greyhounds. Dozens of these dogs used to come over from Ireland and what they were running on was the kill of a live hare. Running round a track, they're not getting a kill, so they lose interest. All they're doing is running with the other dogs and not fulfilling their potential. So the trainers would ring me up:

'We can't do nothing with this dog, d'you want to take it over?'

I'd have a good look at the dog first – see whether it could be worth taking on. If I took the dog, I'd bring it out and drag it – put it down the drag on a dummy hare to see if it had pace. I can tell the agility of a greyhound on the gallop, if it's putting everything into it, if it's chasing the lure or not, if I can bring it on or not. I have the knowledge to see if a dog's got it, running up that drag, chasing the lure. If it has, it's worth bringing on.

It takes a lot of time and money to keep a working greyhound. They're not like a little house pet that you feed a tin of chummy-chum or horsey-hearts and take for a five-minute stroll in the park once a day. They're mad to run and they've got to be exercised and trained properly, just like an athlete. There's an old saying: 'If you got a grief against someone and you don't want to fight them, give them a greyhound.' Because they'll be broke in a month. If you get a dog that ain't up to standard, you're going to waste a lot of time and money. You can spend more hours buggering about trying to make a bad dog good than you would with six decent dogs.

The racing fraternity and, back when it was legal, the coursing fraternity, would go through a lot of dogs to find one that was right and there'd be many dodgy greyhounds they could do nothing with. I'd take scores and scores of dogs like that off trainers and try to save them – I was known for bringing difficult dogs on. I had ways of getting its full potential out, with techniques and tricks I knew through hunting and poaching. I used to have loads of 'chuck-outs' given to me from people who didn't know how to bring dogs on, even though they were supposed to be professional trainers – right through from the late 1970s until I got my trainer's licence. I'd get a call:

'D'you want a dog? I got a dog here two years old. He done this and he done that in Ireland, but nothing over here, except win a couple of trials.'

After the drag, I'd take it to a flapping track somewhere and give it a trial. Then take it round the fields on the scent of rabbits. Just flushing up the rabbits and letting the dog see them dashing into the burrows, not letting it off after them – just something to get its attention. I'd do other stuff like that to try and make the greyhound genuine. And I was very successful with many dogs that got returned to track racing when I was finished with them.

Others I took coursing after the live hare, when it was legal, to see if they were worth the work I was putting into them. First of all, the dogs had to be fit and tough enough to run three courses on the trot in an eight-dog stake – assuming it got to the final. If they were, then I'd persevere with them and take them to a few meetings to see how they got on. If they turned out to be no good for either flapping or coursing or hunting or poaching, then I'd dig a hole and shoot them. What was I supposed to do, give them to Battersea Dogs Home? I didn't breed them in the first place so, if there were too many dogs, that was the greedy breeders' fault, not mine. I provided a service for those dogs that would otherwise be abused or abandoned or starved and spend weeks or months on death row in some dog rescue place, only to be put down by a vet at the end of it.

But every greyhound is chipped now; they're all accounted for, like a car having a log book. Dogs are checked at regular intervals throughout the year and, when one dies or has to be put down, you have to have a form filled out by a vet, so there's no way you can take them out into the woods and shoot them no more. In the old days, after I shot a dog and buried it, if I'd been a religious man I'd have said a prayer. But I'm not and I'd just stand for a while with the sky all a blackness and no stars shining their lights – except for the silver satellites beaming their pitiful pictures across the whole world and sending message pulses out into the deepest part of space, hoping for some acknowledgement from a higher life form. And I'd think to myself – God forbid that we're the best there is!

We used to have upwards of thirty greyhounds of our own at any one time, that we tracked and coursed and hunted and poached with, and it was hard enough work. It's something a man does with muscle and sinew, as well as his skill and wits. And I got nothing against people who spend all their time in front of computers, living what they call virtual lives. Imagining all the things they dream of doing, but never taking no risks, never feeling the heat nor the cold – all safe and sound in their armchairs. Never running through a wood or climbing a tree or wading across a stream, except in their minds. I got nothing against them either who go to expensive gyms and do all kinds of exercising to pass the time and lengthen the life and hang on by the fingernails to the final few hours of heart-breaking humdrum. The lazy ones who won't, need to be chained to a chair and forced to watch the same television programme being played over and over again, where half a ton of shite's being cooked by celebrity chefs. I got nothing against none of that.

As long as they got nothing against me.

They say too that someday the computers will invent robots

to take all the interesting stuff out of life, so the salesmen can fill it with drudgery. More time for the masses. 'Course it all depends on whether they decide to divide up the profits of that brave new world and give us all a little share. Or will they tell us it's been swallowed up by invisible overheads and unmentionable expenses? The coppers will be alright – need the likes of them for a good while yet, to keep law and order and send the malcontents like me, who believe in alternatives, away to where we can't corrupt the rest of society. Just like they used to do to me at school. They'll keep control the way it's done now – by printing political correctness and doling out the opium of television to the people – until identity cards are hanging round all our necks and chips inside the brains. Spit into a computer and it'll know your whole history, back to the beginning of time. It makes me shake!

Hopefully, I'll be gone before all that happens. In the meantime, as a licensed trainer, I work under rules and regulations and they can come out and do an inspection at any time. The welfare of the dog is the most important thing and I agree with that. But, from the point of view of shooting dogs, there was so many reject greyhounds and I used to give them a chance at least, which was more than many people did. Shooting them was quicker and more humane than taking them to the vets, because they thought they were going out for a hunt or a run. Then they'd be dead before they knew it. At the vets, they're in strange surroundings on a table waiting for the injections to work – they can be frightened and distressed and shivering and shaking. Unlike us poachers, some people make a lot of money from dogs – breeders and trainers and vets and insurance companies and dog food makers that turn out tins of processed crap. They live in big houses on prosperous pavements, wearing words of honour – and the walls built of the best brick with money for mortar. Yet they'll criticise the likes of us for cruelty. No wonder the world's in such a state!

I had to take a greyhound down at Christmas time – it broke a hock and so, as I'm accountable now, I took it to the vet. There was nothing the vet could do. I knew that. I knew it was a waste of time. Through experience, having had dogs for a lifetime, you get to know illnesses and injuries and what can be done about them and what can't. And some vets are grasping buggers and charge as much as solicitors these days, fleecing people out of their money. All this one did with the dog I brought down was put him on an expensive drip for a few days and the dog died anyway, like I knew he would. I still get calls from people, but I can't do anything for them now. Just recently, a dog got tore up by another that managed to get its muzzle loose and ripped into its shoulder area. A lot of blood was lost and the greyhound was in pain and deep distress. The owner called me.

'I got an old dog that was running on the flappers down in Wales.'

A flapping track is an independent unlicensed track. Anyway, he asked me if I'd shoot the dog for him. But I couldn't. What was more humane, for me to go over there and shoot it in familiar surroundings, or take it a long journey to the vet and have to wait with it while it got more and more distressed and then put it up on a table trembling and traumatised and knowing something bad was going to happen to it?

Even now, you can go over to Ireland, buy a dog, put it in the back of your van and run it on a flapping track that night. There's no rules and the welfare of those dogs ain't monitored. Dogs get dumped in woods – drowned, with concrete blocks round their necks – tied to trees and left to starve – all sorts. I shot them humanely but I don't do it any more, can't do it any more. Nowadays, a reject dog's supposed to be rehomed by The Retired Greyhound Trust or, if it's badly injured or wicked, it can be 'euthanised' by a vet. But it don't always happen like that.

Like I said at the beginning of this chapter on greyhounds, we don't keep so many dogs any more – neither greyhounds nor spaniels. Just one hound at the moment and I'm thinking about maybe another – and a spaniel. But I couldn't be without them completely. I wouldn't know what to do with myself, because they're part of what I am and always will be. And what I am don't make me a bad person.

That's all I'm saying!

'Solo Concorde' in action, Cotswold Coursing Club, 1993

© E. WALSH

17

Bob – Drag Coursing

I don't believe in anything I hears no more and what I sees sometimes makes me wonder if the world ain't, after all, completely bloody witless. And it's never been much different. The world I grew up in was like a mad dog, always snapping after my heels. Most of the time I managed to keep it at bay and didn't give it the chance to savage me. But once or twice it caught me off guard, when I was sitting back thinking about things and not paying proper attention. And I hates it when that happens.

Dragging's about pulling a lure along a 400-yard track on a gradient for the dogs to follow. It's a straight win system and not a matter of 'turning' the hare like on traditional open or park courses. And people come from all over the country to run their dogs on our drag track – even a lot of Pakistani and Indian blokes; they loves having a bet on their dogs and they loves the sport of it. They does a lot of coursing in Pakistan. They're proud of their dogs and don't like being beat by someone they considers inferior, and they got that class thing from the British during the days of the Raj and now they're stuck with it. But back in the 1970s, when Asian faces weren't all that familiar in this part of the world, just like us they could never get membership of the coursing clubs, no matter how highfalutin' they believed themselves or their caste to be. So they liked to give their dogs a run out in the countryside after a live hare – that way, they'd be keener for the track or the drag.

I met a couple of them at a coursing meet and we got to talking and I invited them down here, so they could come out with me. I told them where to meet, over at Bagstone, near a stream called the Ladenbrook, where there's lovely open ground that's good for a run with the dogs. Anyway, me and Brian, who's only young at the time, goes over there on a Sunday morning in a van I had back then, with three dogs. I'm waiting there for them, thinking maybe that one or two will turn up, if any at all. The next thing, this minibus pulls up and eighteen of 'em gets out, all with dogs. Brian takes one look at 'em and bursts out laughing.

'What you laughing at?'

'We can't take all them across the fields, we'll get nicked in five minutes.'

One of them overhears him.

'Nicked?'

'Don't mind him, Ahmed, he's just a boy.'

They thought I had permission and it was all legal, like, and how could I tell 'em now that I hadn't, after they'd come all the way from Birmingham?

There was two farms down the end of the fields where we were, and you can imagine what the farmers must have thought, in a remote part of Gloucestershire in the 1970s, with eighteen

Asians with dogs crossing their land – and us with them. Probably thinking some refugees from a Rudyard Kipling book are on the warpath or something. We has a few runs and catches a hare, before one of the farmers calls the police and I can just see him hysterical on the phone to the coppers.

'Come quick! I've locked the women in the cellar!'

Anyway, six squad cars surround the place. Police everywhere. I send Brian off with our three dogs to make an escape across the fields and walk the four or five miles home. Me and the eighteen Asians hides under a bridge across the Ladenbrook called the Summer Bridge and they're all shaking in their shoes because they don't want no trouble with the law. On the way out the other side of the farmland, Brian gets stopped by the local policeman, copper Harris.

'How are you, young Tovey?'

'I'm alright.'

'How's your father?'

'He's alright too.'

He asks Brian what he's doing and the boy tells him he's out walking his dogs, giving them a bit of roadwork to keep their toes up.

'And where's your father?'

'He's at home.'

'You sure?'

'Yes.'

'What's his van doing parked over there, then?'

Brian looks across and pretends he knows nothing about it.

'Is that his van?'

'It is. You sure you don't know where he is?'

'No.'

So he lets Brian go on his way with the dogs.

Meanwhile, the Asians decide to come out of hiding and give themselves up. I has no option but to come out too. The coppers are from Thornbury, not local men.

'What you buggers doing?'

One of the Asians tells him 'Mister Bob' invited them down for a run on his land.

'*His* land?'

I intervene and push the bloke to one side.

'Don't mind him, they come down to buy some goats.'

'Goats? What about all these dogs?'

'What dogs?'

'These greyhounds.'

'Oh them, they're not greyhounds, they're goathounds. Needed for the herding back home.'

By that time, copper Harris has made his way over and tells the Thornbury police he'll deal with it and they can get back to their station for a cuppa. He checks out the motors, but finds no game on us, so he has to let us be on our way, but not before he gives the Asians a lecture.

'Mister Bob is a bad man. Keep away from him. You'll only get into trouble coming down here.'

Then he turns to me.

'You got no tax on that van and a bald tyre. I got to pay tax, Tovey, so you have to as well. Get it done!'

And he leaves it at that.

He was alright, copper Harris – one of the few that was. But every time I saw the Asians after that, they'd say to me as they moved away:

'Police told us "Mister Bob is a bad man!"'

Thirty odd years later, and they still call me a 'bad man' when they comes drag racing.

As I told you, we has our own drag course now. A field full of hard hands holding on to long leashes in the rain and the shine. Sly tout voices scowling 'ten pounds for a punt on any dog you fancies now?' Mutton sandwiches with mustard to keep out the chill and heat up the blood. Toughs and gruffs and dog-fanciers and shit-kickers and all sorts of other strange shite-hawks – if you gets the gist of it. Cans of beer and curses and a commotion of shouts and shrieks and snarls. Drag coursing's also called lure coursing – where a lure is tied to a line that runs through several pulleys onto a specially made wheel, fitted onto a jacked-up van. The lure we use makes a noise like a hare, a squealing sound that gets the dogs going. But no live game is used and the lure's drawn into an escape of hay bales at the end of the course. Brian runs the lure, because he knows how to keep it just the right distance in front of the dogs, and we has 400-yard and 280-yard courses. There's normally four eight-dog stakes with a few trials beforehand, and there's cups and trophies and prizes of up to £1,000 and people can lay bets on the dogs if they wants. We charge an entry fee of up to £50 for each dog, depending on the prize money. And that might seem a bit steep to some, but not to them who loves the sport – and it only covers the costs; we don't do it for profit or pay.

You might think the greyhounds wouldn't have the same enthusiasm running after a lure as they would after a live hare on an open course, but that's not so. People have pegged out rab-bits on the drag course field, but the dogs would rather chase the squealing lure than go after the live coneys; that's how much it's in a greyhound's nature to chase something that's running – or it thinks is running. We've had some good times on the drag, and the licensed track people can piss off, with their frowns and their inflated prices. Even though it had its detractors, I considered it my right to go on doing it and living this little life as I see fit – and to allow my sons to do the same. If they wants to.

But time and tide, as they says ... we don't run the meetings ourselves no more – just rent out the drag and let other people do the organising, print the race cards and stuff. Brian still operates the lure, because he's been at it for twenty-seven years and he knows what he's doing better than anyone else. We takes care of the equipment and makes sure it's all in good working order and we'll act as officials on the day, if they wants us to. The organisers, especially the Asians, like someone who's impartial to operate the drag and slip the dogs, so there's no cheating. They also has an independent judge standing on the finish platform with a white flag and a red flag, to adjudicate which dog's first over the line. Sometimes they use cameras as well, to decide a photo finish.

This has nothing to do with drag racing, but I'll mention it here, because it's as good a place as any. You know the old saying 'poacher turned gamekeeper' – well, I was a gamekeeper for a while in my later years, for a private shoot on the edge of the Duke of Beaufort's estate. Me and Brian was already lamping their pheasants so they thought, by getting me as gamekeeper, they'd kill two birds with one stone, so to speak. I agreed, because I wanted to see what it was like on the other side of the law for once. I put up pens for the young birds and placed feeders around and organised the shoots and beaters and drives and looked after the birds and kept 'em safe from other poachers. I could walk round and have a shot and do anything I wanted, but there was no fun in it. There was too much work and not enough freedom.

I lasted one season – then I was clearing away some stuff for the pheasants when I got bit by an adder, which if you don't know is Britain's only poisonous snake. I never knew it was an adder at the time, just thought it was a thorn or something, so I didn't go to the hospital to get it treated. I never got bit by nothing when I was poaching but this time I bled like a pig and could have died. I was bad for a few days with swelling and vomiting and dizziness, but I recovered and I took it as an omen that I wasn't meant to be on the right side of the law. I went back to poaching, so I could roam where I wanted and when I liked and have the freedom of a poacher's domain.

Anyway, that's a bit of a sidetrack from the dragging I was talking about – and so is this. There was one man called Alf who used to come to the drag racing, but he wanted to go out poaching, just to see what it was like. He was a big talker and thought he was a very hard man and he kept asking me to take him out of a night. I didn't want to because I know that them who makes the most noise is usually the least tough. Anyway, he kept on at me, so I takes him this night just to put an end to it and, when we gets to the woods, I'm looking up in the trees for a bird. But Alf keeps talking and talking – like he's nervous or something. This is getting me nowhere, so I think I'll shut him up. I put a finger up to my lips.

'Shhhh!'

'What is it, Bob?'

'Did you hear that?'

'What?'

'A cough . . . and something stepped on a dry twig.'

I can see he's beginning to flap a bit now. I tell him to get hold of a stick or a small tree branch and wait under cover to see if somebody comes along. I know there's nobody about, but he don't.

'What do I do then?'

'Trip him up with the branch and then sort him out.'

'Where will you be?'

'I won't be far.'

Anyway, he's sitting trembling in a bush with a big stick and I move off. I circle round behind him and whisper ,'He's getting closer.'

He whirls round, but can't see me.

'Who's there?'

I whisper again.

'Closer.'

He's shitting hisself by now, so I pick up a big stone and throw it into the bush right beside him. He nearly dies of fright and starts calling out for me.

'Bob! Bob!'

I circle back round and come over to him. He's shaking like a leaf and I think he might have wet hisself.

'What's up, Alf?'

'There's something in the trees.'

'What is it?'

'Dunno . . . but it's whispering.'

'Whispering?

He's nodding his head like a demented pigeon.

'Could be the whispering Wodwose.'

'The what?'

'The furry man of the woods. I think we better go take a look see.'

'No, no. I think we better go home.'

He never asked to come out with me again.

But, getting back to the drag – there's something in the air this Sunday morning, as we set up the equipment and test it to make sure it's all working well and there'll be no problems – it's like I got this bad feeling something nasty's going to happen. It's only a little after daylight and I can see the early morning lights of the village in the distance. Our helpers turn up after a while and we has some tea out of the warm flasks and a chat about this and that. Then the dogs start to arrive. There's a few Asians too, not the ones who calls me Mister 'bad man' Bob, but some I ain't never seen here before. They has this Chinese fella with them and they tell me his name's Kan. I see him looking at my communist hat, so I gets talking to him, just to be sociable, and he's not a Chinaman at all, but a Mongolian. I speak to him in pidgin English and he answers me with a posh Oxford accent. He tells me he went to school under the Soviet system back in his home country and, after Mongolia got its independence, he came to college over here. He works now as an advisor in some financial institution.

I tells him about how Ernie got me the hat and how I wears it a lot just to wind people up. The Asians brought him along today because he misses the closeness to nature he had back in Ukulele.

'Ukulele?'

'Ain't that the capital of Mongolia?'

'Certainly not! It's Ulaan Baatar, which means "red hero" and I come from the Mountains to the north of Uliastayi.'

He says it's a lucky country, with gold and copper and cashmere and camels and many, many horses. And in the mountains they has wild boars and wolves and snow leopards and elk that see humans so seldom they're almost tame.

'Great hunting country, then?'

'Perhaps you can come and visit sometime?'

'Is it hot there? Don't like it too hot.'

'Sometimes . . . in summer. But cold in winter.'

'Colder than here?'

'Much!'

Well, you certainly learns something new every day. He's an eloquent speaker and he tells me the trees there are eternal and the high hills are the axis of the world and the bridge between heaven and earth and the spirits of the mountains and the forests provide his people with everything they needs.

'Why are you here, then?'

'My father insisted.'

He's some talker, this Kan fella and, now that I've started him off, I can't get him to stop – going on about how his race is the best handlers of horses in the world and how a blue wolf and a fallow doe were the spiritual ancestors of all the Mongols. And how his country's a land where the wolf and wild horse runs free and eagles hang in the bare blue sky. I gets a bit fed up with all this flag-wagging and bragging and say why don't he go back there if he misses it so much.

'Because I like your English tea.'

And he'd love to come out hunting with me sometime to renew the closeness to nature that he lost in Oxford. But vans and pickups are arriving now, so I leave him to his half-baked homesickness. Dogs is yelping in anticipation of the chase and gruff voices growling and kids running round and women setting up their food trestles. There's all sorts here, West Country people like ourselves and the Asians from Birmingham and Welsh from over the border and others I couldn't tell you the origins of. All waiting for the racing to begin.

It's an eight-dog stake, which means four runs to begin with, with the four winning dogs going through to the semi-finals, then two runs to determine the finalists. The two finalists will have to run up that drag three times – it's a hard task and takes a lot out of an animal. We has our own dog running in the first race. He's a black two-year-old greyhound called 'The Coalman' and he's wearing red, which means he'll be slipped on the left. I'm confident of our dog though I don't bet on him because I'm here for the sport and the spectacle, not to make money. Brian starts to wind the lure. The dogs can see it and they're going mad. The slipper lets 'em go and they comes flying up the field. They're neck and neck for the first hundred yards, urged along by the shouting, cheering, cursing crowd. Halfway up the course and The Coalman takes a slender lead. I'm at the finish and I throw my hat into the air as he crosses the line first. One course down and two to go. The Coalman takes a rest while the other three races is run off and I slips a raw egg down his neck and washes his feet with warm soapy water.

He's drawn agin' a large, fawn dog in the second course. But the bigger greyhound's slow getting into his stride and The Coalman builds up a nice lead over the first half of the field. But then the big dog gets going and he's closing fast. My heart's in my mouth and I'm screaming at him to hold on. The big dog keeps gaining, gaining, and it seems like they're running in slow motion. Then they flash past the line and I'm waiting to see which flag the adjudicator will raise. He takes a lifetime. But it's red! There's bedlam in the crowd, with swearing and squawking and objections being raised and calls for enquiries and threats and the shaking of fists. But the decision stands. The other semi-final is run and there's a break for refreshments and for the dogs to get their breaths back. The Coalman's breathing heavy and I know the first two courses has taken it out of him. I just hope he has enough energy and stamina left for the final.

The two victorious greyhounds go to slips for the last race. Brian mans the winder. The lure starts to move. The dogs see it and go mad. The slipper's ready. Away they go. The other finalist is a brindle dog called 'Blinder' – and he is. He's away first and leading up the course. Halfway and the brindle dog's ahead by nearly a length and it seems like the race is lost for The Coalman. Then, coming up the gradient, Blinder starts to slacken. This is the test of a true dog, to see who has the most heart, with three gruelling courses taking it out of them. Blinder slows again; the sting's gone out of him. He's had it. The Coalman passes him twenty yards from the finish. The race is won. Double delight and delirium tremens. All hand-shaking and back-slapping and three cheers for the Chinese!

Then it happens – what I was feeling uneasy about. The bad feeling. There's a commotion in the crowd: men shouting and women screaming and dogs growling and barking. A fight's broken out between a group of hard-looking farmhands from Malmesbury and the Asians. I'm over to intervene, but it's escalating quickly and Brian's in there as well, trying to break it up. The Asians is coming off the worst and there's sticks and bottles being used and blood being spilt. Them not involved is panicking and gathering up their coats and children and running from the field. The biggest and mouthiest of the farmhands is swinging a short axe-handle and the Asians are lashing out with their legs and trying to kick the ploughboys away. Pandemonium. This ain't good publicity for our little track – nobody wants to come out of a Sunday and get involved in a riot, except maybe the habitual mayhem-makers.

Then this Kan fella steps forward and grabs the arm of the big shit-kicker. The rest of the fighting stops and it's a face-off between the two of them. A straightener, so to speak. The farm-hand swings the axe-handle at Kan's skull, but the Mongolian dodges the swipe. He swings again and again fails to connect. He growls now and swings wildly back and forth with the stick, but not one of the swipes connects, because Kan moves like mercury. After a few minutes of this, the big fella's exhausted and Kan easily takes the axe-handle from his grasp. The he chops him to the side of the neck with his hand and the man collapses onto the ground. The other shit-kickers carry their half-unconscious mate away, none of them anxious to mix it with the Mongolian, while the Asians lick their wounds and get ready to go. And some days can disappoint like that, no matter how hard you try, and people can turn like dogs on the innocent bystander. I approach this Kan.

'What started all that?'

'A private bet. The farmers wouldn't pay.'

'You can handle yourself, Kan.'

He tells me that his ancestors were the Mangudai, a fierce tribe of Mongols, and his history's a history of blood and savage con-querors – but he learned how to fight at the Oxford Emporium of Martial Arts. I apologise for the behaviour of the farmhands and ask how much the bet was for, but he's philosophical about the fight.

'What's money, my friend? Here today and gone tomorrow. In fact, the present itself is a fleeting thing, if it exists at all.'

I don't know what he's talking about and he asks me how I'd go about explaining the present – is it a day or an hour or a minute or a second, or even less than that? I can't say for sure.

'There really is no present, Bob, only past and future. Once the future appears, it immediately becomes the past. There's nothing in between. And life, therefore, is a complete illusion.'

The Asians are leaving and he has to hurry after them. But he hopes we'll meet again.

'Toodle-oo.'

We never do.

Bob in his element, hare-netting at Dunley, near Andover, 24 February 1990. That day we caught 124 live hares

18

Brian – Country Activities

Everyone wants to complain – it's a national pastime. Some bright spark could earn a fortune: 'Sympathetic ears for hire, fifty quid an hour. Pour all your troubles in one and watch them disappear out the other.' Five minutes guarantee. Or make a mountain of money by singing a little love song. Or maybe set sail some day on a first-class star to the outer reaches of the universe. Never again come back down to swim against the stream of shit in this sewer-world. But wishful-thinking ain't all it's cracked up to be – so never look back, in case, like Lot's wife, you get turned into a pillar of self-pity.

Country traditions have changed over the years. There was once a way of life that had lasted for centuries, but villages are just towns with a bit of rustic trimming now and farms and estates are big businesses. Beagling was one of those old country sports and we had the Wick and District Beagle Pack around here. They used to hunt up and down the area for miles and miles. But it's been banned now, like all hunting with dogs after the Hunting Act came into force in 2005 – except when just following a scent or after rabbits. The traditional quarry of the beagle packs was always the hare and us Toveys supplied those hares for the beaglers. Unlike fox-hunting, beagling's done on foot rather than on horseback, with a pack of twenty to forty beagle hounds. The beagle looks like a foxhound, but it's smaller, with shorter legs and longer ears, and the dogs have a higher pitch to their cry when hunting a line. They're what's called scenthounds, bred for tracking. They have a great sense of smell and are intelligent and even-tempered. But they're not fast enough to catch a hare, like a foxhound would be able to outrun a fox, so the hares were rarely caught by the dogs and mostly lived to run another day.

But the banners of hunting with dogs didn't see the point, that beagling was mainly a sport of tracking, rather than killing.

All the famous public schools had beagle packs in the old days, along with the universities and the military, and there's still about fifty or so packs registered in England and Wales. But there's less country available for hunting now, due to roads being built and small villages growing into small towns to accommodate the city people who come out here to live when they're not working in their glass offices and call centres. Since the banning of beagling after live hares, many packs now hunt artificially, which means following a pre-laid scent, or hunting rabbits, which ain't banned. Sometimes they're used for flushing hares to guns or the retrieval of injured animals following hare shoots, which ain't banned either. But it's all just a pale imitation of the real job the dogs were bred to do.

There's also a handful of basset hound packs still operating today. They hunted the hare too, before it all got banned, and the dogs have even shorter legs and longer ears than the beagle.

Their sense of smell is nearly as good as a bloodhound's and they're a great tracking dog, though a bit too slow to be much good for any kind of poaching. They have a strong, deep voice and great stamina and they're more headstrong than the beagle or the foxhound. The hunting or English basset has a longer leg than the traditional breed you see in dog shows like Crufts and that. This gives them greater speed to hunt with and a slightly higher pitch when speaking on a line. They're difficult to control, though, and hunt more as individuals than as a pack. I'm talking about these scenthounds, as opposed to greyhounds which are sighthounds, because they're all part of the lore of the countryside, going back generations. Although we never used them for poaching, just the greyhounds and spaniels, it's only fair they should get a mention because they were once a common sight, baying and bowling across the land.

Another pack hound we supplied hares for was the harrier. The harrier looks like the foxhound, but it's smaller, though not as small as the beagle. Someone once described a harrier as a 'beagle on steroids' because of its muscular physique and short, hard coat. It has big bones for stamina and strength and is longer than tall. It's a cheerful dog, even-tempered and good with other dogs and it's a first-class tracker. Harriers could push a hare faster and straighter than beagles and, for that reason, they were sometimes followed on horseback. They were used to hunt foxes too, but not round here, the West Country packs where we live always kept to the hares. There's no harrier packs left now, to my knowledge; the last of them disbanded in the 1990s when the harrier bloodlines died out.

With this kind of tracking sport, it's mostly beagling now since the hunting ban, following trails and rabbits – at least, that's the official line. But, as the only long-netters left in the country, we still supplied hares to beagle packs up until recently, even if those hares were rarely killed because the beagles could catch bugger-all, except maybe an old or weak animal. It was all about the following for miles, just for the fun of it. Getting out there and doing something different, instead of sitting inside watching your neighbours through the window. Or driving down to the do-it-yourself shop for a grouting tool and a gallon of pastel paint. Or drinking ten pints of IPA in the pub with your mates – and your whole world turning into a great cauliflower while you slide into a stupor.

Beagling was different to saddle-bumping, even if them who organised it were just as snooty. But it can still be a sport to participate in, if that's what you want. Foot-followers can watch it from a distance or get more involved. The hunt officials wear uniforms, but the rest can dress how they prefer. Unlike fox-hunting, the main purpose of the hunt ain't a kill, but to experience the hounds at work and to get some fresh air and exercise and enjoy the countryside. They usually meet at a pub in the morning, have a few drinks and then move off. They watch the hounds working for three or four hours, or until they get washed home by rain. And what hares were killed by coursing and beagling was nothing compared to how many were shot or died from disease or got run over by mad motorists.

Apart from providing the hares, we never really got very involved with the beagling – too many stick-seats and tweed twin-sets and hysterical haw-haws for our liking. We'd watch them, though, and, in summer, maybe lie in the meadows with a donkey or two grazing round our ears – elderflowers laced in their bridles to keep the flies away. Bees buzzing and butterflies flitting across the clover and eyelids heavy in the heady air. Sometimes it's therapeutic to just hazel in the sun like that, with no bastard bothering you – you could even make a hollow promise to God that, if he don't ask you to get up and do something, you'll behave in future and never find fault with blind faith or make a savage of yourself on a Sunday. And us poachers ain't like normal people – we work to live, not live to work. And sometimes, when the world's bright and fragrant and warm, no man should have to toil – but only lie back in the long grass and dream. And they say in some parts of the world there's a millionaire made every minute. How?

We'd follow mink hounds now and then too, between April and October, through the streams and small rivers all around Berkeley. Mink hounds were once called otterhounds and they have a shaggy coat and are as big as a Labrador. The hunt would draw waterways, searching for the mink and, when one was found, the chase was on and the foot followers would often have to take to the water to keep up. The mink we have here in this country ain't native; they're American animals that were brought over here for fur-farming in the 1920s and here's a bit of history for you. Fur-farming was at its peak in the 1950s, with four hundred farms in the UK – and there were also many illegal backyard operators. Plenty of the animals escaped and established themselves in the wild by the 1960s, reverting to their original chocolate-brown colour and spreading over England and Wales. The government tried to eradicate the wild mink population in 1964, but it was too little and too late. Animal activists attacked the fur-farms in the 1990s and released loads more of 'em and fur-farming was banned altogether in 2000.

We rented out an old abandoned mink farm near Bradley Stoke and we kept about a hundred greyhounds there – I think I told you how Bob used to make me walk there if I was up late as a boy. Bradley Stoke is a new town in South Gloucestershire now, on the north side of Bristol. It was built in the 1990s and people who bought properties there were hit by the housing crash of the same decade, so the town got the nickname 'Sadly Broke'. Anyway, we coursed the dogs across the farmland that was there before all the building and, not so long ago, the body of a young boy was found on a rubbish tip, not a stone's throw from where we had those kennels. He was abducted in London and abused and murdered by a paedophile, before his body was discarded. As far as I know, they caught the culprit – but I can't be sure. I could never understand how a man could hurt a child like that – or a woman either. But then, I suppose the world's a twisted place at times and it might be something to do with the shit food people eat, or some subliminal sickness they see on the television.

To get back to the mink – they're still spreading in some parts of the country and nobody knows how to deal with them, especially since the banning of hunting with dogs. Mink are bad little buggers – they kill everything. When a company of mink, or a gang, as they're sometimes called, goes through an area, they'll kill mollies [moor hens] and coots and take the eggs and attack domestic fowls and water voles and other wildlife. They hunt over several miles, in ones and twos mostly and, when they've eaten everything, they'll move on. They used to be valuable for their pelts but women ain't wearing fur coats no more, and although they're expanding out to more remote regions, there's not as many round here as there used to be – just like all the other wildlife. We used to hunt them along the Little Avon, following the hounds and setting fenn traps that would snap shut and most times kill them instantly.

This is how we'd do it with the traps – it's natural for mink or stoats or weasels to go through holes, so we make a tunnel out of stones or bricks and put a top of small logs on it and cover it over with dead grass and little twigs. We set the trap in there, baited with a bit of mackerel. Fenn traps baited like that also draw rats and squirrels. They're all classed as vermin – they'll destroy pheasant nests and have the eggs and kill the chicks and they'll kill rabbits as well. The fenn trap is humane – it snaps shut and, like I said, most times it kills them instantly. There's a safety catch on the trap so you don't break your fingers. Pull the catch down and open the jaws, then lift the plate up and slide the pin across – now it's set. You can adjust the trigger for different levels of weight needed to spring the trap, then take the safety off and that's it. Simple.

Years ago, poachers used gin traps a lot of the time – though Bob says he didn't – but they were made illegal. A gin trap is a mechanical device with teeth and they were good enough at doing their job. There were different sizes – for fox and badger and rabbit and smaller ones for rats. The name 'gin' comes from the word 'engine', which was used in the old days to describe any mechanical device and the word was just abbreviated for convenience. There's no safety on them, so you had to be heedful or you'd lose a few fingers or even a hand.

You got your jaws, you got your plate, and you set it – carefully. The reason the gin got a bad name is because most people set them in rabbit runs in long grass and, more often than not, they caught an animal by the leg instead of killing it outright.

Rabbit comes along and, snap, its leg's caught – and it can wear the leg down to the bone trying to get free. Sometimes I found keepers' traps with just the leg left in there. But that's people who don't know how to use them properly. The right way was to set them in the burrow entrance – making sure the jaws had enough room to close and the rabbit got caught by the head and killed instantly.

I glue corn to fenn traps to catch pheasants nowadays. This is how it works: I feed the pheasants under a bin first – put feed down every day for them. Then I put the fenn traps down, keep the safety on and chuck corn around them. The pheasants get used to the traps – pecking around, pecking around, but the traps don't go off because the safety's on. Then, when the birds are used to them, I glue corn to them with super glue and take the safety off. The pheasants peck at the corn, but it's glued down – so they peck harder, until they spring the trap.

Like I've been saying, the trouble with traps is, you got to keep checking them in case what you've caught gets taken by predators or other poachers. Or, if a keeper comes upon them, he'll lie in wait and try to catch you when you come back. But they have their uses if you don't want to risk the noise of a gun – they're silent and you can just leave them to do your work for you. Traps and snares have been used by tribes of people since we first crawled up out of the slime and many places still use them so people can catch what they need to eat. Bob met a Mongolian once, who came over here to be further educated and lost all touch with who he was and what his homeland meant to him. He was a sad man, Bob said, who dreamt about his roots and was wandering the world like a lost soul. And maybe I'll go to Mongolia someday. Start in the south and tramp north across the Gobi Desert and the sea of grass they call the Steppe. Stop beside the turquoise waters of Lake Telmen and listen to the dull drone of the insects being all the time eaten by the busy birds. Sit by a cool stream at the foot of some hillside with the scent of strange flowers and the colours of the kaleidoscope world all around me.

Who knows? Maybe.

Getting back to country activities, a cockfight's a blood sport between two gamecocks, or fighting cocks, which takes place in a ring called a cockpit. Two mature male birds will fight to the death, or until one of them's so badly injured it can't fight any more. Game fowl ain't like ordinary domestic chickens, that's because they're bred for fitness rather than egg production or meat. The territorial instinct of the males is what gives them their aggression; they'll fight each other no matter if they're trained to do it or not. It's their natural instinct. 'Gameness' is the term for the aggressiveness of a bird – the more aggressive it is and the more willing to fight, the gamer it is. A 'game' bird will keep on fighting, even if it's badly injured.

We used to keep twenty or thirty fighting cocks in trios, two hens to lay eggs and a cock to fertilise them. We kept them in separate pens in the garden and fought them between ourselves for the sport, not for money or betting. To fight them out with other people, like Gypsies, brings trouble. Then you get asked where you live and the next thing people are coming round stealing your birds and dogs too, if you have any. We kept Old English game birds, which was one of the oldest strains of poultry. The breed was developed through the Middle Ages by the English nobility for its fighting traits and eye-catching colours.

And although cockfighting became illegal in England in 1835, we still kept and fought the birds while others just kept them for showing. Fighting's what a gamecock wants to do. It doesn't need to be forced into it; it'll just fight no matter what.

We free-ranged the stags [young males] because it was better for their diet and fitness and immunity against disease, although it was riskier if there were foxes about. No matter how game a young cock was, he'd be no match for a fox. When they began to fight with each other, we'd have to separate them to prevent injuries. They'd have to be kept away from other fowls like ducks or geese as well and that didn't mean just putting up a piece of chicken wire. A young stag will go through wire mesh and this could result in injuries to his feet and legs.

Cocks ain't fought until they're nearly two years old. We'd spar them first, covering their natural spurs with a soft cloth to prevent injury to the sparring birds. This would give us an idea how good a bird was going to be. Natural spurs grow to about two or three inches and if the bird was going to fight 'naked heel', they'd be left as they were. Otherwise, the natural spurs would be sawn off and the bird would be armed with metal spurs, called gaffs, which have a socket that fits over the butt of the natural spur.

At about a year old, the comb and wattle are trimmed back – this is called dubbing and is done to prevent the opponent bird from getting a bill-hold and gaining an advantage during a fight. The sickle feathers of the tail would be trimmed too, along with any other long feathers that the cock might trip on during a con-test. Along with that, bulky feathers can overheat a bird in a long fight and hamper its agility. A couple of weeks before a fight, the cock will be conditioned like a professional athlete with what's called the 'keep'. It's a special diet and exercise and it gets the cock used to its handler, so it can be picked up during the fight without causing damage. Cocks that are aggressive towards their keepers makes for problems during the keep, and if it turns on its handler in the pit the other cock will take advantage of it. Like I said, cockfighting's been banned for a long time. But it still goes on during the year, apart from the autumn, when the cocks moult and grow new feathers.

You may or may not agree with blood sports and that's your prerogative. There's some I hold with and others I don't. Badger-digging's one I don't, even though I did when I was younger. I liked the terriers and was of the mind that each should be left to his own. But I don't hold with it now – it's a countryside activity that's not for me and I don't bother with, no more than I bothered with fox-hunting when the bum-bouncers were at it up and down the land. You could eat a badger one time, but you could never eat a fox so, unless they're doing damage to your livelihood, like killing lambs or chickens, then leave them alone.

Illegal badger-digging with dogs goes on a lot in Wales, just over the border from where we are. It's at its peak between January and June, when a sow badger can fight for up to eight hours to protect her cubs. Because the badger's such a fearless animal and a ferocious fighter, it's a prime target for terrier men who want to test their dogs. Lakelands and Patterdales and Jack Russells and all kinds of cross-breeds get sent down into the sett to locate a badger and keep it at bay. The men listen for where the noise is coming from, much like with ferreting, then dig down and drag the badger out. Sometimes the dogs and badgers can die if the sett collapses and suffocates them.

If they're just there for the dig and a bit of sport, the diggers will set their dogs on the badger there and then and the badger's usually outnumbered and killed, but the dogs can get seriously injured too. Badgers are normally shy animals and keep to themselves, but they become very aggressive when cornered or provoked. A badger has great strength and a bite or a blow from one of its claws can do a dog proper damage. Many dogs that get badly injured during badger-digging are shot, because their owners are nervous about bringing them to the vet in case the vet gets suspicious about where the injuries came from.

If the diggers are into baiting, then the animal will be picked up with badger tongs, because they're strong creatures and can have a hand off someone, and put in a heavy box and taken away to be baited later. This involves going somewhere quiet and remote where the noise won't be heard – maybe a barn or a big shed or a cellar or a derelict building of some kind. A ring's set up that the badger can't escape from and dogs are set on it. Even if the badger fights off the first dog, it has to fight a second and a third and a fourth and so on, until it's too injured and exhausted to fight on. The baiters will then kill the badger with a gun or club or let their dogs kill it for the blooding. There's always a lot of betting involved and a winning dog's value will rise – and so will the value of its pups. Badgers being caught and sold for baiting can fetch as much as £500, so you can see why lots want to be doing it.

Badger-digging and-baiting were once seen as true country sports but both are banned now like a lot of others. Personally, although I did a bit of it a long time ago, I never got involved to a great extent, because it's not a real sport to me – and it can be just cruelty for the sake of making money. Nowadays, they say badgers spread tuberculosis to cattle and the ministry men set cage traps with peanuts for the animals they want to tag or cull. I've nicked some of the traps over the years and used them for catching foxes that were taking my pheasants or rabbits. Foxes will take game from land rented by us. We'll take the pheasants off the estates and release them on land where we have permission – if foxes come and start taking those pheasants, then I'll trap them and shoot them. I'll shoot any vermin I come across as well – crows and magpies and squirrels and feral cats and the odd Conservative councillor. Ha ha!

A farmer came to me once and told me that foxes were killing his lambs and could I do something about it. I didn't normally kill foxes, except when they came after our ducks, but I agreed to help him in return for him allowing us to shoot on his land. I took an earthing terrier with me and I soon found the fox den. I sent the terrier in and started to dig. After about twenty minutes, one of the foxes bolts, with the terrier clinging to its back by its teeth. I'm trying to get it with my gun, but it's a tricky shot – a moving target with a small dog hanging from its back, which I don't want to shoot. I take aim and pull the trigger. The fox falls and so does the terrier. I run to where they are, but the dog's alright, still clinging to what it believes is its kill. It's a good shot – and a good dog! In the next field, there's a nine-inch land drain, fenced off. It comes out in a ditch about a hundred yards away. The ditch is flooded – the water must've been backed up in the pipe for quite a way. After about five minutes, another fox comes out of the pipe in a big bubble and starts to run away. I let him get about thirty yards then shoot him dead. I think it's strange that the foxes would be in a flooded drain but what's happening is some animal rights people are cage-trapping city foxes

and releasing them in the countryside, to stop them being shot
by pest controllers. There's a sudden increase in fox activity in
this area and the city foxes have mange, which can spread to the
country population. Country foxes wouldn't be in a drain like
that and the ones I shoot are scrawny things, used to scavenging
for food and not hunting. I get four foxes out of the one earth
that day.

Now, I know a lot of people won't want to read about me
shooting foxes. Townspeople think they're nice cuddly ginger
dogs. And I've got nothing personal against the fox, but if they
were coming into where you worked and affecting how you were
able to make your living, you'd soon be asking someone like me
to get them out of there. Or if they killed your pet cat, or bit
your baby, or dragged the rubbish out of your bins, or shat all
over your nicely manicured lawn. Because foxes look so hand-
some, not ugly like the rat, people are never going to agree on
how to control them.

Like I said, it's not personal.

That's just a few of the country activities of years ago. Most
of them ain't allowed any more – because everything changes
and nothing's certain these days and friends and foes are all
mixed up and indistinguishable. Except for some of the buggers,
who'll never be any different. But the world evolves, if that's the
right word, and us in it must conform in the end, with the winds
of change that continue to blow. And, like the Mongolian said to
my father, outsiders won't be tolerated forever.

19

Brian – Into the Wild

Some people say China's soon to become the world's leading producer of consumer goods, but it'll all probably be a load of old nonsense that nobody needs, to add to the mountain of useless waste straining the world's natural resources. They've already got the billionaires and the shining stars and I wonder if they'll have a Xiznyland and a Xolywood too? But it's not all progress and promise in the world; there's reports that the Yanks are making it compulsory for the biblical account of creation to be taught in all secular schools – born-again brain washing.

Nowadays, I like to travel further afield than just the West Country. Every October, I go with my brother Robert up to Aberdeenshire in Scotland, decoying geese and ducks and teal. We stay on a farm and go wildfowling on the foreshore along the eastern seaboard of an evening, before it gets dark. Or we trek inland and set up our hide and decoys in barley stubble and wait for the geese to fly in from the likes of Cotehill Loch or the Loch of Strathbeg to feed on the gleanings. There can be up to eighty thousand geese flocking at that time of year, before the weather hardens and they move on down the east coast to places like Norfolk and even across to Normandy. If we see them out in the fields, provided they've not eaten everything and are ready to move on, they'll fly in again the next day.

We get out there early, set our hide up with camouflage netting and grass and stubble over it and shoot them. If we're shooting a field where geese want to feed, we don't need a lot of decoys to bring them into range, but if we want to pull them into a field they're not directly feeding on, it helps to have a bigger pattern of decoys. I had a hundred and eight birds over three mornings one season, using about twenty decoys and a good caller. I breast them, bring them home and freeze them, for eating during the year ahead.

I've always been a good fit runner. I've outrun gamekeepers and dogs and Land Rovers – so, when I see a picture of people running in front of bulls in Spain, I think I'd like to have a go at that. I find out as much as I can about it and go over there for the first time in 2005. Pamplona's the capital city of Navarre, in the foothills of the Pyrenees, and they hold the Fiesta of San Fermín there every July. It's an eight-day festival and I arrive a couple of days into it, with all sorts of music and dancing and fireworks and frivolity going on. But I'm only interested in the bulls. I find out where I'm supposed to go to take part – the town square – then I go get a white rig-out with red sashes like the runners wear and I kip down in the park that night in my sleeping bag. I'm up at dawn the next morning and have a light breakfast of strong coffee and a sweet roll because I don't want a full belly weighing me down while I'm running.

I get to the square at 7:00 a.m. and there's already crowds of people milling all over the place. Some of them look like they've been partying all night and are only there for the spectating and not to get anywhere near the bulls. Most of the runners are dressed in white, with the red bandanas round their necks and the red sashes round their waists, just like me. They're called *mozos*, which I think means 'boys', and red and white are the colours of the butchers who began the running tradition years ago. As my grandfather was a butcher, it seems appropriate for me to be here – like I deserve my place. The bulls represent power and life and danger to me, and running with a wild dangerous animal will be primeval in its very essence. I'm jostling for position in the crowd of runners and I try to get to the front, where we're being held back by the police until the official start time of 8:00 a.m. Then a rocket goes off to signal that the bulls are running.

The sea of *mozos* begins to jump up and down, trying to locate the rampaging animals, in order to time their run. Suddenly it's like a tidal wave of bodies washing down the narrow streets and everyone around me begins to gallop. It's a red-and-white cauldron – voices shouting, spectators screaming, the ground quaking. I'm not the tallest of blokes and I don't see the bulls coming until they're almost on top of me. I'm running as fast as my feet will move and I can feel the beasts' breath on my back, smell their steaming bodies right behind me, their horns only inches away from my spine. Most of the *mozos* only run for a few seconds, scrambling to stay in front, then diving out of the way at the last moment. A bull becomes most dangerous when separated from the herd, so they run a few slower steers to keep them company, but I don't want to be caught on a steer's horns either, so I keep going.

As the seconds tick by, I'm finding it more and more difficult to make my running way through the throng. People are falling all around me and getting trampled on by those coming behind, and it's more like an obstacle course than a bull run.

I turn into la Estafeta now, which is downhill, and a couple of the bulls behind me lose their balance and start sliding. I jump out of the way to avoid being upended and I pass them again before they manage to get back on their feet. I can see the bullring up ahead, which is the final destination and, although I've only been running for a few minutes, it's at full pelt and my breath's coming in gasps and my heart's pounding. The entrance to the bullring's narrow, like a funnel, and all the runners are trying to get through at once and jamming it up. The bulls are closing fast behind me and I've got nowhere to go. Then I fall to the ground, having been accidentally tripped by some careless idiot. I try to get up, but it's impossible. Panic-stricken people are crushing me, trying to get through the bottleneck, trampling me underfoot. Then the bulls arrive and pound over me. I'm hit by hooves in the head and stomach and arms and legs, and the screaming and snorting is deafening. Until it all goes quiet after the pandemonium passes and I'm lying motionless on the ground. Some people come to see if I'm alive or dead and I struggle back to my feet. A medic checks me out and there are no broken bones, although I have extensive bruising to my body and find it difficult to walk for the next four days.

Since then, every July, I go back to Pamplona for the bull running. I either go for a day or two or sometimes for the full week – and every year I do the run. But I'm more crafty now and don't get hemmed in and tripped up, like I did that first time. I go on my own, flying over to Barcelona and bussing the rest of the way and sleeping in the park, but they come from all over the world to have a party and sometimes I link up with people I've met from previous years.

The running of the bulls is called the *encierro* and it's something that couldn't be done anywhere else. It originated with the need to get animals to the bullring from outside the city. These days the *encierro* starts at a corral in Calle Santo Domingo when the clock on the church of San Cernin strikes eight in the morning. The Spanish sing a prayer to Saint Fermín for his blessing, then two rockets are launched, one to signal the release and another to signal the animals are all out and running. Then about a dozen bulls and steers charge behind the runners for a distance of just over half a mile. Most of the runners wear their red and white and carry rolled-up newspapers, and I fit right in with the rest of them – just like I did the first time.

A double row of barricades runs along the length of the route to allow runners to escape if they're in danger – the gaps in the barricades are wide enough for a human to get through, but not a bull. There's little chance of being gored by the bulls – being trampled by the hundreds of idiots that take part is the biggest danger. Most of them don't have any bottle and they panic when the bulls get close and they can cause chaos – like what happened to me in my first run. But I call it running *with* the bulls now, rather than running in front of the bulls, because that's what happens with most of them. Personally, I try to stay ahead of the beasts for the full three or four minutes and I always have done, except when dickheads get in the way. Blokes called *pastores* run behind with long sticks, to stop the idiots from antagonising the bulls from behind and making them turn round and run back the way they came. But this is sometimes impossible because of the amount of people that get overtaken, then they start grabbing the bulls by the tails and doing stupid things, just to prove how macho they are. Trained bullfighters are positioned in the bull-ring, to help the runners get out and to guide the bulls through and into another corral. When that's done, everything settles down and the whole thing's over.

It's not as dangerous as the television programmes make it out to be. At the same time, not everyone can do it. It takes cool nerves, quick reflexes and physical fitness. If you're not up to it, stay away. Which the vast majority of the runners should do and leave it to people like myself, who're fit enough to stay in front of the bulls and not be endangering everyone around them. If you want to have a go, you have to be over eighteen and you got to get to the City Hall Square before 7:30 a.m., that's when entry to the run closes. Harassing or maltreating the bulls ain't allowed, but the morons still do it – neither is drunkenness or the taking of any kind of drugs. But who can tell if an entrant's high or not? They all seem to be on something to me! It's just an adventure that I've taken part in for a few years now and maybe I'll continue to do it for a few more – or maybe I won't.

Another place I've been going to regularly for a few years is Ireland. During the coursing and racing days, I used to go over there buying and selling greyhounds. I'd bring dogs back, get them going good, then sell them or sell a share in them – but I've not been doing that for a while now. Instead, I go over there and rent a cottage on the wild west coast, just to get away from it all and savour the solitude. I don't go to hunt or fish, but to take a break and explore remote areas, from Bloody Foreland in the north to Roaringwater Bay in the south. And once I saw a ghost.

It's when I was staying in a lonely part of County Mayo called Blacksod Bay and I'm up early this morning, watching a strengthening sun out over the raw Atlantic, walking alone along the ancient clifftops, listening to the calls of the curlews and the searing cries of seagulls as they glide over the glistening water. Standing on the edge of a continent, surrounded by acres of milkwort and lyme grass and creeping willow – when, suddenly, a thick mist rolls in and blots out the sun and the luminous sea. For some reason, although I ain't never been a superstitious man, a shiver runs up along my spine and a cold chill flows through my bloodstream.

I move inland, hoping to find my bearings and not fall over the edge of the cliff, but the mist thickens even more as I trek in along the lanes. There's no people nor houses anywhere near this place, so no way to get directions, and I'm completely lost now. I'm looking for high ground to get up above the fog and see where I'm situated, when I come to a gradient that turns into a hill. I follow it until I run out of road and find myself in an over-grown churchyard, with subsiding stones and a small fire of elderwood and leaves burning and an eerie silence all around. I've seen no animals on the way here and now not even the sound of a birdcall can be heard. The air's dead, no breeze blows and it seems like time's standing still. The church looms out of the gloom like a menacing monster and I'm wondering if there's a priest inside who could point me in the right direction back to my little cottage. I pass by old Celtic crosses with weather-worn inscriptions, to a heavy wooden door that creaks when I push it open and step cautiously inside.

It's dark in the old church, with just a haunting of light from the high stained-glass window and a single candle flickering in front of a menacing crucifix on a dark altar down the end of the aisle.

'Hello!'

No answer.

'Anyone here?'

Nothing. I'm moving down the church towards the candle, when I hear the sound of rustling movement behind me. I turn to see something fading into the air. An image. An emanation in the shape of a woman with flowing hair and a long, shift-like dress – just a glimpse, before it evaporates. And I think it's a trick of the shadows in this relic of a church. Then the door I came in through slams shut and I put it down to the wind, even though there's no wind to speak of. I retreat and try the old iron handle, but it won't open, no matter how hard I pull. It's jammed tight. Time to calm down and gather my giddy thoughts. There must be another way out – and somebody must've lit the candle and the fire outside. The window's too high to climb through, but maybe there's another door behind the altar.

I move towards the ghostly candle again, sideways, keeping a lookout behind me in case I'm crept up on. I'm level with the flame now and I see a face reflected in it. Not my own face – a woman's, with lips drawn back across her teeth in a threatening smile. Her eyes are blood red and I jump back away from them. Then a sudden breeze blows the candle out and the apparition disappears and I'm alone. I notice a little door behind the altar, leading to an old sacristy. I move quickly along a low corridor and out onto the coast road. The mist's lifted and the sun's shining again.

Later I learn from the locals that the church was abandoned long ago, when the priest moved to the new ministry in the village of Dooagh. And there's a story about a banshee – banshees are women who were hired to howl at funerals – haunting the place. Even now I can't say for sure if I really saw her, or if it was just a figment of the flickering candle and my frightened fancifulness. But what I'd like to know is this – *who* lit the candle in the first place? And the fire outside? And they say Judas hanged himself from an elder tree and the burning of that wood unleashes the devil.

I visit Ireland every now and then and maybe I'll go back some day to the old church near Blacksod Bay, to see if the banshee's still there.

Besides Ireland, what I like doing most of all is going off alone to places like Romania and Estonia and Poland and Belarus and other Eastern European countries, between the months of April and November. I go for a few weeks at a time and trek into the big forests and national parks and onto the mountains to find wild animals – bears and wolves and bison and elk. These ain't hunting trips, and I don't have a gun or any other weapon. I just go to see the animals, to be out there with them and to share their space. It's not all about killing, it's about observing animals.

When the communists were around in Eastern Europe, they stopped the shooting of wolves and bears, so there's a good population of them there today, and I've seen them all, up close – wolves and wildcats and bears and European bison. I've no wish to shoot them – what for? I couldn't take them home to eat them! It's just a chance to be part of their environment, living for a short time the way they do – being close to nature and the essence of what it is to be a real human being, not a whining artificial imposter. I never take a guide with me because I have tracking knowledge. I know how to find animals. I have that instinct: where they prefer to lay up to get out of the cold; where they water; where they go to find what they need to survive. I'm usually days from civilisation, in hundreds of square miles of forest. Sometimes I camp out and other times I use cabanas, which are mountain huts where I can get a bunk and a bite to eat.

Once, back in 2008, I'm out in the Byelavyezhskaya Forest, which spills over from eastern Poland into western Belarus. It's one of the largest areas of primeval mixed woodland in Europe, with pine and beech and oak and alder and spruce growing over an area of nearly five hundred square miles. I don't stick to the National Park with its guided field trips – too many idiots with mobile phones taking pictures and shouting to each other and crashing about like a bunch of demented bears, so no animal will come near them. I get off the beaten track and onto more rugged terrain, away from the trails altogether. On this trip, I want to get up close to the wisent [bison] and watch them graze in the clearings and on the hay meadows at the fringes of the forest. They stay in the trees in summer and it's easier to come across them at this time of year, in early winter.

It's an embryonic experience, wandering through the November trees with no one near me for miles, and knowing I'm surrounded by wild animals like elk and lynx and wolf, even if I can't always see them. I can smell snow in the air, coming from the northern regions of this little spinning-top world, where my father once hunted with an Eskimo. I move along the border between Poland and Belarus, through country that's as close as any to how it was when the woods were inhabited by Vistulans and Kryvians and Steppe Nomads and a man could understand who he was – before it all got clouded and confused. I want to see the bison before I go home and I hope the experience will keep me going until I can come back again.

I like being out here alone in the wild and I'm drawn south, kept company by buzzards and black woodpeckers and long-eared owls. The leaves of the deciduous trees are falling all around me and the forest floor's a carpet of russet colours. I set up my tent close to a clearing, as night's beginning to fall and I want to get a small careful fire going so I can cook my beans and sausage and make a mug of strong tea. The clearing's large; there are signs of bison around and I hope I'll be able to see them tomorrow. I relax in the gloaming, lying quietly in the seclusion of the forest and the comfort of my own company.

Next morning I'm up early and in cover at the edge of the tree line. Then I see them, emerging cautiously into the open: a small herd – a couple of young bulls and about half-a-dozen cows and some calves, maybe a year or two old. The mature adult bulls tend to stay solitary for most of the year and only rejoin the herd during the mating season in August and September. I'm watching them for a while and it's a majestic sight, when I notice that something else is watching them too – a grey wolf. It's an adult male of about a hundred pounds in weight and maybe forty inches tall at the shoulder. I'm downwind, so he can't scent me. Then I see some movement and another wolf becomes visible, and another, and another. It's a pack – on the hunt. The bison sense the danger somehow and stampede off across the clearing. The wolves don't follow, just watch them go, and I think they'll probably circle round through the trees and try to catch the wisent by surprise and maybe bring down a calf.

Later in the day I pack up my gear and trek further south, hoping to come across an elk or a bear or a wildcat. Tomorrow's my last day and then I have to head home to England. The weather turns colder and snow starts to fall as I pitch my tent and make camp that night. I think about the wolves as I sit by the fire. They're rarely seen and I've been very lucky to encounter them like that today. I wasn't afraid because, as far as I know, there ain't a single case of a human being killed by a healthy wolf. But they've always been labelled as vicious and bloodthirsty and they've been hunted and trapped and poisoned to the point of extinction for hundreds of years, based on religious superstition and irrational fear. They're the ancestors of all dogs, no matter what shape or size, even the greyhound and the fox. They're intelligent, tactical hunters that work together to bring down prey, even though they're all different, with their own personality. The strength of the pack's in each individual wolf, and the strength of each individual wolf is in the pack. The wolf's emotions and behaviour patterns are similar to ours – affection and loyalty and jealousy and anger – and they communicate through sound and smell and body gestures. Just like us. But howling's the thing that mystifies and frightens most people, especially when more than one wolf's doing the howling – like now.

That night I sleep restlessly, being woken at regular intervals by the sound of the wolves. They seem very close, but I know they could be as far as five or six miles away. I get up at dawn and emerge from the tent to find there's been a heavy snowfall during the night and the early morning takes on a strange sort of luminescence, reflected in the drifted snow. Overhead, the sky's clearing and still alive with stars, with the ghost of a moon gradually giving way to the day. The enchanted half-light sparkles like dancing fireflies, filling the place with an air of unreality, like in some child's fairy-tale. I feel strange and stand transfixed, head raised and arms outstretched, and it seems like all that matters is here – nothing's gone before and nothing needs to follow. I walk towards a tree to relieve myself and, suddenly, I'm flying through the air and land with a breath-blasting thump on the steep side of a ravine. I begin to roll – over and over and over and over, bouncing off snow-hidden boulders and young saplings and crashing through thorns and undergrowth. I seem to roll forever, until I finally black out and everything fades to soothing darkness.

When I open my eyes again, I can't see anything, just a kind of whiteness. I wipe a thick covering of snow from my face and see that it's still day, with a blizzard falling so hard I can't make out the boundary between land and sky, nor can I see further than a couple of feet in front of me. There's a searing pain in my head and I put my hand up to find congealed blood on my left temple. I try to stand, which I'm able to do only after several shaky attempts but, as far as I can tell, no bones are broken. I feel feverish and completely disorientated and I'm shaking from head to toe. The ravine wall's too steep to climb back up for my gear and I won't last long without my coat and hat. I can't see the sky to know which direction's east, or west, or north, or south, and I don't know how far I am from a trail. Then I hear the wolf howls again, and I decide to follow them.

I move off slowly and, after a while, it begins to grow dark and I know night's approaching. I swallow some snow to slake my dried-up and blood-encrusted mouth. Although I'm an experienced woodsman and have survived in some very rough terrains, I know this ain't good. Without hard-weather clothes and a sense of direction, I might not make it. The night, when it comes, will finish me off for sure if I don't find cover. But I keep following the wolf howls – it seems to be the only alternative I have. I must go west, back into Poland, but my legs won't stand no more and I find myself back on the ground. I crawl through snowy under-growth, pushing myself forward. Time's passing and the sickly light from the sun's fading. Then I hear water close by. I crawl towards the gentle lapping and the smell of the river until I can see it: some tributary of the River Bug that runs through this region – maybe the Lesnaya or even the Narev? There's a boat moored about a hundred yards along the bank and I get myself into it and cover myself over with a heavy tarpaulin. Darkness comes and I'm exhausted and I fall into a fretful sleep.

I wake to a rocking motion and, when I stick my head out from under the tarpaulin, I can see the boat's come adrift during the night and I'm moving along a fast-flowing stretch of water. The snow's stopped and I can make out from the position of the sun that I'm heading west, which is where I want to go. There's no oars or paddles in the boat, so I can't control it, as the tribu-tary opens up into a bigger river, and it ain't long before I have company on the water.

'Help!'

I'm close to civilisation and some villagers take control of my boat and bring it ashore. They can see I'm sick, with some kind of virus, and maybe that's what disturbed me in the tent and dis-orientated me when I came outside. They lift me out of the boat and I'm taken to a local hospital. I can't understand what anyone's saying to me – until a doctor comes who speaks English.

'You got forest fever.'

'What's that?'

He tells me it's caused by the bite of a mosquito that's unique to the area I was trekking in. The effects are flu-like and can cause mild hallucinations. It ain't a serious condition if it don't develop into malaria, and it wears off after a couple of days. I was more at risk from hypothermia and I was very lucky to find cover in that boat.

I've been back to the forests of Eastern Europe several times since. But I never found out who owned that boat – or if the wolf howls led me to it.

Speaking of boats, I've been out fishing on the Danube Delta for carp and perch and roach and eels. There's freshwater sturgeon there too, and many other kinds of fish I don't even know the names of. And three hundred and twenty species of wild birds – pelicans and herons and egrets and cormorants and all kinds of exotic ducks and geese and the water's lovely and so clear you could drink it. Animals inhabit the banks on either side – otter and mink and raccoon and wild boar and fox and wolf – and there's times, I must admit, when I wish I had a gun with me, so I could take home some rare meat to the family.

The Lofoton Islands is an archipelago off the coast of Nordland, in Norway. They're inside the Arctic Circle and lately I've been going up there following the killer whales. I don't go with any tour operator, just under my own steam, like with all the other places I go to. I fly up to Bødo Airport, then sail out on the trawlers. The killer whales come after the herring that spill out of the trawler nets and I go out on a Zodiac speedboat and come right up alongside them to take pictures. All these things I do just because they're there to be done. I see a picture of something or read about it in a book, then I want to go and do it. And I get there however I can – by plane or boat or motorbike or horse-and-cart or whatever. I hope to keep on doing these things for as long as I can – till I'm at least ninety.

Along with the poaching, of course.

And they say that evolution and the genetic code have brought the world along to the state it's in today. How far have we come? Or are we still as savage as when we first fell from the tertiary tree – with a hatchet in our hand?

Brian in Pamplona, 2012

20

Brian – The Last English Poachers

They say there's big money to be made on the internet these days. Danger is, some smart bugger might identify your password and intercept your stash before you retire to your rocking chair. Or else the military laboratories might accidentally unleash some deadly disease or the God-botherers might find the key to nuclear technology and blow us all to bits. It only takes some disillusioned scientist who's hit the skids to post the formula on Facebook. This planet's an unsteady place now, what with the super-rich frightening the moronic classes into believing the world's in danger of being overrun by reason. And it's hard to say if good will triumph over evil or vice versa – I mean, who knows, these days, which is which?

Just to recap a bit on what we've been saying in this book and sum it all up: until the 1980s, when you had land with a titled person on it, like the big estates around here, all the farms and houses were full of estate men. All under the lord's boot – all cap-tippers to the lord. Tenant farmers and anyone in an estate cottage, paying estate rent, owed their allegiance to the earls and

dukes. The main preoccupation on those estates was the shooting. The toffs thought more of their sport than they did of
people. They had millions of pounds' worth of houses and land
and farm buildings and crops and tractors, but the thing they
valued most was their game – and poaching it was what stung
them the most. However, they always had this army of cap-tippers to come after you and grass you up to the police and try to
beat the shit out of you. And that was the 'us-against-them'
game we played all our lives, and are still playing to some extent.

After the '80s, all these villages got built up and commuters
moved in – plastic people, bought people – following the false
promise of money and mundanity. All they do is go to work
every day for their bosses, come home, sleep, go to work, and on
and on and on. So, it's not so much of the old class system any
more, where everything revolved round the estate. A lot of
estate cottages got sold off and the people living there now are
mostly city people who wouldn't know anything about shooting
or rabbiting or hunting or poaching.

'I heard some banging in the night . . . what was that?'

You still get hospitality shooting, where companies will buy
a day or a weekend. And corporate shooting's big business in
itself and has to pay its way and ain't so much the exclusive pursuit of the gentry. Although most of the estates round here are
still owned in name by the aristocrats – like the Duke of
Beaufort, whose family name's Somerset, and others as well,
who try to hang on to the old days and the old ways. In reality,
they were never that much different to the rest of the rabble.
They've always been ordinary, even if they thought they were
extraordinary – and now they're accountable to the law, just like
us poachers. They've always blamed us for thinking we're above

the rules that they made themselves – rules that applied to everyone else except them. And even still they believe they're above those rules and sometimes they are.

Sometimes they get away with murder, like Lord Lucan, and sexual deviancy, like Lord Podge, and all kinds of other frauds and fiddles, like giving land away to the National Trust to save on death duties. Have to account for it all someday I hope – because there must be more in the universe besides this contaminated little planet, full of wastrels and wishful-thinkers.

The Earl of Ducie once owned most of this village and nearly everyone in it, except for us. Berkeley Estate, with its big deer park, is still owned by the Berkeley family and there's a lot of other titled families still strong in this area. You still have foreign kings and queens and princes and princesses going up the estates for shoots and horse trials and stuff, and they still have some say-so and we still have to go a bit careful. But it's not like it used to be, when they could get gamekeepers and estate workers to come out mob-handed and patrol the village streets armed with clubs and cudgels looking for us poachers. If they came upon us, they'd chase us and try to trap us; surround us and give us a good beating. And Bob told you about the six police cars with dogs coming out in response to some silly saddle-bumping earl, just over a few rabbits.

You'd get in the local papers quicker now for being up before the magistrates for a simple motoring offence than you would for poaching. They'd be hard put to even know what poaching was – probably think you were being done for grooming kids on the internet or something. But poaching was a big crime once, and we had the full force of the law against us because of who we were taking from. I remember when that rural copper who discovered the truck used by the Great Train Robbers at

Leatherslade Farm was interviewed, he said: 'We ain't used to this sort of thing, just arresting poachers.'

And arresting poachers was their main occupation. What else did they have to do – stopping a fight outside the local pub? Catching kids stealing potatoes? Farm workers nicking batteries from tractors? Drunks coming pissed out of the pub on a Saturday night and pointing their plonkers up against the church wall?

But poaching ain't their priority no more and the lords ain't got the same power as they used to have. There's no local police cap-tipping to the earls now. That system got diluted in the '90s. All the old boys who sucked up to the toffs and worked for them for forty years or more have died off. Now it's all commuting and credit cards and mortgages and social media and idiocy like that, and they have too many other things on their minds. Our village ain't such a closed community. We still got the farm workers and the hangers-on up the bigger estates like Beaufort, where they say the King of Spain comes to shoot – and rich Yanks pay £50,000 for two days' sport and stay in Beaufort House, then go back to America and tell everyone they stopped with one of the bastard descendants of King Henry VII. A gamekeeper bragged to me about how much they paid. And I said, 'I hope they left some for us; we don't pay anything.'

So, you see, things are changing, even though the land's still owned by the rich – maybe not the same rich as in days gone by, but the rich nevertheless. Some would say the change is for the better and others would say for the worse. To me it makes no matter, I still live my life the way I always did. I just have to make adjustments every now and then. These changes affect rural areas all over England, not just south Gloucestershire, where the old agrarian feudalism of the countryside's being swallowed up by the new economic feudalism of the towns and cities.

And it's not just the social changes – the landscape around the village is evolving in step with the modern obsession with banality and conformity. A lot of the local shops and pubs are gone, priced out of existence, and there'll soon be a Starbucks on every sheep trail, and a Burger King on every bridle path. The village is getting bigger and bigger, with outsiders coming in and private houses being built for people who commute to Bristol and other cities for their livelihood.

We used to know everyone in the village; now we know nobody. There's no character to the area any more – no local coppers who understand the lore of the poacher, despite being set on catching us for their lords and masters. The ponds are all being filled in to reclaim land for housing, and farming methods have changed, with more sheep than ever before. Nothing likes living with sheep, no wild animal – they graze everything down to the root and stink the fields up with their piss. They attract ticks that can take the eyes out of hares and send them blind. Once the sheep moved into this area, the hares moved out and, along with the hard winter I told you about, that might have been another cause of their disappearance. There's no ground cover for wild animals, with it all been nibbled down bare, and we've caught hares with no eyes from the ticks. Only good thing about sheep is their shit – it thickens the grass when they thread it into the close-cropped earth. And they say a sheep's fart's better than a ton of farm manure.

Bob has almost come to the end of his poaching life, due to health reasons rather than any loss of interest. He still comes out as a lookout for me when I'm after the pheasant, but he's pushing on for eighty now and, although he's not had a drink for well over forty years, the alcohol he drank when he was young has taken its toll. The old illnesses have come to stake their claim on him, along with the other things that age brings. He still has the scarring on his brain from the accident in the Navy and now he can't piss proper and has to have a catheter. But he has no regrets. He wouldn't have lived his life any other way. He's always believed in treating with respect those who treat him with respect, and tried to live life a day at a time and enjoy his family. In any case, there's little space left in a politically correct world for men like him, who've spent their whole lives on the land, hunting wild animals that people who've never been to the countryside now feel they need to protect.

Despite all the things that've changed, I still go out all the time and I'm flexible enough to adapt. In some ways it's easier to poach now because the police station's been closed and there's no village coppers keeping an eye on me. I can move about of a night and the newcomers wouldn't have a clue what I was doing. On the other hand, the keepers have night-sights now and mobile phones with cameras and satellite navigation systems and all sorts of electronic equipment. And there's these constant news reports of rampant tabloid phone-tapping and secret letter-opening and computer-bugging and all kinds of unmentionable surveillance – and apprehension growing daily among us fugitive classes that anonymity will soon be as dead as the dodo.

And what will it be like when the buggers invent telepathy?

But what's in the blood to begin with stays in the blood forever, and I just have to adjust my methods and my means and on I go, away into the mist beyond the hill. Between us, me and Bob have been poaching for eight decades and I want to make it up to a hundred years before I'm finally finished.

I never got married, even though I had many a girlfriend when

I was younger and even one or two now – some long time and some short time and some I might have married, but it didn't work out that way. The thought of losing my freedom to be able to go where I want and do what I want kept me back from marriage. I didn't want to be tied down; I wouldn't have been able to stick it. It'd be like being in jail the whole time, wouldn't it? There can't be more to love than lust or more to marriage then madness. Can there? In any case, I was never an ideal ticket for a woman – alright to muck about with and have a hidden huddle, but not a good long-term proposition. Not a municipal misfit like me, who didn't want to work eighty minimum-wage hours a week to make some tax-dodging entrepreneur rich. I'm probably too old for it now and the thought of being penned up still don't appeal to me. There's too many things I still want to do before I'm on a Zimmer frame.

I'm over fifty now, but I can still run and climb a mountain and wrestle a stag and fight a gamekeeper. Once I'm over seventy I probably won't be able to do so much of that any more – so maybe I'll get married then. But, for now, I'm doing the same at fifty as I did at five. And I like the freedom of it. I'll carry on poaching till the day I die. I'll never stop. There'll always be land and wild animals – rich buggers with their gormlessness and their game – and there'll always be me, taking it from them. And if I can't walk I'll get myself a wooden leg.

We've always been known as men who stood up for what we believed in and were never afraid to say what we thought. I hate freemasons, lords, earls, vicars, yes-men, and anyone else who believes they're better or bigger or bullier, who think they're special in some way. But we're in a minority these days, free-thinkers – people who ain't been brainwashed by the system, who see things a different way from the stampeding herd. And most of the old poaching skills are being lost. Young people ain't brought up to have to kill animals for food any more, so they don't know how to hunt with dogs or nets or traps – and all they want to do with guns is shoot each other. Times are different, just like Bob's before me, and I remember the village the way it was. Nothing much changed between his time as a boy here and my time as a boy here. His time was in the 1940s, before he went into the Navy, my time was the 1960s – twenty odd years apart – and nothing much changed in those twenty years, apart from going from horses to motors.

We held the same parties at Christmas in the village hall, to make sure every kid got at least one present, no matter how poor they were. But it stopped when the population grew and the middle-class kids were seen chucking the toys away and saying, 'I don't want that rubbish' – spoilt kids from the new houses; a different kind of kid. With their mountain bikes and mobile phones and promises – gifts of greed and gimme and gollop, to stand them in good stead for their future in the never ending cycle of slaving and shopping. Hark, the herald angels sing, glory to the Christmas fling! We never had anything much, so it was nice to go to a Christmas party and get stuff you wouldn't get at home – jelly and ice cream and cake, and everyone excited about the present they were going to get at the end of it. There was an annual outing to Weston-super-Mare and we all looked forward to paying our couple of shillings to Mrs Blizzard up the road and getting taken to the seaside on a coach once a year. There were rambles in the woods, all the way round and back for a big tea. Jelly and ice cream means nothing now, everyone can have it any time they want, but we used to run hopping and skipping for such a rare treat.

The village held a sports day once a year, just like in my father's time, and you'd get a shilling for coming first in a race –

egg-and-spoon or sack or piggy-back or three-legged. I'd enter every race I could, because I was a good runner and a lot of the time I won. And then there was a big communal nosh-up out on the playing field. There was fancy dress and me and two of my mates once went as the butcher, the baker and the candlestick maker. I was the butcher, like my grandfather; or we'd go as Bill and Ben the Flowerpot Men, or Laurel and Hardy. Cora always made the costumes for us and you got a prize if you won. We had pram races in the summer and 'penny for the Guy' in November and carol-singing from the back of a trailer at Christmas. And nothing much changed for years and years and years.

But it all has now.

Everything lost its character with the mass influx from the cities and towns. The village, the land, the people – it all became sterile and anonymous. Everything became consumerised, televisionised, cloned with no individuality and no real heart. Once we were known here as poachers; the police kept a sharp eye on us, the landowners hated us, the village people knew us and had game off us. Not many people really know us now. You might say anonymity's a good thing in our game, and maybe it is, but it comes at a high price. And, anyway, I never really cared about being called a blackguard – a few months in jail never bothered me, a fine never bothered me, and what people thought never bothered me neither.

I'm one of the few who's been able to stay in this village and whose family goes back generations here, to the 1800s and even before. Whereas most of the kids I grew up with have had to move because there's no social housing here and you need half a million quid to buy a property, or up to £1,500 a month to rent one. You need to be a banker or a fancy football player or a confidence trickster to be able to afford to live here now, so where can ordinary village kids go? They all had to move to places where accommodation's cheaper – shithole towns and urban areas and city slums.

It started when that old trollop Thatcher brought in the Right to Buy scheme. Everyone wanted to own their own council house – they had to go to work to pay the mortgage and became bought men. And women. Owned. In debt. Enslaved. Under the whip of the so-called entrepreneurs. Then Thatcher's mates cut wages and increased working hours and everyone had to get two or three jobs to keep on affording the mortgage until, finally, they had to sell their houses to the people who live here now, and move off somewhere cheaper. So now there's nowhere for local people to live in these villages.

The people here now deliver Peter and Petra to school in Range Rovers and race round the lanes in Mercs and BMWs – anxious, uptight, jittery people, oblivious to country ways. The aristocrats were a bit like that years ago, aloof and arrogant, but they knew about the countryside and respected it. These people think they're the new aristocracy and us Toveys are a little island in our little house, surrounded by sharks – property values and shiny cars and tinny accents and shrillness. All swimming round us, hoping to swallow us up. We don't fit in any more in a place where we've fitted in for hundreds of years. There's no room for us in an upwardly mobile society with values that ain't ours.

We were always different and people never knew how to deal with us. They were wary of what we represented – afraid of our freedom, our disregard for authority. It was dangerous, like the very lore of the countryside was dangerous, unpredictable. Steeped in the ancient and the strange and the essence of all things natural.

Bob has a stuffed white hare in a case that he caught while long-netting on an estate at Andover, belonging to Eagle Star Insurance. There's an old West Country legend that tells of a witch who took the form of a white hare and went out at night looking for the souls of broken-hearted maidens who couldn't rest and who haunted their unfaithful lovers. If that's true, then he has that witch here in our house, safe inside a glass case. Ha ha!

And, at one time, there was a white fox in the area and I saw it once when I was out near Lutheridge Farm. I was in the middle of a field and all these magpies were making a hell of a racket. I looked across and caught a fleeting glimpse, before it disappeared. I tried to squeak it back into sight, but it didn't respond, and it reminded me of the old stories about the white fox-woman of folklore who was beautiful, but skittish and dangerous and not easily tamed.

> Fire and frost in your eyes
> Are you woman, are you wise?
> Wild and sly, hunt by guile
> Tooth and claw, falsely smile
> Mouth blood-red, for your prey
> Slow to love, quick to slay.

And that's the countryside for me, how it used to be – wild and seductive. The feel of the giving ground under my feet and the wind on my face and the sky above and the trees and the meadows and the streams and the lakes and the light and dark of it all. And the animals – mostly the animals, with which I feel such an affinity – just a millimetre above on the genetic scale. They kill each other to survive and I kill them. I'm top of the food chain.

But it was never all about killing. Life has to be given a chance to breed and recover. We put down rabbits and relocate hares and bring on gamebirds and wildfowl. We look after our environment. So, I suppose we're conservationists in our own way.

I have no son to pass this passion down to. And if I did, what would he say to me in these days of creeping disillusionment?

'Who said you had the right to make me?'

So, when my father dies, and I die after him, we'll be gone forever. And I think of these words I read once:

> *The rain across the woodland*
> *Is playing with the night*
> *And if it ain't wrong*
> *It must be right!*

Bob with pheasant

A Poacher's Glossary

Albino – A deer with no pigment in its skin or hair

Balance of the day – Remains of the day

Bagging – Loose netting

Bang railer – A dog that likes to run on the rails – on a greyhound track

BB – Big ball lead shot

Beaters – People who drive hares in for open coursing

Bee nettles – White nettle (plant)

Blind-eyes – Hogweed (plant)

Cage trap – A baited cage, used for catching vermin

Chal – Gypsy word for boy or child

Chitlin – Guts (of a pig)

Chopsy – Mouthy – gobby – too much to say

Clap net – A spring-loaded net

Clobhead – An idiot

Coney – Slang for rabbit

Covey – small flock

Creeping jinny – Moneywort (plant)

Dap – A tuft of grass that isn't worn down, where rabbits jump

Deckhead – The underside of a ship's deck (naval)

Dibby – Merry or drunk

Didicoy – A Gypsy, but not a true Romany

Ditching spade – A tool used for digging down into rabbit burrows

Drag-coursing – Running two greyhounds after a lure on a straight course

Drag-net – Net about twenty-five yards wide and four yards deep, with a line coming off each of the front corners – it gets dragged along over stubble and grass and short kale to trap game

Droppers – Live rabbits, used for spot-(drop)coursing

Duckerer – A Gypsy fortune teller

Duck frost – A light, early frost

Fallow – pale brown / reddish (deer)

Fenn trap – Spring-loaded mechanical trap – modern substitute for gin trap (now banned)

Flankers – People used to control hares in open coursing

Flapping track – An independent, unlicensed greyhound track

Foreshore – The part of a shore between the water and cultivated land

Form – Where a hare or rabbit quats (lies down in the grass)

Funnel net – A net with a wide circular opening at one end, tapering off, to trap fish

Gaff – A hook for landing fish

Gavage – Method (instrument) used for force-feeding animals

Gin trap – A mechanical trap with jaws and teeth for trapping a variety of animals

Goatsfoot – Device used for cocking a crossbow

Gone to bricks – Gypsies who live in houses and don't travel any more

Gralloch – The entrails of a dead deer

Grunty – A tough guy, or someone who thinks he is

Hazel – To rest, relax

Hedge-mumper – Nosy parker

Hind – A female deer

Hingle – A snare made of wire and attached to a stake in the ground

Hob – A male ferret

Hotchi – Gypsy word for hedgehog

Jill – A female ferret

Joe-cockys – Boasters and Braggers

Jug / Jugging – Roost / Roosting

Landing net – A net used for landing fish, once hooked

Long nets – Adjustable nets that are four to five feet high and a hundred to a hundred and fifty yards long, used for netting hares and rabbits (and other game as well)

Lure – A manmade imitation (rabbit/hare), sometimes covered with fur and with a squeaker inside

Lurgy – Slang word for disease or fever

Mist net – Fine-mesh net, suspended between two poles

Mitched – Bunked off school

Molly – Moorhen

Monkey-men – Con men

Myxomatosis – An infectious viral disease affecting rabbits

Night line – A baited fishing line, left overnight

Nut stick – A straight stick from a hazel tree

Open coursing – Running two greyhounds after a hare on open ground, where the hare has to be driven in by beaters

Paddling – Flock (of ducks)

Park coursing – Running two greyhounds after a hare in an enclosed park or field with an escape at the end for the hare

Pastore – Bull shepherds (Pamplona)

Pluck – The heart, liver and lungs of a dead animal

Pompey – Naval slang for prison

Pricker stick – Stick used for holding the noose of a hingle (snare) off the ground

Priest – Short club, weighted with lead

Purse net – A net with a draw-string, used when ferreting for rabbits

Quarry – An animal being hunted

Quat / Quatting – Lying down in the grass (a rabbit or hare)

Quean – A female cat

Roost / Roosting – Birds settling down for the night – a place where they do this

Sally tree – Acacia (resembling a willow)

Shackles – U-shaped metal links, closed by a bolt (naval)

Shy – A hide, where the slipper waits with the dogs in greyhound coursing

Slipper – Someone who slips the greyhounds in hare or drag coursing

Slip snare – Similar to a hingle

Spot coursing – Dropping a live rabbit on a spot and giving it a head start before letting a greyhound or lurcher after it (also called drop-coursing)

Spring-gun – A mantrap, used by gamekeepers to ambush poachers

Spur – Bone or metal protrusion on the ankle of a fighting cock

St Stephen's Day – Boxing Day

Stud-tailed – Feline Acne

Tup – An awkward person or thing

Umiak – Eskimo canoe

Widgeon – A dabbling duck with reddish brown and grey plumage

Withy trees – Willow

Wisent – European bison

Yawney – A fool

Ya-Ya – Toff

Yoikes – Tally-ho brigade

Bob Tovey, poacher

Cora's Game Recipes

Please note all animals need to be skinned (or plucked) and cleaned before cooking

Hare – Lightly Fried

Place whole hare in large pot on top of cooker.

Bring to the boil.

Turn down to simmer.

Place lemon, cut into four pieces, into pot.

Cook until meat falls off the bones.

Take hare out of pot and place on a plate or dish.

Remove all the meat from the bones and place in frying pan with just a little oil.

Fry on low heat until browned.

Serve with creamed or jacket potatoes, carrots and onions (or alternative vegetables).

Roast Pheasant

Place pheasant in roasting dish.

Place whole onion or apple inside bird to keep moist.

Place streaky bacon over breast and legs and sprinkle with pepper.

Pour oil over pheasant and allow to run into roasting dish.

Stuffing can be prepared separately in a dish or placed inside bird (my preference is separately).

Cover pheasant with foil.

Place in pre-heated oven, then turn down to 150–170°C (elec).

Baste well while cooking until meat is well done.

Remove bacon and foil to allow pheasant to brown – turn off oven while browning.

Serve with potatoes and choice of vegetables.

Rabbit Hotpot

Place legs and jointed back of rabbit in large pot.

Add thick slices of potato, carrot, whole shallots or small onions, parsnip, leek and any other choice of vegetable.

Cover with cold water and place in bottom of pre-heated oven.

Cook until the meat is nicely tender.

Make dough-boys out of flour, part milk, part water, pepper mix.

Add to pot about 20–25 minutes before dishing up.

Roast Partridge

Place partridge upside down in roasting dish.

Pour oil over bird and allow to run into roasting dish.

Cover with foil.

Place in middle of pre-heated oven and turn down to 130–140°C (elec).

Cook for approx. 30–45 mins.

Take foil off and turn bird upright and allow to brown – turn off oven while browning.

Serve with potatoes and choice of vegetables.

Afterword

Bob working spaniels in Lower Woods, Wickwar, carrying his postman's

Bob Tovey was taken ill with pneumonia on 9 November 2014. He died on 7 February 2015, just as this book went to press.

My father and I were out poaching for the last time together on Bonfire Night, 5 November 2014. We poached the Duke of Beaufort's estate and shot twenty-seven pheasants. Bob got ill shortly after and spent time in hospital, before slipping away two weeks before his 77th birthday. He lived his life right up to the last minute and was talking about going out long-netting again on his very last day in the world. He said he'd had a good innings, considering all the things he'd done and the amount of alcohol he'd consumed in his younger days. He was a man who lived life his own way – he did what he wanted to do, not what others wanted him to do. He'll be missed by his family and friends.

Brian Tovey

I was so sorry to hear of the death of Bob Tovey. He was a unique man with an indomitable spirit, a rakish sense of humour and an elemental outlook on life. I had the great privilege of meeting and working with Bob on *The Last English Poachers* and it's an experience that will stay with me for a very long time. Loss is an abstract concept – it can be relative, great or deep or gradual or unquantifiable. A glorious piece of the heritage of this country has been lost with Bob's passing. I'm just glad I was able to know him personally, before he passed into legend.

John McDonald

I went out long-netting again on 7th March 2015. It was a lovely spring day and I netted thirty-one live hares at Ballington, the last place Bob and I netted together nearly three years earlier to the day – mentioned at the end of Chapter 11. It was a poignant coincidence and I could feel my father with me.

Brian Tovey

Bob with Biddy, the last spaniel he owned, spring 2011